TOM HARDY

RISE OF A LEGEND

JAMES HAYDOCK

JOHN BLAKE

Published by John Blake Publishing Ltd,
3 Bramber Court, 2 Bramber Road,
London W14 9PB, England

www.johnblakebooks.com

www.facebook.com/johnblakebooks 🅕
twitter.com/jblakebooks 🅣

First published in hardback in 2012
This edition published in 2015

ISBN: 978 1 78219 756 0

British Library Cataloguing-in-Publication Data:

A catalogue record for this book is available from the British Library.

Design by www.envydesign.co.uk

Printed in Great Britain by CPI Group (UK) Ltd

1 3 5 7 9 10 8 6 4 2

Papers used by John Blake Publishing are natural, recyclable products made
from wood grown in sustainable forests. The manufacturing processes conform
to the environmental regulations of the country of origin.

Every attempt has been made to contact the relevant copyright-holders, but some were
unobtainable. We would be grateful if the appropriate people could contact us.

'When I started out, I just wanted to be on *The Bill*. When I went to drama school I was like: "If I can just be a police officer on *The Bill*, that will do me." So I've done very well, thank you God and everyone else.'

ACKNOWLEDGEMENTS

Huge thanks to everyone at John Blake Publishing for their support and especially to Allie Collins who has been very flexible with deadlines!

Enormous gratitude also to Graeme Andrew at Envy Design for a slick cover and page design.

Thanks, too, to my two amazing secret proofreaders – you know who you are!

Finally, thanks to my family who were always there with encouraging words when I needed them.

CONTENTS

CHAPTER ONE

THE MEAN STREETS OF EAST SHEEN

It was the summer of 1977 and the mood was one of celebration. Throughout the land, red, white and blue bunting fluttered in the warm breeze as the people of Great Britain threw street parties to honour the Queen's silver jubilee. The joyous mood intensified when the country was presented with another, very different, reason to put the flags out: Virginia Wade clinched the Women's Singles title at the Wimbledon Tennis Championships, in a welcome display of British sporting achievement. The dying days of the Labour government and the winter of discontent were still some way off and, for now, the nation was on a high.

During these summer months, Edward and Elizabeth (née Barrett) Hardy were preparing for the birth of their first – and, in the event, only – child. Elizabeth, who goes by her middle name of Anne, had grown up in the north of England and was descended from a large Irish-Catholic family. Edward – or 'Chips', as he is better known – was born in Ealing, London.

A propensity for the creative arts was present in both parents: Anne is an artist and painter and Chips, having read English Literature at Downing College, Cambridge, from 1969 to 1972, became a successful advertising creative who, in his career, has notched up some award-winning campaigns. In 2006, for example, he was the creative director on the campaign for the health supplement Berocca, which won the Best Fashion, Beauty and Healthcare award in the Campaign Media Awards. Chips is also a successful author and playwright who specialises in comedy writing – he has collaborated on numerous comedy projects and even won a British Comedy Award for his work on *The Dave Allen Show*. His plays include *There's Something in the Fridge That Wants to Kill Me*, a black comedy that was staged both in London and at the Edinburgh Fringe Festival.

The entertaining biography of Chips that appears on his literary agent's website gives some clues as to his family history: it declares that 'recent contributions to his gene pool include an Ealing Studio Fire-chief who rounded the horn aged 12'. Delving further back in time, it states that his ancestors apparently include 'river men, pirates, horse-breeders in England and France...'

On 15 September 1977, Chips and Anne's son, Edward Thomas Hardy, made his entrance into the world. Like his mother, he goes by his middle name – and perhaps by doing so has avoided the confusion that can occur when a father and son share a first name. Though born in Hammersmith, West London, it was in the idyllic surroundings of East Sheen, a quiet and leafy suburb of the city, where Tom grew up. It's an area where schools are good, crime rates are low and there is an abundance of green open space – the perfect place to bring up a child.

The cosy atmosphere of SW14 was something against which Hardy would rail in his adolescence, but in more recent years he has chosen to move back to its comforting surroundings. 'People walk around in chunky sweaters, wearing bright smiles. I did leave once, but I soon came back – it's a state of grace,' he commented when asked about his neighbourhood. 'It feels like such a special and calm place amid the sprawling metropolis of London – a bit like an imaginary village where you'd expect to see Postman Pat.'

Although East Sheen is a far cry from areas of London that you would more readily associate with celebrities, such as affluent Hampstead or funky Primrose Hill, Tom isn't the only star who has chosen to hang his hat there. Back in the nineties, East Sheen was buzzing with excitement at the news that Tom Cruise and former wife Nicole Kidman were to purchase an ivy-clad mansion in the area. (The mansion had, in fact, also once been the home of ballet dancer Rudolf Nureyev).

These days, should you choose to sit and sip a latté in one of the local coffee shops, you might encounter 007 himself, Daniel Craig, veteran newscaster Sir Trevor McDonald or the BBC's political bloodhound Andrew Marr, all of whom are residents. 'It's heaven for the middle classes,' adds Tom, 'the duvet of the south west. It's not trendy and cool, but it's still a great place to live.'

Tom's start in life was secure and privileged and he admits that he had, 'all the signs of a middle-class upbringing, where every opportunity was provided for me to do well'. His parents were intelligent, creative folk who recognised the value of a good education and were fortunate enough to have the means to choose private schooling for their son. Rather than a state-funded primary school, Tom attended local prep school, Tower House. Situated close to Richmond Park, Tower House was founded in 1932. It is a small independent boys' school that supports pupils in all areas of their development and places equal importance on both academic and social growth. Like so many private preparatory schools, it prides itself on providing a foundation for pupils whose parents want them to progress to reputable secondary schools via the 13+ exam. Notable fellow Tower House alumni include actor Rory Kinnear and Jamie Rix, successful author and son of actor/producer Brian Rix. More recently, the school has attracted attention thanks to one former pupil in particular: before gaining an unhealthy vampiric pallor and a hordes of teenage fans, Robert Pattinson quietly went about his primary education at Tower House.

From here, Tom progressed through the private education system to boarding school. Reeds School is in the pretty Surrey town of Cobham and boasts every educational facility a pupil could wish for. Its academic standards are amongst the highest in the land and it also prides itself on its sports and drama facilities. High achievers who have passed through its gates include former tennis champion Tim Henman and skier Louise Thomas.

Tom has described his younger self as 'boring', but he maintains he was a child with a vivid imagination and one who loved stories. His lively mind was not always engaged in positive activity, though, and he has confessed that he learned the art of manipulation early on in life. His grandfather apparently recalls that he was a bit of a 'Walter Mitty' character, meaning that he spent much of his time escaping the mundane reality of his own existence by inhabiting a world of fantasy – something Hardy would later indulge in through the medium of acting. Apparently he also developed a keen sense of humour early on, a trait surely inherited from his comedy-writing father.

It didn't take long for the enquiring and imaginative boy to want to shake the foundations of the charmed life he had been born into. 'From a very young age, I was flagrantly disobedient,' he told the *Evening Standard* in 2006. 'I got involved in anything that was naughty. I wanted to explore all the dark corners of the world, partly to see if I could control it.' He was also not averse to a bit of scrapping and can remember '…being kicked in the balls at school when I was about nine. That was a miserable outcome.'

One upshot of his involvement in all things 'naughty' was his expulsion from Reeds for stealing sports kit. And although he left under a cloud, the school now seems proud to count Tom Hardy as one of its old boys, heralding him as one of their 'former pupils who now excel on the stage and screen'. The expulsion didn't signal the end of Tom's school career, though. He went on to attend another exclusive educational establishment in the shape of the independent sixth-form college Duff Miller in South Kensington, London.

Private schools invariably channel pupils towards going on to further, traditional academic pursuits, but this was something clearly not on Tom's agenda. He has admitted that he 'couldn't really get to grips with school work' and left school without any clear idea of what he could do next. His antics and irrepressible nature were far from conformist and he didn't quite fit the mould of student that private schools are so good at churning out.

Like many adolescents, Tom struggled to feel comfortable in his own skin. The agonising quest for identity is something every teenager goes through but how this angst manifests itself depends on the circumstances and personality of the individual. Tom's discomfort was twofold: he was uneasy with both his own susceptibilities and his surroundings. In an effort to disguise the former, he did what so many teenagers do and changed his appearance. While some might dye their hair or alter their clothes in an effort either to stand out or to blend in, Tom's actions were more extreme and he began what would become a lifelong obsession with tattoos. At 15 he acquired his first, which was of a leprechaun by way of a tribute to his mother's Irish roots. In an interview with Canada's *The Globe and Mail*, he remembered his mother's dismay upon the discovery of his first piece of body art: 'She kept saying "my beautiful boy, my beautiful boy…".'

He also explained the psychology behind his desire to decorate his body to the *Guardian* newspaper: 'When I was a kid, people thought I was a girl, but I wanted to be strong, to be a man. My vulnerabilities were permanently on show when I was young, I had no skin as a kid. Now I'm covered in tattoos.'

Here was an angry young man who was deeply frustrated with his lot: nice, well-educated, middle-class Tom from the suburbs was simply not what he wanted to be. He needed to experience danger, to knock the edges off his comfortable existence. The tattoos and minor transgressions, therefore, soon developed into more destructive behaviour such as drinking, drug-taking, getting into fights, robbery and even carrying weapons. He also started to keep less-than-desirable company and hung around with, as he puts it, 'lads that looked like the guys who were on trial for the murder of Stephen Lawrence'.

Tom has also referenced his father when speaking of what drove him towards seeking out the more dangerous side of life in his youth. According to Tom, Chips is not the kind of man to resolve a problem by getting into a physical fight about it. He was a highly intelligent man and this was simply not his way. So Tom felt obliged to try and create a persona that was the exact opposite. 'The point is, my father's not really into throwing his fists. He's got lightning wit, backchat and repartee to get himself out of a scrap – and nothing else... so I had to go further afield and I brought all sorts of unscrupulous oiks back home – earless, toothless vagabonds – to teach me the arts of the old bagarre,' he revealed to the *Mail & Guardian* in 2011.

In his teenage years, Tom was no stranger to a police cell, though surprisingly he was never actually charged with an offence. Speaking to the the *Observer* about what drove him to such acts of rebellion he commented, 'It's the suburbs. The life is so privileged and peaceful and so bloody dull, it gives you the instinctive feral desire to fuck everything up.'

And, for quite some time, that's exactly what he did. When he was 15 years old, he was arrested for joyriding in a stolen Mercedes and being in possession of a gun. The consequences of this could have been disastrous but, mercifully for Tom, he happened to be in the company of a diplomat's son, so the problem was made to disappear. According to Hardy, he was prepared to do the time but in the end was able to walk away from the incident without further repercussions.

The drinking, the drugs and the criminal behaviour were apparently all symptomatic of a person filled with 'self-hatred'. Speaking to *Attitude* magazine in 2008, Tom reflected on his wild, wayward years with his trademark self-awareness: 'I was an obnoxious, trouble-making lunatic. Not comfortable in my own skin and displacing that into the world. A complete twat. A knobhead. Mostly because I'm a middle-class white boy from suburbia. Growing up I was deeply ashamed, I was like "I'm not street and I'm not rich". A classic case of suburban kid…'

The anomaly of tearing it up on the streets of slumbering East Sheen is something that Tom has been asked to explain on more than one occasion. How could a teenager really live life on the edge and put himself in harm's way in a place that seems so safe, so normal? Scratch the surface of respectability and you might be surprised at what you find lurking beneath. 'Behind those Laura Ashley curtains there are a lot of demons. East Sheen is a middle-class area, Trumpton or Sesame Street, but there's trouble if you want it.' And he certainly did.

Through his late teens and into his early twenties, Tom continued to have brushes with the law –'I was looking at 14 years when I was 17, I was looking at five years when I was 21 for something else' – and what started as casual drinking and recreational drug use eventually developed into more serious alcohol and substance abuse. In the midst of all this chaos, Tom achieved something typically bizarre and incongruous: he entered – and won – a modelling competition.

That Tom's looks are exceptional is in no doubt. He has been blessed with the kind of face and physique that makes people sit up and take notice. The raw ingredients of a cover boy are all present: smouldering eyes, fine bone structure and, of course, those lips. His lips have, in fact, been the subject of much media scrutiny and have been described as both 'pillowy' and 'bruised-looking'. The alluring looks are just part of the attraction, though. He has something else that makes him stand out from the rest: his looks have an edge, a hint of menace, something that both modelling scouts and casting directors have been quick to pick up on when seeking a certain kind of brooding, dangerous look for either a campaign or a role.

Whatever his motivation – most likely to fulfil that need for attention he so often refers to – in 1998, he entered *The Big Breakfast*'s 'Find Me a Model' competition. At the time, *The Big Breakfast* was a hugely popular, energetic early morning television programme aimed predominantly at the youth market. It had launched in 1992 and enjoyed huge success under the guardianship of presenters Chris Evans and Gaby Roslin. When they left the show, so did a number of viewers and ratings dropped. The producers finally found a winning formula in Johnny Vaughan and Denise van Outen, who co-hosted successfully from 1997 for a number of years.

'Find Me a Model' appealed for gorgeous young hopefuls from all over the country aged between 16 and 24 to enter a series of regional heats for the chance to win a modelling contract with major international agency Models One. There were two contracts up for grabs, one for a female model and one for a male model. Back then, Tom sported long hair and a skinnier frame than the one we are familiar with now, but his unique brand of looks appealed to the judges and he scooped the top spot. His female counterpart was pretty blonde Kirsty Richards. Speaking to *Arena Homme* in November 2010 about the competition, Tom recalled unhappily: 'I stood there with this hair, this really big quiff the hairdresser had done and this ridiculous jumper while they went on about me not liking football but liking Steven Berkoff.'

With a contract in the bag, Tom set about his fledgling career as a model and got some high-profile shoots under his belt, including *Male Vogue* and fashion shoots with photographer Gino Sprio. And never let it be forgotten that he was also once Mr July in *Just Seventeen* magazine.

It will come as little surprise that Tom was a fish out of water in the world of photo shoots and catwalks. He had a huge desire to be noticed and appreciated, but he was putting himself in front of the wrong type of camera – his heart was a million miles away from modelling. 'I tried to be a model when I was 19 and I was shit,' he told the *Observer* in 2007. 'I can only function when I become someone else.'

Tom had always been fascinated by acting and felt it was something at which he might succeed, but had never actively been pushed in that direction. He maintains that while he was at school, his aspirations as an actor were not encouraged – acting was not viewed as a profession, but rather as something to be pursued as a hobby. But to have acting merely as a part-time recreation was not an option for him.

'I didn't get any GCSEs or A-Levels,' he said in an interview with the *indieLondon* website. 'But everyone was like: "Please, will you do something?" And I was thinking: "Well, I kind of like the idea of joining the French Foreign Legion." But my mum said: "That's never going to happen because you can't even wash your own socks..." Then some angel somewhere said: "Have you ever considered going to drama school?" And this sounded like the solution to all my problems.'

He initially tried and failed to win a place at Drama Centre (which he would later attend) and so remained in a quandary about how to turn his thespian dreams into reality. It was his good fortune that, at the same time as he was trying to figure out the best way forward, his mother was studying Art at Richmond Adult Community College. She happened to notice that the college ran a one-year drama school access course and encouraged her son to audition. Reluctantly he did so and, in what would prove to be one of the turning points in his life, Tom secured himself a place on the course.

The purpose of an access course such as the one offered at Richmond is to teach pupils the basic tools of their craft. On completion of the course, students might choose to move on to a degree at drama school or they might follow a different acting-related path. Pupils who have completed the course have gone on to study at establishments such as LAMDA and Italia Conti as well as Drama Centre. It is also a good foundation course for students who wish to pursue a degree in drama via a university. The course at Richmond provides important training in the areas of text and voice work, physical theatre, movement, stage combat and preparing pieces for audition.

Tom has nothing but the highest praise for the course, recognising that, without it, he might not be where he is today. 'I really needed that string to my bow,' he told the BBC in 2006. 'It was a make or break year – I didn't get into acting school the first time around and this was the stepping stone for me.' He also recognises that the skills he acquired there were vital to a young actor learning his trade. He was taught 'how to walk, transfer ideas to an audience, how to speak clearly, sing and dance, but perhaps most importantly, to strip a script down to the syllable and get down to the basics of what is being said.'

He describes the place as 'a goldmine' and, while he was a student there, relished the fact that professional actors would come and share their knowledge and experience with the pupils, giving them a genuine insight into the reality of their chosen profession. 'It was a bit like having a soldier come in and tell you what weapons to use.'

In more recent years, Tom has chosen to repay the favour and has returned regularly to help teach students in the 'Acting for Camera' module of the course. He is passionate about giving something back to the profession he adores and, equally, the college has been more than happy for him to do so. As well as helping a new generation of actors he feels that, by teaching, he is able to build on his understanding of his profession. 'I love my craft and I don't like to see it abused. But I have to give it away to keep it – in doing so I can learn it again.'

To say that the course was the saving grace for the troubled youth, however, would be overstating it. Although he had been presented with a chance to do the one thing he felt he could have a shot at, the ruinous impulses were still very much in evidence and eventually he was kicked off the course for not turning up to classes. To complete any kind of qualification requires a level of discipline and a certain willingness to adhere to the rules – something that Tom still fought against. His addiction to excess was always lurking in the background and, only a few years later, he would hit the self-destruct button in a spectacular fashion. But, for now, his potentially lethal energy had found an alternative conduit.

Despite being too cool for school, the training that Tom undertook at Richmond Drama School enabled him to progress in his chosen sphere. Second time lucky, in 1998, he got himself a place to study for a degree in Drama. He originally had his sights set on the much more conventional RADA (Royal Academy of Dramatic Arts) but having failed to get in, he found himself at Drama Centre which, it could be said, was more of a fit for him. 'With my physique and bow legs, I ended up going to the Drama Centre, which is full of characters and dysfunctional types,' he commented in an interview in 2009. Step right in, Mr Hardy.

Today, Drama Centre is part of Central St Martins College of Art and is located in Clerkenwell, near Sadler's Wells Theatre. Back when Tom was a student, the college was housed in the unconventional setting of a former Methodist chapel near Chalk Farm station, a stone's throw from bustling Camden Market in North London. Although the aspiring actors have long gone, the building still stands and now houses a thriving exhibition space.

Drama Centre came into existence in 1963, when co-founders Christopher Fettes and the late Yat Malmgren broke away from the Central School of Speech and Drama to form their own acting school, taking a small group of students with them. Amongst this initial intake – imaginatively labelled Group 1 – were formidable young talents such as Jack Shepherd and Frances de la Tour.

Over the years, Drama Centre has developed something of a mythological status to those outside its walls, even those who are themselves in the business of acting. It is different from any other drama school and, to the uninitiated, it can appear at best exclusive and at worst somewhat cultish. The rarefied atmosphere it projects owes itself to the unique and specific method of teaching adopted there.

Its intense approach to the craft is based around the work of Malmgren, who developed his own methodology, marrying the movement analysis of Rudolf von Laban and the psychoanalysis of Carl Jung. This prescribed approach to acting became known as 'character analysis'. Drama Centre was – and is – the only drama school to teach in this way. 'Because it's only done at that place, it creates a lot of suspicion,' said a former Drama Centre student, who joined the school the year prior to Tom. 'There's masses of jargon, so the words I would use to describe a character would not be understood by someone who has not attended the Drama Centre. When you come out, you need to unlearn being there to get on with "normal" people.'

The school is undoubtedly a tough place to study. The hours are long, the work is intense and students are not necessarily nurtured in the same way as at other institutions – the faint-hearted need not apply. When Tom was a student, a typical day would start at 10am, with classes going on until 5.30pm. Once classes were finished, rehearsals for that session's end-of-term show would take place from 6pm until 9pm. In addition to coping with such a demanding time-table, students had to be hardy enough to deal with the feedback from tutors, which was often brutal – the ethos being to break a person down in order to build them back up again. Said the former student, 'They can be hideous to you the whole way through and then, by the third year, think you are marvellous.'

In an interview on the subject, famous Drama Centre alumnus Colin Firth recalled: 'I chose the Drama Centre because it had a reputation as a hard school, and I thought my resolve should be tested. Either you bend under pressure or you respond to the challenge. I can be very lazy and complacent unless I'm pushed, so I knew I'd be weeded out very quickly if I was making a mistake.'

Unrelenting it may have been, but for those with talent, resilience and determination there were huge rewards to be reaped. Some of the finest actors of their respective generations learned their trade there and have gone on to do remarkable work. Simon Callow, Tara Fitzgerald, Anne-Marie Duff and John Simm are all products of Drama Centre – some of whom Tom would find himself working alongside later in life.

So how did the young Tom Hardy, who had fought against applying himself in previous educational establishments, fare as a student in this fabled institution? It has been widely reported that he didn't stay the full three years of the course and was kicked out at the end of the first year for being, in his own words, 'a little shit' (though he did return to study for the second year). His personality and behaviour, however, were not actually markedly different from any of his contemporaries. He may have carried his share of troubles with him but he was in good company.

The fellow student observed: 'He was quite intense, but mostly he was an entertainer – he's a really funny guy. Much more known for telling jokes than for being dark and moody. He was a really positive person to be around, even if he was a bit tortured about stuff. He's mentally really fast and hungry for everything. He's a really intelligent guy whose brain ticks over at a rate of knots.'

When asked about Drama Centre, Tom acknowledges that the reputation of the place is, in part, founded upon the myths circulated by drama students from other schools. But he does confirm that a young actor there is stripped down with a particular intensity, which could be seen as a kind of 'tough love', as a preparation for the insanely competitive arena of acting where only 2 per cent of actors are ever in work. 'It's about terror. And the terror is actually about honesty – terror that is, in the term not to do with terrorism but in the term to do with: why do you want to be an actor? There are millions of people out there who want to be an actor. And even if you are any good at what you do, what makes you think you should be doing that? How hard are you prepared to work?'

And, for a while, Tom was prepared to work hard. During his time as a drama student, he appeared in productions of *Measure for Measure*, *Tartuffe*, *The Matchmaker*, *Ivanov*, *Filumena* and *Anatol*. In *Anatol*, it was Christopher Fettes himself who directed Tom. According to the fellow student: 'They didn't give Tom the easiest time but they obviously really liked him. He knows what to do. He knows what's funny, he knows how to time things. He seems really comfortable in it, intense as he is... he was always bloody good.'

Though Drama Centre was steering Tom towards the one career in which he truly felt he had a chance of success, he was still falling prey to his addictions and throughout his time as a student there, was drinking heavily and using drugs – as he put it, his vices were 'anything I could lay my hands on. You name it, I took it.'

As if the intensity of an acting degree at Drama Centre and the chaos of his addictions wasn't enough to keep Tom distracted from himself, he then experienced another life-changing event. True to form, it was erratic and spontaneous. As 1998 drew to a close, while he was out and about in London's Covent Garden, Tom met a production assistant (now producer) Sarah Ward. Something clicked between the pair and, three weeks after setting eyes on each other, they got married. It was, according to Tom, 'pretty crazy but very exciting at the same time'.

Whatever the circumstances surrounding this whirlwind relationship, there can be no doubt about the strength of Tom's feelings for Ward. Although the marriage would, in the end, not withstand the insurmountable obstacle of Tom's addictions, his feelings for her were genuine. 'I loved Sarah and I still do and we married for all the right reasons,' he told Nick Curtis of the *Evening Standard* in 2006. 'I feel she saved my life on numerous occasions. But in hindsight, we didn't have the best reasons to stay married, for the health of everyone involved.'

Like so many of those who are dear to Tom or who have played a significant part in his life, Ward has been commemorated in one of his many pieces of body art. On the right-hand side of his lower torso, roughly parallel with his belly button, is inscribed in large letters 'Till I die SW'. The dragon on Tom's left arm is also a tribute to Ward, who was born in the Chinese year of the dragon. In recent years, Tom has admitted that the dragon tattoo was 'a mistake' and has even tattooed over some of the places on his body where her initials were etched, in one instance with a rock design.

For Tom, however, his tattoos are more than mere decoration. He has admitted that, in his younger days, they existed as a way for him to disguise who he really was, a means of drawing attention away from the unease of his existence. As he has gone through life, he has continued to add tattoos to his body and they now collectively serve as reference points to his life. 'Every tattoo I have means something to me. Each one is something that I've been through in my life or I've done, or I've been. So I map that out on me, where I've been and where I'm going.'

Despite such a multitude of distractions in his personal life, Tom did in fact return to drama school in order to complete his second year. True, he had been thrown out at the end of year one, but this was not an uncommon occurrence. During the second year, though, things changed for Tom in quite a major way, thanks to a casting director called Gary Davy.

The previous year, Davy had seen a photo of Tom in *Male Vogue*, from his modelling days. He had spotted something in Tom's look that he felt would be right for the lead role in a forthcoming film he was casting. At the time, however, Tom was in the throes of his degree course and turned down the role in order to continue with his studies. A sensible move, but the young actor must have made quite an impression on Davy and, the following year, Davy contacted him again. This time, he was working as the casting director on an HBO miniseries with Steven Spielberg and Tom Hanks at the helm. He wanted to cast Tom in the show and, this time, the offer was too tempting to refuse. Serendipity, and of course raw talent, had propelled Tom straight from drama school into the world of high-profile, big-budget television drama. *Band of Brothers* was to prove both a critical and ratings success and is a project any actor would be proud to have been involved in, however large or small their role.

In a prescient comment made to *The Stage* in 2004, Davy reflected on why he pinpointed Tom for the role: 'From the moment I met him, I knew how important he was going to be. I simply knew he was going to be a star.'

How right Davy has proved to be. In recent months, with Tom being cast in bigger roles and teetering on the cusp of breaking into Hollywood, it is obvious that he is set to be one of the most prolific actors of his generation. While continuing to gain critical acclaim, he is also now starting to be something of a box-office draw – if his name is attached to a film, cinema-goers are starting to sit up and take notice. Back then, however, it was the expert eye of a professional who had the foresight to see the natural, raw talent which could, if harnessed correctly, go on to create a superstar.

The route to success is seldom easy and Tom was to encounter some major setbacks on his way. To all intents and purposes, he was making inroads into acting and even finding himself attached to worthy projects – to be plucked from drama school and land a role in a major television series is quite a rarity. On the surface, he was throwing himself into a new career; just below, however, still lurked his addictions and insecurities. It would not take long for the balance to shift and for the dark to eclipse the light.

CHAPTER TWO

SOLDIER, SOLDIER

The first ever glimpse of Tom Hardy on screen is one that still brings delight to his legions of female fans should they choose to seek it out on YouTube or pause it on their DVD player. His first appearance in *Band of Brothers* is in a rather unexpected bedroom scene in which his character, Private John Janovec, gets to know a member of the local female population in Sturzelberg, Germany during the final months of World War II. Blink and you might miss it, but eagle-eyed devotees of the Hardy physique are even treated to a brief glimpse of the actor's backside.

Tom's role in the ensemble drama was not a major one and he only appeared in the final two episodes of the 10-part series. However great or small a part, it was the most amazing start for an actor who hadn't even completed his training. To be cast in a Steven Spielberg and Tom Hanks television production is a dream come true for any actor – and for one just starting out, it was the luckiest of breaks.

Band of Brothers is one of the most revered and respected television miniseries ever broadcast. Based on the best-selling book by World War II historian Stephen E. Ambrose, it follows the journey of Easy Company, 506th Parachute Infantry Regiment, 101st Airborne Division, and charts their experiences from the start of their training in Georgia, parachuting into Normandy on D-Day, taking part in Operation Market Garden, the Battle of the Bulge, the discovery of one of the concentration camps at Dachau, through to the capture of Hitler's Eagle's Nest and the end of the war.

At the time it was made, the series broke the record for the most expensive television production, costing $120 million to put together. Hanks and Spielberg, fresh from the success of the movie *Saving Private Ryan* (which Spielberg had directed and in which Hanks had starred), were originally intending to make separate World War II dramas but eventually decided to collaborate rather than compete and began work on Hanks' project of the adaptation of *Band of Brothers*. They had drawn on Stephen E Ambrose's wealth of knowledge of the period for *Saving Private Ryan* and, as well as providing the original material for *Band of Brothers*, he was also enlisted as Executive Producer on the show.

Hanks and Spielberg were actively involved in the casting of the actors who would make up the 50 soldiers whose stories would be followed through the series. It was critical for them to find exactly the right actors to play each man for two reasons: firstly, the men needed to bond as a unit, and secondly, each actor needed to be able to do justice to the experience of the real veteran they were portraying.

One key aspect of casting was the desire to use little-known actors to fill the roles of the men of Easy Company, a decision which helped to give the show the all-important feeling of an ensemble piece. It also meant that audiences wouldn't have preconceived opinions of the actors playing the men of Easy Company. One notable exception to this was the casting of *Friends* star David Schwimmer as Captain Sobel.

It is well documented that, during casting, Spielberg was in charge behind the camera and Tom Hanks staged the acting, keeping his eye on actors who seemed to bond and who appeared appropriate for particular roles. Apparently, though, when casting the leading roles of Major Dick Winters and Captain Lewis Nixon, they knew they had found their men almost as soon as they entered the room. Tom Hanks had met and spent time with Dick Winters and knew he needed a certain kind of actor to do justice to such an outstanding soldier and leader: the role went to up-and-coming English actor, Damian Lewis. The part of Lewis Nixon went to American actor Ron Livingston. As it turned out, the series proved to be a springboard for a number of lesser-known young British actors who have since gone on to become stars in their own right: James McAvoy, Michael Fassbender, Simon Pegg, Marc Warren and, of course, Tom Hardy, to name just a few.

All of the actors, including Tom, appreciated that they were portraying real people and that they had a duty to the men and their families to make sure they gave the best and most accurate performances they possibly could. Speaking to *IGN Movies*, Tom reflected on his approach to the part: 'I was in two episodes and had 12 lines. That was the sum total of the work I had to do. But nonetheless, I would work just as hard trying to portray someone whose relatives are still around. Obviously, nobody wants to go out there and say, "This is my big moment". And I'm playing John Janovec, who is dead. He died for freedom. So, yes, you have to approach that.'

The bond between the men who fought side by side in Easy Company was an extraordinary and unique one and it was vital that the relationships between them were understood and felt by the actors in the ensemble. To achieve the feeling of unity, the final group of 50 actors who constituted the men of the company were sent on an intensive 10-day bootcamp under the command of Captain Dale Dye, who was also the military adviser on the series. They endured 18-hour days and military drills and what had started as a group of actors transformed into something else – it gradually became a functioning unit.

The plethora of young Brits cast in the American drama might have had something to do with the location for filming. The series was made at the Hatfield Aerodrome in Hertfordshire in the South East of England. Now no longer in existence, the lot was then over 1,000 acres in size and housed disused hangars that proved ideal spaces for building sets. The producers were already familiar with the aerodrome, as parts of *Saving Private Ryan* had been filmed there. At the time, Tom Hanks said: 'England is a wonderful place to make films, and as the experience of making *Saving Private Ryan* made clear to us all, it is an ideal place to make this ambitious miniseries.'

Shooting took place in 2000 and lasted eight months. Each episode of the series had a different director at its helm, with Hanks himself directing Episode Three, *Crossroads*. Despite the array of directors, great care was taken to ensure that there was continuity in character and style for the duration of the ten episodes.

For Tom Hardy, to be plucked from drama school and plunged right into the middle of such an epic production was at once breathtakingly exciting and incredibly daunting. As well as this being his debut on screen, Tom had the added pressure of knowing that he had to film his first bedroom scene – a nerve-wracking experience even for a seasoned actor, let alone a rookie. 'Everything was happening fast and it felt wonderful,' he said to the *Evening Standard* in 2006. 'I had never acted for the camera. It's a huge set, it's Tom Hanks, it's Steven Spielberg, and no expense spared. I felt very exposed, isolated and vulnerable. I had to do my first sex scenes, which were terrifying. But at the time I thought I should never ask for help, and I kept thinking, "If I cock up, I'll never work again".'

Speaking about the awkwardness around his opening scenes, Tom revealed to *Esquire* magazine: 'I was terrified! It wasn't half as closed a set as I thought it was gonna be. They kept saying they could see my pants, so I wound up with a flesh-coloured pouch gaffer-taped over me balls! Took a load of hair out when I ripped it of after. Band of Brazilians, more like!'

The soldier whom Tom was portraying, Private John Janovec first appears in Episode Nine, *Why We Fight*. There are so many intensely emotional moments in *Band of Brothers*, but this particular episode contains one of the most poignant scenes of the series. Easy Company by this time (1945) is in Germany during the last days of the war. The statement that forms the title of this episode is one pondered amongst the soldiers who begin to ask themselves if the sacrifices they have made have been worth it. The question is answered for them when they discover a concentration camp that formed part of the Dachau complex and come face to face with the atrocities committed by the Nazis.

Episode 10, *Points*, the final episode of the series, centres around Easy Company entering Berchtesgaden to take Hitler's Bavarian mountaintop retreat, the Eagle's Nest. By this time, the war was all but over and the men were left with time on their hands and were anxious to get home. Before his turn comes to return to the USA, Private Janovec is involved in a road accident, suffers a fractured skull and subsequently dies. His conversation with a fellow soldier, Webster, just before the accident is of how many 'points' he has accrued on his service record and how soon he might be able to go home. It was a significant scene to include in the drama and one which demonstrates another heartbreaking injustice of war: in this instance that, even when the men were no longer in combat, there were still casualties.

The miniseries was first aired in the United States in September 2001, shortly before the attacks on the World Trade Center. Its debut in the UK followed in October. While audiences and critics, particularly in the UK, marvelled at the expense that had gone into making the show, most agreed that it was a remarkable achievement. Of course, there was the inevitable criticism from British audiences that the show was another example of Americans giving a biased depiction of events during World War II – but to offer this up as criticism is to rather miss the point of what was at the heart of the series. It succeeded in what it set out to do, which was to offer a faithful and compelling portrayal of what this particular group of men experienced when they went to war. Those men who had fought with Easy Company and were still alive when the series premiered confirmed that the show was an authentic representation of what they had been through.

With his first small-screen outing under his belt, Tom was hungry for more work. Luckily for him, the next job in his diary was a part in a Ridley Scott movie – the young actor really was on a roll. Once again, Tom would be playing an American soldier, but this time he would be recreating a more modern chapter of US military history.

Although set almost 50 years and thousands of miles apart, there are common threads running through *Band of Brothers* and *Black Hawk Down*. The subject matter of both is drawn from actual historical events and uses the recollections of the people who participated in those events. They also share similar themes such as comradeship, loss, a sense of belonging and a desire to be the very best at what you do.

Black Hawk Down tells the true story of a battle between US forces and Somali militia. In 1993, Somalia was a country torn apart by warring factions. Relief was not getting through to starving civilians, with much of it being hijacked by warlords. General Mohammed Ali Farrah Aidid was widely considered to be the worst of the warlords and challenged the presence of the UN and US troops in Somalia, even specifically targeting American troops. A previous attempt by US forces to capture Aidid in a safe house in Mogadishu had failed and, in October 1993, a task force was deployed to capture some of Aidid's key men. The mission went catastrophically wrong and, during its course, two Black Hawk helicopters were brought down by Somali RPGs (rocket-propelled grenades) and went crashing into enemy territory. Elite US Ranger and Delta regiments were then engaged in a 15-hour effort to rescue their own men. During the course of the mission, 18 US soldiers lost their lives. *Black Hawk Down* recalls the events of the disastrous mission and the men who were involved.

The film was a major production, boasting big names and a big budget to match: it was produced by Hollywood big-shot Jerry Bruckheimer and directed by Ridley Scott. An accomplished director held in high regard, Scott was clear on what he wanted the film's focus to be – it was to cover the insertion of the troops into Mogadishu, their exit and what they felt afterwards. The narrative was kept simple: no back stories were given for the soldiers, nor did they talk about their personal lives. It was a film that dealt purely with the horror of the events that took place and the actions of the men who were involved.

Just as authenticity had been paramount for *Band of Brothers*, so it was for *Black Hawk Down*. Just as the *Band of Brothers* actors had attended bootcamp, so the actors who were to play the soldiers in *Black Hawk Down* were required to attend 'Ranger Orientation' in order to experience the kind of training that real soldiers have to undertake. They also needed to understand the ethos of the Rangers: the respect they have for authority and the bond they have with their fellow soldiers. As Eric Bana's character Hoot puts it in the film: 'It's about the men next to you. That's it. That's all it is.'

The actors weren't spared at all when they turned up for bootcamp: the first thing they had to endure was having their hair shaved off. Once they had been made to look like soldiers, they then underwent days of gruelling combat and movement training, as well as gun skills so that they gave the impression of being real soldiers on screen.

Just as he had been when making *Band of Brothers*, Tom was acutely aware that he was representing a real soldier, Lance Twombly, and that he had a responsibility to that man when it came to portraying him in the movie. 'Lance Twombly, who is still alive, he still lives with the demons. There are these people who have fought and will fight and will die. It's a responsibility if you're going to go in there and play a character like that, and the pressure is enormous.'

A desire for realism fell not only to the actors but also to the director. He was all too aware that he was dealing with relatively recent events and that he couldn't take liberties with accuracy. 'When it's so recent and vivid, you can't diddle around with it, you can't romanticise it,' Scott expressed to the *Guardian* in 2002. His desire to adhere to the truth also manifested itself in his attention to detail. He was determined to use real Black Hawk helicopters in his film, as to have anything else would have compromised authenticity. Only the US government have Black Hawks and in order to gain permission to borrow their 'birds', protracted negotiations about how the military were represented in the film had to be undertaken with the Pentagon. It was only at the eleventh hour that Scott found out he had permission to use the helicopters (and in fact had to rearrange the shooting schedule to accommodate this delay).

Ridley Scott is a director who always has a clear idea of what he wants to achieve when he's shooting and, according to one of *Black Hawk Down*'s stars, Ewan McGregor, he shoots as he wants to edit the film. He wanted the combat and the reactions of the soldiers in the film to look as realistic as possible. This was partly achieved by the actors not being aware of when or where exactly there would be explosions and gunfire while filming was taking place. Therefore many of the reactions you see on screen are ones of genuine shock and surprise. And even with the explosions and gunfire and other background noise, they were all expected just to get on with delivering their lines and filming the scenes. 'It's massive,' commented Tom during the filming of the movie, 'a huge barrage of orchestrated violence.'

During the film, Tom's character, Lance Twombly, and his friend, Nelson, played by Ewen Bremner, become separated from the troops they are with when some of the Rangers leave their position in order to secure the helicopter crash site. For quite some time the two characters are left on their own and the light-hearted dialogue between them provides some relief from the incessant gunfire and explosions occurring throughout other scenes in the film. At one point, Twombly accidentally deafens Nelson when he fires his rifle too close to his head.

The realism of the combat in *Black Hawk Down* was something critics picked up on when the film hit cinemas at the start of 2002. While they noted the film avoided venturing into the territory of political comment or international relations, they acknowledged that, technically, Scott had achieved something remarkable. In fact, the grit and relentlessness of the combat was compared to the realism of some of the fighting recreated in *Band of Brothers*. Philip French of the *Observer* went so far as to say that *Black Hawk Down* was 'one of the most convincing, realistic combat movies I've ever seen, a film presenting a confused event with clarity and involving us as if we were there in the thick of the fray.'

Tom shared his director's desire for realism and embraced the reality of his role wholeheartedly. In one scene, just as Twombly is reunited with his fellow rangers and is running across open space to rejoin them, he is fired upon by the enemy and catches fire. Ordinarily, this action sequence would have been undertaken by a stunt man but Hardy was desperate to do it himself and, in the end, Ridley Scott agreed. Since his teens, Tom had thrived on risk-taking behaviour, from alcohol to drug-taking to criminal activities, and now that he was acting for a living, he still seemed to crave the thrill of living dangerously. 'I begged them to blow me up and they blew me up and I feel great – I feel born again. I want more, though, I want it to be bigger,' he commented while working on the film. Speaking to the *Observer* in 2007, he was philosophical about his motivation for carrying out this dangerous stunt himself – '...it's about feeling alive – and maybe that's only possible in the presence of death.'

Some years prior to landing his first acting jobs, Tom had expressed to his mother a desire to go and join the French Foreign Legion. She persuaded him not to enlist, on the basis that he wouldn't last five minutes. In 2001, Tom found himself cast once again as a soldier in an adaptation based on true events – and, ironically, he was to play a Legionnaire.

The filming of *Black Hawk Down* had taken place on location in Morocco and Tom found himself back there enduring the scorching heat of the desert for this next role in

Simon: An English Legionnaire (also called *Deserter*). While the film gave the young actor a much bigger role and the opportunity to flex his acting muscles a bit more, as a production it garnered much less attention than either *Band of Brothers* or *Black Hawk Down*.

The film is based on the memoirs of Simon Murray's time spent in the French Foreign Legion in Algeria at the time of the Algerian War of Independence (1954 to 1962). Murray enlists in the Foreign Legion after being rejected by his girlfriend, Jennifer and arrives in Algeria to find that life as a Legionnaire is far more brutal than he had imagined. Nevertheless, he befriends some of his fellow soldiers, including the Frenchman Pascal Dupont, played by Tom (this time losing the American accent and gaining a Gallic one).

Although the opening of the film did not attract vast swathes of media attention, by contrast, the nature of the film's inception did. It was reported that Sarah Ferguson, Duchess of York, had read the book and passed it on to her friend, director Martin Huberty, urging him to bring it to the big screen. At the time of the film's release, she commented: 'I recommended the book to Martin, and am delighted to have played a small part in the film's coming to life.'

Though beautifully filmed and effectively recounted, the film proved to be a tough sell and although Tom's role was a supporting one, his reviews were more positive than those for Paul Fox who had taken the title role of Simon. 'As played by Fox, Simon is disconcertingly passive, especially when compared with the angry and more driven Dupont,' was the comment offered by *Variety*.

While Tom was dramatising the events that had changed

the path of Algeria's history, the international landscape as it was in 2001 was about to change beyond recognition. The 11 September terrorist attacks sent shockwaves around the globe as people struggled to comprehend what had taken place in the USA and how it would affect the world in months and years to come. Events of these proportions remain seared on the consciousness for a very long time and most people can remember exactly where they were and what they were doing when they learned of news of this magnitude, and Tom was no exception, particularly given his location at the time.

'We'd just done *Black Hawk Down* and they shelved that immediately,' he recalled when speaking to *The Wrap*. 'There were a lot of war films that year being made. A lot of work was being done in North Africa. Everyone had started panicking. And I was executing holy men in a scene three days later in a mosque in Morocco. It was a thing called *Simon, French Foreign Legion Deserter*. So it was a very odd situation to be in because there I was playing a soldier in North Africa. We had a plane on standby to get us out if anything kicked off.'

Tom went on to reflect on the effect the attacks had on him on a more personal level, too. 'Immediately, it was a life-changing event. I have friends who serve, I have a lot of friends in special forces, I have very, very close friends who deal in very serious operations all over the Middle East that were affected post-9/11. I'm still really thrown by the loss and the amount of people on that day, and that whole situation, to be honest. I'm a bit thrown. I've got friends who were in the building, in the twin towers. I have friends who are servicemen, what can you say?'

Years later, in 2007, Tom found himself coming a bit too

close to a genuine soldier's life for comfort. He had auditioned unsuccessfully for an American series called *Generation Kill* – the part he wanted was that of a Marine during the 2003 American invasion of Iraq. By this time, Tom had a bulkier and more toned physique and was training regularly. Plus, he was being recognised for his tough guy characters, so it would be fair to assume that he would be a dead cert for the role. Sadly, it was not to be, but something about the rejection made Tom determined to prove to himself that he was made of the right stuff to be a solider. In a decidedly impulsive move, he took himself off to an induction with the Parachute Regiment in the Territorial Army. Fortunately for all concerned, when Tom realised the scale of the commitment – and that he may well be sent into active combat – both he and the military recruiters realised it was not really an option for him. 'I started to ask questions, so they soon got me out. That finished all that macho bollocks for me. But I sucked up the environment, I absorbed a few more characters,' he explained to the *Observer*.

Tom's part in *Simon, An English Legionnaire* had rather gone under the radar, along with the film itself. Just around the corner, though, lay a part that would draw more attention to him than he could possibly have imagined. He was about to embark on a starring role in one of the biggest television and movie franchises in the world. How would the up-and-coming actor cope with the scrutiny of die-hard fans? And how would he cope with the responsibility of a major Hollywood role?

CHAPTER THREE

THE GUTTER AND THE STARS

For any actor, taking on a role in a long-established franchise is an endeavour that brings both pleasure and pain. On the one hand, it is a sure-fire way of raising the profile and is usually a lucrative pursuit. Johnny Depp, star of the blockbusting *Pirates of the Caribbean* franchise, has stated that he is paid 'stupid money' for making the movies and chooses to justify the pay cheque on the grounds that he is earning the money for his children's futures. On the other hand, fans of established franchises tend to have strident opinions on the direction of the series and are notoriously choosy about which actors are cast in certain roles. Daniel Craig is a prime example of a fine character actor who found himself thrown into the limelight in 2005 when it was announced he was to be the new James Bond. Before he'd even had a chance to prove himself, Bond aficionados made no secret of their doubts over the choice of Craig as the next 007. As it happened, Craig was arguably one of the best

Bonds ever and rapidly hushed the naysayers with his rebooted spy. It takes a resilient actor to handle such pressure and an intelligent one to silence the critics.

Coming into a franchise as long-standing and with such a fanatical following as *Star Trek* was never going to be easy, and any actor doing so would be sure to elicit a vociferous response from Trekkies. The original television series aired back in 1966 and, since then, the format has been reinvented for new generations of fans. After the original series, the show was recast as *Star Trek: The Next Generation*, which ran from 1987 to 1994.

The 2002 film, *Star Trek: Nemesis*, was the 10th film in the *Star Trek* franchise and the fourth (and final) one to feature the characters from the television series of *Next Generation*. The plot of *Nemesis* unfolds as the Starship Enterprise undertakes a journey to a planet called Romulus, the Star Fleet crew believing that the Romulans want to broker peace and negotiate a truce. As they head towards the Romulan Empire, they discover a villainous clone of the Enterprise's captain, Jean-Luc Picard (played by Patrick Stewart) who is planning an attack on Earth. The clone, Shinzon (played by Tom), is the result of an experiment conducted by the Romulans in an attempt to take Picard's place on the Enterprise and use the clone as a spy – but after a change in Romulan government, the clone plan is shelved and Shinzon is sent to Remus as a slave. Having been cast aside on Remus, Shinzon plots his power grab. According to Patrick Stewart, the original intention was not for there to be a clone but for Picard to find a long-lost son, but the actor, amongst others, felt that this might make for too sentimental a storyline.

The story raises interesting issues, such as how far a person's character is formed from their genetic blueprint and to what degree they are influenced by their environment. Shinzon is theoretically the same as Picard but has grown up surrounded by beings from different races – and has been treated badly by them.

From the outset, director Stuart Baird and producer Rick Berman had clear ideas about the kind of actor they were looking for to play Shinzon. For a start, the character is a clone of Picard (albeit 25 years younger), so the right candidate had to bear some resemblance to him. He also needed to be an actor with the ability to tap into the darker side of human nature in order to portray a complex and tortured villain. Additionally, the actor in question had to be assured enough to star opposite not only one of the most respected actors of his generation but also the man who had so successfully inhabited the skin of Captain Picard for 16 years.

The search for Shinzon was a lengthy one, with the part at one point apparently being intended for Jude Law. Baird ultimately decided, though, that he wanted an unknown actor for the part. Also paramount was to find someone with sex appeal and who would attract younger fans to the film. Casting directors scoured the UK for their man and six actors were screen tested for the role before they eventually alighted upon Tom, who turned out to have just the right ingredients for the part. 'He had an edge ... a street feel,' said Baird.

The audition process, though, was anything but easy. At the time of casting, Tom was still out in Morocco filming *Simon, An English Legionnaire*. It transpired that his agent had been contacted by Patrick Stewart who wanted to find out if she knew of any actors who would be a reasonable fit for the part of Picard's evil clone. She knew just the young man and, naturally, Tom jumped at the chance to take on a major Hollywood role. Particular pages from the script were sent out to him in Morocco but, true to his non-conformist style, he managed to get hold of the script in its entirety and elected to use other parts of it for the audition tape he was making. Even more unconventionally, he chose to deliver some of the dialogue to camera in the nude. The maverick nature of his tape appealed to Stuart Baird and also to Patrick Stewart, who commented: 'I was riveted by it and Rick [Berman] was too... I said, "There's something very odd about this fellow, but I think we should see him."' Having made quite an impression, Tom got the call to go to LA for a screen test.

Poised for what could be his big break into Hollywood, Tom was understandably nervous and, on his arrival in LA, was unexpectedly given the full Tinseltown star treatment. The night before the screen test, he was whisked from the airport to a sumptuous hotel in a chauffeur-driven limousine. Unable to believe his luck, he got out his video camera and excitedly filmed his luxurious room as a memento to show his wife, Sarah, and family back at home. 'And then, suddenly, I realised it was a school day next day. I had serious work to do. Prepare. Panic, panic. So I filmed myself doing my serious work – which is something I do – going through the script again. It was just in case... Whatever happened in this screen test, I've got this on tape, doing my stuff in a relaxed environment – how I want to play this character,' he explained to *SFX* magazine.

Unfortunately for Tom, the following day, his nerves got the better of him and the screen test turned out to be little short of disastrous. 'I was supposed to be this incredible villain and instead I'm a quivering nervous wreck, waiting to be exposed and sent back to Britain. Then Patrick Stewart comes in dressed as Picard in his Star Fleet uniform and we did the scene and it was terrible, I mean awful, I was appalling,' he told the *Sun* in 2002.

Despite the disappointing performance, Tom was determined not to lose out on the part and insisted that Baird take a look at the character and script work he had recorded on his camera the previous night. His preference would have been for the director to have seen only his acting, not the part of the tape in which he had been showing off his Hollywood hotel and, as he put it, 'messing around in my boxers.' Unfortunately, there were no videotape editors on hand at the studio to extract the relevant part of the tape, so Tom was obliged to hand it over in its entirety, scantily-clad antics and all. One can only imagine the dreadful sinking feeling he must have experienced as the handed over the tape. Having resigned himself to having blown his big chance, he was pleasantly surprised when he was offered the part a few days later.

Winning the part was just the first step of a challenging process. Tom has admitted that, while he was aware of *Star Trek*, he had never been a Trekkie, so had to immerse himself in the programme's history and characters. He was also acutely aware of the pressure that came with a major role in a big-budget franchise film: 'To be 23 or 24 and have that kind of money on my shoulders... I thought, if you f**k this up, Hardy... to be aware you're holding that kind of weight

– it was a huge deal for me,' he explained to the *Sunday Times* in 2006.

When it came to taking Shinzon from script to screen, it was clear that he would not succeed as a character in his own right if he was played as simply an impression of Picard. While Tom did pay attention to certain physical aspects of the Picard character, when it came to the essence of Shinzon, he brought his own interpretation to the nature of his villainy. In an interview with *IGN Movies*, Tom explained how he set about differentiating Shinzon from Picard so that he might give him some depth: 'In order to make this gentleman three-dimensional as opposed to one-dimensional, I had to find a human issue on him. And that means I don't have to copy or mimic anything that Patrick does at all. Which is very free, because then all the sudden [sic] you have a foundation to develop a character.'

Later in his career, Tom would garner huge acclaim for his powerhouse performances as dark or disturbed characters (*Oliver Twist*'s Bill Sikes, Charles Bronson, *The Take*'s Freddie Jackson). His success in bringing these kinds of characters to life is in part down to his skill at seeing both the light as well as the shade in the characters he plays. He has explained that, if a character he is studying is essentially a dark character, he searches for the light in him and vice versa. Preparing for Shinzon – one of the first of such types he was to take on for the big screen – was no different. A hard worker and an actor who always strives to do better, Tom threw himself into capturing the opposing forces that made Shinzon complex and three-dimensional. Speaking to the *LA Times*, he commented: 'He's a monster, but he's also a product of circumstances who's deeply in pain.' Thankfully, the new *Star Trek* villain was in very capable hands. There would be no pantomime baddie performance from Tom.

Looks-wise, Tom and Patrick Stewart were not dissimilar – Stewart even commented that Tom was 'the spitting image of me as a young man' – but Tom's physical appearance still had to be tweaked so that he genuinely looked as if he could have been created from the same DNA as his nemesis. One of the most noticeable things about Patrick Stewart's – and therefore Picard's – appearance is his baldness, so the hair clearly had to go. This was not a problem, as Tom had not long had his hair shaved off for his role in *Simon: An English Legionnaire* and so was no stranger to sporting a hairless pate. Tom's lips were, unsurprisingly, slightly bigger that Stewart's and this difference was addressed by making a fake scar for Tom's mouth which gave his lips a look that was, as he put it, 'slightly beaten'. The make-up team then went even further and took a cast of Patrick Stewart's nose and chin to make latex replicas of them for Tom to wear. Tom explained the lengths to which they went in order to achieve the likeness to *Trekweb.com*: 'We moulded the nose – several thousand noses, I think – before we got the right nose. Then, because my lips are slightly larger, we added a scar to take down the size of my lips. We had all this ready to go in latex but we had gelatine as well and under the lights my nose would sort of grow – and then sag.'

And while the costume Tom had to wear for the film was somewhat uncomfortable, he claimed its restrictive design actually assisted with his embodiment of the character of Shinzon. 'It was incredibly uncomfortable, and within that being uncomfortable it added to the character for me. You know what I mean? Because he's a very bowed and repressed young man. That whole suit was very constricting and it didn't allow much movement because his whole life hasn't allowed much movement,' he explained to *IGN Movies* website. It certainly looked impressive on screen in all its rubber glory, but its spectacular appearance came at a price and Tom admitted that he'd needed physio on his back after spending so many hours encased in it!

Naturally, when it came to being on set, Tom spent the majority of his time working alongside Patrick Stewart. The young actor was conscious of the fact that he was relatively new to the game and, while it was a daunting prospect to star opposite someone as esteemed as Stewart, he took the opportunity to benefit from the wealth of the older actor's experience. The pair took the time to sit and talk through their thoughts on what would work for their characters and Tom allowed himself to learn from the more seasoned actors around him. While on set, Stewart had plenty of time for Tom, but was mindful of the fact that, because of the nature of their on-screen relationship, it would be wise to keep a bit of distance between them: in other words, it wouldn't benefit the dynamic of the film if they were to become best mates. 'I didn't want him to be someone I could have a beer with. It would have showed. But I liked him a lot,' Stewart remarked.

As well as being relatively new to professional acting, Tom also had to cope with being a late addition to a long-established family of actors, the majority of whom were all *Star Trek* old hands. Although they were inclusive and welcoming, Tom realised that, by stepping into the scenario as a villain, it was slightly easier for him to establish himself amongst them. The nature of his role meant that it was acceptable for him to fall outside the camaraderie of the main group of actors. 'It was a group who are very accepting … It was quite bizarre having so many people who knew what they were doing – it was lucky that I was a villain, in many ways,' he said.

There was one cast member in particular with whom Tom got on like a house on fire. Ron Perlman, who plays the Reman viceroy Vkruk in the film, is an experienced Hollywood actor who has appeared in countless movies and television series. Since *Star Trek: Nemesis*, Perlman is best known to cinema audiences for his role in the *Hellboy* movie franchise. Tom found it a pleasure to work with Perlman and has stated how generous and funny he was as a colleague on set. In more recent years, Perlman has expressed how much he enjoyed spending time with Tom and how delighted he is that Tom is now so in demand as an actor. Speaking to *Startrek. com* to commemorate the eight-year anniversary of the release of *Star Trek: Nemesis*, Perlman reflected generously: 'Tom has become probably one of the most sought-after actors in the world. Did you see this movie he did, *Bronson*? It was brilliant. And now Tom is in everything. I loved him when I first met him. I loved working with him. I found him to be really smart, really a great kid. He was much younger then. He was also really humble and knew that he was kind of living a charmed life by playing major roles in major motion pictures. Everything I like about an actor was in this kid, and I'm so happy to see what's happening to him now.'

Once the film had wrapped, Tom had a promise to keep before he flew home to the UK. He had told his agent, Lindy King, that if she got him into Hollywood, he would honour her by having her name tattooed on his arm. If you look closely, on the inside of Tom's left arm, just above the elbow joint, you can see Lindy's name just below a tattoo of a crown.

Amongst the *Star Trek* fraternity, there exists a theory that even-numbered *Star Trek* films are always good. Sadly, this theory didn't hold water when it came to their opinions of *Star Trek: Nemesis* which, as the 10th movie in the series, should by rights have been a cracker. Amongst Trekkies, there were rumblings of discontent when it came to light that director Stuart Baird was not intimately acquainted with existing material and apparently hadn't attempted to do any research in the same way that other new *Trek* directors had in the past. On the whole, fans seemed to find the film bland and unimaginative.

For critics, their disapproval largely arose from the fact that the *Next Generation* part of the franchise was now past its sell-by date, and *Star Trek: Nemesis* seemed to have made no effort to breathe new life into it. As Anthony Quinn quipped in the *Independent*: 'It's another *Star Trek* movie, the 10th in a series that's still boldly going where most franchises would have called it a day.'

In fact, the film did signal the end of the *Next Generation* series and was judged by Patrick Stewart to be 'a suitable farewell. A number of us feel we don't want to outstay our welcome.' It appeared they may have already done just that.

Although the film did not fare well from the sharp tongues of the critics, Tom was widely praised for his performance.

He even won himself a nomination for a Saturn Award from the Academy of Science Fiction and Fantasy in the Best Supporting Actor category (the award was ultimately won by Sean Astin for his part in the third instalment of the *Lord of the Rings* trilogy, *The Return of the King*). The British media jumped on the role of Shinzon as being Tom's big break and proclaimed him to be the next big thing in British acting. *Variety* wrote that he showed 'charisma in a stock villain role that should (given the circumstances) have been written with more dimensionality.'

One American critic, Michael Kleinschrodt described him as the film's 'best surprise,' going on to say: 'The young man has no trouble holding his own in scene after scene opposite Stewart, a fair indication that he might just have a stellar career ahead of him.' It was a reasonable assumption to make, given the awesome show of talent from the young actor so far. And Tom did have a 'stellar career' ahead of him – but it would take almost a decade for him to get everything in the right place and show the world what he was capable of.

Star Trek was not the only project Tom had been working on at this time, but it was without doubt the most high profile and it brought with it the burden of expectation. Unfortunately, the next few releases with his name attached to them were either unremarkable or Tom's role in them was something of a 'blink and you miss him' experience. None of the films provided that vital stepping stone he needed to capitalise on his new-found recognition.

The Reckoning, released in 2003, is a medieval murder mystery with an impressive cast headed up by Willem Dafoe and Paul Bettany. The plot concerns a priest (Bettany) who flees his village after being caught having sex with a married woman. Whilst on the run, he encounters a travelling theatre troupe that traverses the country performing morality plays. They reluctantly allow him to join and subsequently find themselves at the centre of a genuine murder mystery. Tom's role in the film is that of a member of the travelling players. It's not a lead role and he's very much in the background of the action. The one thing that may just spark a bit of interest among Hardy devotees is that his character is more often than not required to take on the parts of female characters in the morality plays, so he is often dressed in women's clothing and sporting make-up on camera. Excerpts for a 'before they were famous' set of clips in the future, perhaps.

In the promotional puff, *Dot the I* was billed as a love story with a psychological twist. While at first it seems to be the intriguing tale of a love triangle, it eventually descends into a rather silly plot in which the denouement takes on more importance than the characters involved. Writing in *Variety*, David Rooney was pretty categorical in his dismissal of the film, commenting: 'Behind its slick veneer and the glibness of its preposterous premise and dark twists, there's a yawning absence of charm or substance in this London-set love triangle, as well as a lack of chemistry between its three leads.' The three lead characters were played by Gael Garcia Bernal, James D'Arcy and Natalia Verbeke, while Tom's character (also called Tom) was a more minor role and was, along with Charlie Cox, Kit's (Bernal) friend. Between the two of them, they provided some light-hearted relief from the mayhem of the rest of the story.

Finally, *LD50* was filmed between October 2002 and early

2003 (also the year of its release). In it, Tom plays a character called Matt, a member of a group of animal rights activists. Having been involved in animal liberation raids on research laboratories in the past, this time the group reunite to rescue a friend who was left behind at a facility when a previous raid was interrupted. The group receives a message indicating that their friend is being subjected to a traumatic ordeal. Their mercy mission takes a sinister turn and they get more than they bargained for as they attempt to track down their missing friend. Classified as a 'psychological horror', the film was probably most notable for the fact it co-starred Melanie Brown, aka Scary Spice. It was first shown in the USA at the Detroit International Horror Film Festival but in most territories it went straight to DVD and made little impact.

Underneath it all, Tom was still a troubled soul. Like many other young actors, he was plagued by insecurity, as he recalled in a 2009 interview with *Daily Variety*: 'I came back from *Star Trek*, and I didn't have any work, and I panicked.' To make matters worse, he was still a slave to his drink and drug addictions. While acting was occupying his 'busy head' to a degree, the only way he could really calm the noise in his mind was by seeking escape into the fug of alcohol and drug binges.

With the benefit of hindsight, he more recently reflected on this period of his life when he met up for a second time with *Lodown* magazine and remembered an interview he had done with them during the press junkets for *Star Trek*. Talking to them in 2011, he looked back on what his state of mind had been in 2002: 'I wasn't even on the f*****g planet. Let's make no bones about it, I was on rocket fuel. Man I was f****d. And I thought that film was going to make me a superstar. How wrong was I?'

Tom is famous for his candidness in interviews and one story in particular (that has been repeated time and again) demonstrates the extent to which he seemed hellbent on derailing a potentially remarkable career. Speaking on *The Jonathan Ross Show* in 2010, he admitted that there had been many occasions on which he'd blacked out whilst bingeing on either drugs or alcohol. He recounted a time when he had been in LA for a meeting with director John Woo about a possible film role. Thanks to who knows what kind of misdemeanours, he missed the meeting, instead waking up in a bed in an unknown location in the city, next to a naked man with a gun – and a cat. It might sound like a scene from *The Hangover* but this was Tom's reality at the time. As he told Ross: 'The safety of the gun was off, so I must have fallen asleep looking down the barrel of a gun.'

As Tom is now acutely aware, talent alone is not enough to build an acting career – it takes hard work and commitment, and his exorbitant behaviour was proving a massive impediment to his progression. 'There comes a point when the world will stop rewarding potential and talent, natural gifts. There's only so long that people will put up with the potential of working with someone who could be brilliant,' Tom told *Men's Health* magazine. Fortunately for his health and his career, his exhausted body forced his hand in cleaning up his act.

Excessive indulgence in potentially lethal substances is a habit that can only be endured for so long before the body – and often the mind – gives up. Inevitably things build towards a critical point and, in some cases, an addict will take heed of the warning signs and choose that time to change their behaviour. For actor and comedian Robin Williams, for example, the wake-up call came in the form of the drug-related death of his friend John Belushi, in whose company he had been the night Belushi died. The tragedy brought into focus the danger of his own addiction to cocaine. He checked into rehab and, since becoming clean, has had the most remarkable film career. In other cases, sadly, these warning signs are dismissed and can lead to tragic and untimely deaths. In press interviews with Tom, the point at which he woke up to himself is repeatedly referred to – and why not? It makes great copy for journalists and it gives Tom a unique selling point: the bad boy from the right side of the tracks who pulled himself back from self-destruction.

Towards the end of 2002, during the nocturnal hours when London's West End truly comes alive, Tom was often to be spotted out and about on the busy streets, chasing highs. The superstardom he had expected had not been forthcoming and he didn't have work on tap to occupy his restless mind. His insecurities piled up and he quietened his inner turmoil by participating in a lifestyle that blurred the hard edges of reality. One night, on Soho's Old Compton Street, his indulgence went too far and he collapsed, crack pipe in hand, covered in blood and vomit. His burnout was so severe that he was taken straight to hospital. Upon his release, he returned to his parents' house in East Sheen and they helped him enrol on a recovery programme. 'That was a lesson to me,' he told the *Mail & Guardian* in 2011. 'I was fed to the Kraken and popped out the other side. In death I was reborn...'

Sadly, one casualty of his breakdown was his marriage to Sarah. For obvious reasons, Tom doesn't go into great detail about this aspect of his recovery but part of his rehabilitation was to make amends to his parents and his ex-wife for his past behaviour. His recovery also signalled that he had finally grown up and taken responsibility for himself and his actions. 'It was the end of a childhood which had gone on too long, that didn't grow into adulthood and wasn't going to work alongside my profession,' he admitted.

What his bad behaviour did do, though, was to give him experience of the terrifying side of human nature. His predilection for dangerous substances and situations pushed him mentally – and often physically – into all kinds of desperate places; corners of the world and of the mind where most would rather not go. And he has exploited his knowledge of these grim recesses of the soul for some of his most spectacular performances.

Although he had ditched the drink and drugs, he was all too aware that there was still chaos inside his head that needed some kind of outlet. 'I can't stand being in my head, that's why I have to get out of it. That's where the drugs and drink came in. I don't do any of that any more, though. That's why I have to act,' he explained to *The Times* in 2007. To the delight of critics and fans, Tom had decided to channel his adrenal fizz into his work – a wise choice, considering the breathtaking results that have followed.

It was fitting, then, that the first role he undertook as the clean and sober Tom was that of a desperate drug addict. Guided by his agent Lindy King, the direction of Tom's rebooted career was to have its foundations on the stage rather than the screen. *In Arabia We'd All Be Kings*, by Stephen Adly Guirgis, is set in New York in 1996, at the time when mayor Rudy Giuliani was redeveloping Times Square. The action of the play takes place around a bar in Hell's Kitchen, where the misfits who constitute the characters of the play gather. The production was directed by Robert Delamere and staged in April and May of 2003 at the Hampstead Theatre in London, which touted the play as 'an uplifting tragi-comedy capturing the vibrancy of a unique precinct under threat'.

Tom's character was the aptly-named Skank, a junkie who turns to selling his body for money to fund his increasing drug dependency. It might seem ironic that this was the role that restarted Tom's acting career, but for him it was a gift: 'After I came out of hospital, my first job was playing a crackhead alcoholic rent boy in a play, which was tremendously cathartic because I was re-enacting a load of stuff I had just lived,' he said in an interview with the *Irish Times*.

It should also be remembered that this was Tom's professional stage debut. Since he left drama school to be in *Band of Brothers*, all his jobs had involved acting for film. For someone who has admitted – and demonstrated – that he has a debilitating fear of failure, to go from rehab straight to a stage performance must have been daunting, to say the least. On the stage, there are no second takes, no re-shoots and the actors have to bring everything to their performance, night after night. Speaking to the *Evening Standard* a few months after the play had ended its run, Tom described how he felt when acting on stage. 'Terrified – every time. You're bringing a character to life in a gladiatorial ring where people want to see you fail.'

When the theatre critics came to assess the play, failure was not a word they juxtaposed with the name Tom Hardy. Quite the opposite, in fact. Whatever their comments on the production itself, they were united in their praise of Tom's performance.

Nicholas De Jongh of the *Evening Standard* described it as 'a remarkable stage debut' and Paul Taylor of the *Independent* described Skank as 'brilliantly played by Tom Hardy'.

Barely had Tom taken his final bow at the Hampstead Theatre than he found himself travelling up to Sheffield's Crucible Theatre to work under the direction of Robert Delamere once more. This time, the play was *The Modernists* written by Jeff Noon, a writer better known for his fantasy novels than for his plays. *The Modernists* is set in Soho in the early 1960s and the drama centres around four musicians who are Mods in the old sense of the word. They live at a time before Mods became associated with violence, parkas and scooters; they follow a strict dress code and they speak using a very specific vocabulary. In fact, they are somewhat dandy and not at all like the popular projection of the Mod. Tom's role was to play Vincent, who is described as the 'alpha male' of the group. Critics mostly agreed that the play had a lot of potential but was lacking in drama. Dominic Cavendish, writing for the *Daily Telegraph*, commented: 'The play's main event proves to be the leader Vincent's psychological collapse, mirroring this hermetic sub-culture's own implosion. But the crisis always feels more aridly theoretical than theatrically true-to-life.'

Once the short run of *The Modernists* came to an end, there was no rest for the reinvigorated young actor and, in the autumn, he went on to consolidate his stage craft by appearing at the Royal Court Theatre in *Blood*, by Swedish playwright Lars Noren. Without wanting to give too much of the plot away, *Blood* is a modern reworking of the Oedipus story and Tom's character, Luca, is a medical student who was orphaned as a child. His psychoanalyst, Eric (Nicholas

Le Prevost), is also his lover and, through the course of the play, Eric's wife (Francesca Annis) develops a sexual relationship with him as well.

The play itself didn't fare well in terms of the critics' reactions. Paul Taylor writing for the *Independent* found it so farcical that he felt the 'most impressive feature of the evening is the heroic way Ms Annis and Mr Le Prevost manage to keep a straight face'. Other critics were less harsh: Michael Billington of the *Guardian* felt the play was flawed but found it 'exquisitely gripping'. He described Tom as giving Luca 'intemperate rage' and Nicholas De Jongh of the *Evening Standard* was even more enthusiastic, stating: 'Superlative Tom Hardy invests Luca with raw energy and suppressed desperation.'

It seemed that Tom had staunch support from the *Evening Standard* camp so it was perhaps unsurprising when his name was amongst the nominations for that newspaper's theatre awards for 2003. The category in which he found himself nominated was 'Outstanding Newcomer' and his shortlisted rivals were Lisa Dillon for her role as Hilda in Ibsen's *The Master Builder* and Amanda Drew for *Eastward Ho*.

The lavish awards ceremony was held at the Savoy Hotel in November 2003. The great and the good of London's theatreland were present and the proceedings were presided over by Rory Bremner. The award for Outstanding Newcomer was presented by Nicholas Hytner, then the newly appointed director of the National Theatre. As a prelude to presenting the award, Hytner gave a light-hearted speech in which he congratulated all three of the shortlisted nominees and quipped that he hoped they would only do enough 'dodgy television' to finance their loft conversions.

The award, of course, went to Tom for his performances in both *In Arabia We'd All Be Kings* and *Blood*. He admitted he was very nervous as he collected his statuette and amongst his obligatory thanks were the Hampstead Theatre and those involved in getting the production off the ground there, as well as his parents, his girlfriend, his agent, Lindy King and all his friends and family, who he referred to as his 'support unit'. And not to be forgotten was his dog, Max, who he said would be very grumpy if he was left off the list. Finally, he expressed his gratitude to the *Evening Standard*, Nick De Jongh and everyone who had voted for him.

To further boost Tom's credibility, his performance in *In Arabia We'd All be Kings* also garnered him a nomination at the 2004 Laurence Olivier Theatre Awards, again in the category of Most Promising Newcomer in an Affiliate Theatre. Sadly he didn't win the double this time and the award went to playwright Debbie Tucker for *Born Bad*, also staged at the Hampstead Theatre.

It is gratifying to observe just how successfully Tom had managed to turn his life around in the space of a year. As 2003 drew to a close, he was sadly without his marriage – but there were so many positives on which he could draw as 2004 dawned. He had conquered his drug and drink addictions and, although recovering from such dependencies are battles that are never truly won, he was in a new frame of mind and could see that his new-found sobriety was bearing fruit on the work front. He had achieved recognition for his acting and was determined to capitalise on this. It was starting to look as though Tom's time might yet come.

CHAPTER FOUR

THE PLAY'S
THE THING

It was no surprise that, towards the end of 2003, the name Tom Hardy started to appear in the obligatory end-of-year round-ups heralding British stars of the future. The *Evening Standard* included Tom in their list of *Bright Young Things*, alongside fellow actors Rosamund Pike, Sienna Miller and Orlando Bloom; and *W* magazine numbered him among their collection of fresh talent that was, apparently, 'filling up casting directors' wish lists on both sides of the Atlantic.' His new-found dedication to his craft had started to pay dividends and, thanks to the canny agent he had in Lindy King, offers of work were piling up. 'I've played a range of different screen and stage characters and it's all because of Lindy,' he told *The Stage*. 'I'm 100 per cent committed to her.'

In March 2004, the play *Festen* opened at the Almeida Theatre in London's Islington. Adapted from the 1998 Danish art-house film of the same name, it deals with the traumatic subject of sexual abuse within a family. In its filmic form, *Festen* had been the first work of the Dogme movement, a group of Scandinavian film-makers whose desire was to produce films in a far more pared-down style than their Hollywood contemporaries. Writer David Eldridge adapted the film for an English stage production, to be directed by Rufus Norris. The simplicity of the film's production and direction allowed for a smooth transfer from the screen to the more intimate environment of a theatrical production.

The action of the play unfolds over the course of two days of festivities as a family gather for the 60th birthday celebrations of its patriarch, Helge. Three of his children are present: Christian, Michael and Mette (Christian's twin, Linda, having recently committed suicide for reasons that later become apparent). During the party, Christian reveals that Helge sexually abused both him and Linda when they were children and, from this shocking disclosure, the tension of the play builds.

In this production, Christian, Michael and Mette were played by Jonny Lee Miller, Tom Hardy and Claire Rushbrook respectively. The production as a whole received unanimous critical acclaim: the writing, the sound staging, the set design, the direction and the acting were all deemed to be outstanding and it was agreed that an intense and powerful drama had been created and executed perfectly. 'This *Festen* is an embodiment of what theatre should be,' proclaimed Paul Taylor in the *Independent*.

Tom's character, Michael, is an aggressive brute of a man who is shown to be a racist and a bully. Once more, the actor's job involved getting to grips with the dark underbelly of human nature and, true to form, Tom gave a captivating and nuanced performance. Michael Coveney of the *Daily Mail* referred to him as 'electrifying' while Tom's long-time supporter Nicholas De Jongh said he turned in a 'remarkable, quicksilver performance'.

Speaking about the succession of troubled characters he had brought to life for the stage, Tom commented: 'I do feel alive when I play these characters, like I owe them something. There's no such thing as a coincidence.' His experiences of the bleaker side of life were still feeding into his work and illuminating his characters with an authenticity that was continuing to attract a lot of positive attention. While Tom's own experiences helped him to have an affinity with some of the disturbed characters he played, he was always aware that it was not within his remit to impose his own opinions or personality on them.

Having finished his stint at the Almeida, Tom journeyed across the River Thames to south London, where he undertook another fringe play, *Roger and Vanessa*, this time at Theatre 503, a small performance space above the Latchmere pub in Clapham. The decision to stage the play had come about when Tom happened to meet the play's American writer, Brett C Leonard. This fortuitous encounter occurred at RADA, where a rehearsed reading of the play was taking place as part of a showcase of American writers' work. Coincidentally, at this reading, the part of Roger was taken by none other than Stephen Adly Guirgis, the writer of *In Arabia We'd All Be Kings*, the play that had been responsible for launching Tom's career.

Tom felt a connection with both the playwright and his

work and, in his typically energetic fashion, decided he wanted to stage the play himself as soon as possible. Getting *Roger and Vanessa* off the ground was a frenetic experience for all involved. The ethos behind the enterprise was for the play to be brought together at lightning speed, and for the professionals involved to fit it in around their usual work commitments. Tom, who would play Roger, had just finished his run in *Festen* and was tied up with filming the TV drama *Colditz*. Linda Park, the American actress who was to play Vanessa, was flown in from LA during a gap in her schedule. Robert Delamere, with whom Tom had worked on *In Arabia We'd All Be Kings*, was enlisted to direct and had a production opening at the Almeida just 24 hours after *Roger and Vanessa* was due to open! No mean feat, but as Tom put it, 'We were all busy but we just jammed the work together. It was a workshop vibe, for the love of the work.'

'It's crisis directing,' Delamere told the *Guardian* at the time. He also noted the contrast between the cheek by jowl nature of the Latchmere production and the rather more sophisticated one he was working on at the Almeida. Although chaotic, it was an exciting experience and he appreciated what was being achieved with *Roger and Vanessa*. 'It's great having such a little space and without all that pressure you get in bigger theatres. This is about the personalities in the room, and that's it.' He also pointed out that the nature of the material Tom had chosen suited the approach to staging it.

The production was billed as 'shotgun' theatre and was 'a crazy idea to put on a show in no time at all'. There were just four performances in all and tickets were free as the company deemed it to be a workshop rather than a polished theatre production. That's not to say that those involved didn't take what they were doing seriously – the aim, according to Tom, was to provide the same enjoyment from a night out as a conventional theatre trip would.

It was in this production that the seeds were sown for the formation of Tom and Robert Delamere's theatre company – named, aptly, Shotgun. Following *Roger and Vanessa*, the Latchmere offered Tom a residency in their performance space and he snapped up the opportunity. In fact, what he created was less of a formal theatre company and more of an actors' co-operative – or as he put it, a 'splinter cell group'. He wanted to establish an informal and safe space where actors, writers and performers of any level could get together, explore their ideas and unleash their creative talent. 'There should be no pressure, no commitment, just talent and immediate response to the material that walks in the door,' he declared, when announcing the formation of the group. From a personal perspective, Tom also felt that, within the confines of pressured production schedules of film and television, actors didn't have enough time to really dig deep into the characters they were to play, and wanted Shotgun to provide them with the chance to share the development of their work with other, like-minded people. There was to be 'no fear, no ego, just good hard clean fun'. The venture did have a whiff of *Fight Club* mentality about it, though – attendance at the Shotgun workshops was by invitation only, 'to keep it safe'.

The project was indeed worthy and showed that Tom was keen both to invest something in the community and to continue learning new ways of keeping his beloved craft fresh and organic. On a more practical level, he also claimed that

Shotgun stopped him and his fellow actors from 'getting upset when the phone doesn't ring during our downtime'.

Although Tom's relationship with his parents had been put under enormous strain during his years of addiction, he had always remained close to them and, once he was clean and sober, his relationship with his father took on a new lease of life. They were both intelligent and creative souls and given that Chips had written plays in the past, it was only a matter of time until he became involved in the creative ventures of Shotgun. Along with Chips and other members of the Shotgun team, Tom undertook a project named, interestingly, the Octoplot Revolution – which sounds rather more radical than it actually was. In fact, it was simply a guide giving instructions on how to write a play (or screenplay) in eight stages. 'It's a simple format and it becomes a way of expressing yourself. Anyone can follow it,' Tom explained to Baz Bamigboye of the *Daily Mail* in August 2006.

The Octoplot Revolution was an idea that extended beyond the confines of Shotgun. Tom, Chips and some of the other Shotgun members were aiming to integrate the Octoplot Revolution into an educational outreach programme for 14 to 16 year olds, which would stretch across 32 London boroughs.

It wasn't long, however, before Tom's working relationship with educational establishments came to an abrupt halt. In November 2006, he and other members of Shotgun were due to go and speak to pupils from 10 schools about their work – and also about Tom's own life and career. The talk was part of a project called London Schools Masterclass funded by the Department for Education and Skills (DfES). Just a couple of weeks before the event, Tom gave an in-depth interview to the

Evening Standard in which he laid bare the problems of his youth, his brushes with the law and his addictions. Within two days of the interview appearing, Tom was informed that the DfES was anxious about the reaction to the revelations in the interview and had therefore decided to postpone the masterclass.

The decision of the DfES could be construed as hasty and reactionary – and its ramifications would certainly be disappointing for the young people who would have benefited from the talk. Granted, Tom had not lived a model life but he was a fine example of someone who had, through hard work and determination, pushed himself firmly back on track. Plus he had made no secret of his past – surely better than covering it up and being exposed further down the line? Speaking to the *Telegraph* at the time, he expressed his frustration at the cancellation, describing the decision as 'quite bureaucratic and quite puritan. All we are interested in is giving something back to the community.' He added: 'We wanted the kids to feel the pleasure and fulfilment we feel as professional performers. If we can help any child leave school with a sense of purpose and usefulness, then that has to be a good thing.' After all, Tom knew better than anyone how disheartening it could be to leave school with no aspirations, goals or direction.

Dispiriting though this was, the endeavours of Shotgun continued apace. Next up was their first production, a play called *Blue on Blue*, written by Chips. The play tells the story of a wheelchair-bound war veteran living with his nephew. The younger character is damaged and forced to confront his problems. The playwright described his play as 'a hard-arsed look at compulsion and co-dependency but... first and foremost, a darkly funny play about people.'

Speaking to the *Evening Standard* (in the very interview at which the DfES took such great umbrage) Chips explained that he had drawn on parts of his relationship with Tom when writing *Blue on Blue*. Speaking about his son, Chips said: 'We've had our ups and downs over the years, but Tom wouldn't be such a good actor if he didn't have those things in him.'

The play was staged at the Latchmere during November 2006 and was directed by Tom. Simon Rhodes, Gideon Turner and Danielle Urbas filled the roles of uncle, nephew and Marta the home help respectively. It was only on for a few nights but its run was a sell-out and the *Daily Mail* review stated that the play 'astutely raises difficult social problems without being preachy'. Being under Tom Hardy's directorship, it would have seemed odd if it had been any other way.

Shotgun followed up *Blue on Blue* with a play called *Two Storm Wood* by Edward Bennett-Coles, staged in February 2007. Perhaps inevitably, though, the indie theatre company didn't stay together for much longer. Work commitments must have eaten up the amount of time that Tom was able to devote to his project, but looking back on the Shotgun days in an interview with *Time Out* in 2009 he recalled: 'Everybody joined up and it was all dope, then everyone went solo and it wasn't as good. I've gotta bring it back for the reunion. Even if it is just a karaoke night.'

Whatever his best intentions were with offshoot projects like Shotgun, with his career now taking off in ways he probably never imagined possible, it seems unlikely that Tom will have the time to revisit his theatre company. Perhaps there lies a project for when the credits have rolled on his last movie.

At the same time as charging around trying to pull together his first 'shotgun' production, Tom had been busy fulfilling professional commitments. His schedule dictated that work on *Roger and Vanessa* had to be fitted in around filming for the television drama *Colditz*, in which he had a principal role.

The two-part ITV drama took its inspiration from Henry Chancellor's book of the same name. The source material for the book was interviews with allied soldiers who had been held in the German high-security prison during the Second World War. The television adaptation centres on the fates of three fictional characters who initially escape from a prisoner of war camp during the war. Two of them are captured and taken to Colditz (Jack Rose, played by Tom, and Tom Willis, played by Laurence Fox) while the third (Nick McGrade, played by Damian Lewis) makes it back to England where he falls in love with Lizzie (Sophia Myles), who happens to be the sweetheart of Jack. The adaptation also boasted a sprinkle of Hollywood stardust in the form of Jason Priestley (star of teen drama *Beverly Hills 90210*) who played Canadian soldier Rhett Barker, also an inmate of the prison. Shooting took place over the summer of 2004, in London and on location in the Czech Republic. 'Colditz' was in fact a medieval monastery in Kutna Hora, a town located about 70km east of Prague.

The character of Jack Rose is essentially the hero of the piece: dependable, honest and brave, he stands in stark contrast to deceitful, selfish Nick McGrade who wants to keep Rose's love Lizzie for himself by any means possible. Tom described Rose as 'an ordinary person in extraordinary circumstances' and this was a change from the kind of role the actor was accustomed to taking. 'I've never played a straight lead before,' he mused. 'I normally get tortured characters and villains and angry young men.' Fortunately for Tom, he did get the chance to delve back into his tough-guy store cupboard, for a scene in which he comes to physical blows with Willis.

Tom recognised that, as in *Band of Brothers*, a delicate touch was required when bringing Jack Rose to life. Although the characters were fictional, he was all too aware that they were representations of people who had experienced incarceration in Colditz. 'People have died in these uniforms. It's important that this drama pays tribute to what those guys did,' he told the *Independent* in 2005.

Colditz saw Tom reunited with his *Band of Brothers* co-star, Damian Lewis. While Lewis was complimentary about Tom and predicted great things for him in the future, he also joked about how, in both productions, Tom's character had been the one who'd had all the luck with women. 'I always resented Tom for turning up on *Band of Brothers* and getting the girl – in fact, the only girl in a cast of hundreds of smelly men! I, on the other hand, spent eight months with my face squashed up against someone else's backside in one sodden trench after another. And it looks as if Tom might have got the girl again, damn his eyes,' Lewis joked to the *Sunday Mercury*. Tom was eager to return the praise, expressing how pleased he was to be working with Lewis again, who had coincidentally also recently appeared in a production at the Almeida. 'I've been on his heels for a bit so it was good to work with him – he's a character,' said Tom.

It's interesting to note that when he spoke about appearing in the drama, Tom made reference to the brief spell of time that actors have to explore their characters when confined by production timetables. As well as shooting, actors would also be reading the script, trying to cram in research and getting to know the story. It was this scarcity of preparation time that had been one of the principal reasons for the formation of Shotgun – it was a space where actors could come and explore their characters in the company of other professionals.

Colditz was broadcast over Easter weekend in 2005, as part of ITV's commemoration of the 60th anniversary of the end of the War. Though the actors had all done their best to be respectful to veterans of the Second World War, some of the men who had been incarcerated in Colditz didn't respond positively to the programme. Amongst the criticisms levelled at it were that it didn't offer a true representation of what life had been like within the confines of the prison. A scene in which German officers carry out a mock execution was deemed to be too far from the truth. 'That sort of mock execution did not go on at Colditz and to pretend it did is just not acceptable,' said a former Colditz prisoner, Ken Lockwood, when speaking to the *Telegraph*. 'Both sides appreciated the other's point of view and as time went on some of the Germans grew to respect us.' It was also pointed out that there were some costume errors and that the set looked far too flimsy to be a high-security fortress from which there was little hope of escape.

Naturally, the producers rallied to its defence, stating that some liberties had been taken in order to broaden the appeal of the drama. They needed to reach a prime-time ITV audience, which was a significantly younger demographic than that which made up the voices of dissent.

Television critics were equally unimpressed with *Colditz*

and adopted a rather scornful stance in their notices about the show. Most agreed that, while the drama had started with promise and had chosen lead actors with discernible talent, by the second instalment, it had rather lost its way and become a bit of a joke. The *Scotsman* described it as lurching from 'schlock romance' to 'a clever pastiche of *The Great Escape*'. The *Daily Mail* was more scathing and declared that by its conclusion, it had 'degenerated into a rather silly melodrama capped by a soppy ending'.

For Tom, though, the experience had given him a chance to try something different from his regular roll-call of villains and maladjusted characters and he remained as determined as ever to make his work shine. He has often asserted that his job is to observe and then depict, not to offer comment. 'I just came to tell a story and be part of a story' he said of his time on *Colditz*. 'There's no wrong, really, there's just bad acting and then there's convincing acting. And somehow I'd like to do the work.'

If you are a Hardy superfan who feels the need to watch everything he's ever been in – and he has a dedicated following of ardent admirers who do – you might just want to skip the film *EMR* when filling your online shopping cart with Hardy goodies. While it's a perfectly watchable conspiracy story with an interesting twist, Tom's appearance in it is brief, to say the least. In fact, if you acquired it specifically because his name is in the credits, you would be more than a little disappointed. For the sake of completeness, it is necessary to record that, in 2004, this independent film was released and Tom had a role in it – there is little more to say than that.

The year of 2004 had, however, been deemed by the media to be the start of a new era in British film. A slew of UK talent was attracting attention from across the Atlantic thanks to a succession of small-budget films that had performed well stateside. This was great for young actors such as Tom who were looking to gain more exposure and good news for Brit flicks looking to attract big investment.

It would be hard to find a more British film than *Layer Cake*. The book on which the film is based was the debut novel of JJ Connolly, and it led reviewers to declare him the new voice in British crime fiction. Set in gangland London in the nineties, the story is narrated by a nameless, low-key drug dealer aged 29 who is desperately trying to extricate himself from the game before he reaches 30.

In 2001, a copy of the book was sent to SKA Films, the production company of Guy Ritchie and Matthew Vaughn (the director/producer dream team behind *Lock, Stock and Two Smoking Barrels*). Originally, it was Ritchie who agreed to adapt the story for the screen and Vaughn undertook his usual role of raising the finance to make the picture. However, after delays in securing the rights to make *Layer Cake*, Ritchie became too busy with other projects to be able to commit to directing it. Vaughn was already heavily involved with the film creatively and was understandably reluctant to hand over the directorial reins to a third party, so he opted to make the film his directorial debut. It was a challenge for him as, prior to *Layer Cake*, had only been involved in the production side of movies; now, he needed to cut his teeth on the creative aspects of film-making.

It was JJ Connolly himself who adapted the book into the

film's screenplay, and shooting took place over the summer of 2003. Cast in the main role of the nameless narrator (listed simply as XXXX in the film's credits) was Daniel Craig. At this stage, Craig was a reasonably well known character actor but had not yet attached himself to the juggernaut Bond franchise. 'When I first met Matthew he fired me up about the film, and I read the script in one sitting,' enthused Craig to Nick Curtis of the *Evening Standard*.

The film was, in fact, awash with a host of familiar and brilliant British actors: Michael Gambon, Kenneth Cranham, Dexter Fletcher and Jamie Foreman, to name a few. Prior to winning the part of Tammy in *Layer Cake*, Sienna Miller had probably been best known for her role as Jude Law's real-life girlfriend. In this movie, she proved that she could be so much more than that. There are also two trusted sidekicks who work as part of XXXX's close-knit team. One is Clarkie, the part played by Tom, who is described in the opening scenes of the film as having a double first in Industrial Chemistry from Cambridge. The other is Terry, played by Tamer Hassan, who provides the brawn to complement Clarkie's brains.

Another, uncredited, star of the film is London itself. Those who call London home and love the familiar sights of their city were delighted to see it make a significant contribution to the atmosphere of the film. Locations that were used for various parts of the story were mews houses in Kensington (XXXX's home), The Regency Café in Victoria (where Morty exacts a violent attack) and the St Martin's Lane hotel in Covent Garden (a memorable scene, where Tammy appears in all her lingeried glory, much to male movie-goers' delight).

The poster campaign rolled out just prior to *Layer Cake*'s

cinematic release was nothing if not striking. The artwork had been the brainchild of advertising executive Trevor Beattie and, if you weren't already familiar with the story, seemed somewhat cryptic. Rather than featuring any of the stars of the film, the posters instead carried an image of a yellow Range Rover with an iron perched on the bonnet, a scorch mark around the iron clearly visible. The producers, Sony, whom Vaughn had persuaded to come on board, apparently disliked the posters but they seemed to intrigue British cinema-goers and were successful in enticing them to go and see the film. And, of course, once you'd watched the film, you could rest smug in the knowledge that you were one of those who understood the meaning of the campaign artwork.

It would have been difficult for the producers to raise too many objections to any part of *Layer Cake* once it had been released: the box office figures spoke for themselves. It took over £1 million in its opening weekend and almost £3 million in the first fortnight. It seemed that Vaughn's worries about not having directed before could be laid to rest: British film audiences liked his style (which was less knockabout than his partner Guy Ritchie's) and he had made a genuine and stylish gangster movie. Tom's role in the film had been a relatively small one, but he had been part of a tremendous success story. Thanks to its favourable reception in the UK, when *Layer Cake* opened in the USA the following year, Sony went all out to promote it. It was a strong, credible piece of work for Tom's CV.

Although he'd had some experience of the Hollywood movie-making machine, Tom was all too aware how difficult it could be to secure the roles for which you were put forward.

You could be the most gifted actor in the world but if you didn't have the right look for a part, it would slip through your fingers. Tom is undeniably handsome and oozes sex appeal (if in doubt just refer to the mass of adoring comments posted alongside any photograph of him displayed on the internet). His looks and physique, though, do mark him out for particular kinds of roles such as misfits, villains and rogues – the kinds of parts that he has spent the majority of his career inhabiting. There is one character, however, you probably wouldn't associate with him too readily, yet who Tom was desperate to play – a character from literary fiction who has become synonymous with one of Tom's fellow Drama Centre old boys, Colin Firth.

As Tom tells it, he came tantalisingly close to winning the part of Mr Darcy in the 2005 big screen adaptation of *Pride and Prejudice*, in which Keira Knightley played Lizzie Bennett. Suited and booted, Tom had duly turned up for the scheduled meeting with Hollywood big cheese Stacey Snider. In spite of his best efforts, she deemed him unsuitable for the role, exclaiming: 'Babe, every woman in the world has an impression of who Darcy is and you're just not it.'

'That hurt, that really hurt,' recalled Tom to the *Telegraph*. 'I'd worn a blue shirt and jeans and a blue blazer and been doing my best Hugh Grant impression. But now I was back to playing the wonky skewiff-teeth kid with the bow legs.'

Poor Tom! Despite being brought up in East Sheen and attending public school, he was too much of a bad boy to be the nation's favourite literary hero. Although he admits his imperfect teeth may have contributed to his not obtaining the role, to date, he has refused to succumb to the Hollywood norm of getting them fixed. And long may that decision last – he wouldn't be our Tom without his characteristic, imperfectly charming grill.

On the other side of the coin, there are also countless productions to which the media attaches actors that they ultimately do not pursue. In 2004, the press was excitedly reporting details of a film in the offing about the death of Rolling Stone Brian Jones. Stephen Woolley was in the director's chair for the movie and Tom Hardy was one of the names reported to be in talks to play the role of Brian Jones. The film, *The Wild and Wycked* [sic] *World of Brian Jones*, had been a decade in development, but by the early part of 2004 was ready to go into production. The *Evening Standard* stated that Tom was 'first in line for the part of Jones' but, as is so often the case – and for whatever reason – as quickly as he had been linked to the movie, he was no longer connected to it. Ultimately, the part went to newcomer Leo Gregory, though established actors such as Paul Bettany and Jonathan Rhys Myers had also been rumoured to be up for the part.

This particular role was not to be the one for Tom, but he had little to worry about on the work front. There was no shortage of jobs for the actor and, at this period in his life, that was a blessing. His breakdown was still the recent past and he was a recovering addict with a void to fill. In an interview with the *Irish Times* in 2009, he analysed his post-collapse career and remarked that, subsequent to his rehabilitation, his priority was to fill his time with work – he needed one job after the next to keep pushing himself forward, away from his demons. 'People say to be careful when you get sober because then you get your feelings back. I was very lucky because I got job after job after job, but I was always working for the next job and I was never really in the moment.'

Indeed, if you were a fan of television drama in 2006, you might have experienced a feeling of déjà vu as one face in particular kept popping up on your screen again and again. Prepare to meet Tom Hardy, darling of the BBC.

CHAPTER FIVE

THE BOY FROM
THE BEEB

There is little to recommend the early days of January in Britain. The Christmas celebrations are over, the population has reluctantly returned to work and there are plenty of cold days and long nights ahead. In 2006, against this gloomy backdrop, the BBC chose to broadcast a grisly, gory, post-watershed drama called *Sweeney Todd*. Despite its gruesome nature, the show was well received and engendered a more positive response than much of the channel's Christmas schedule had.

The legend of Sweeney Todd has its roots in the early nineteenth century. Though it has been posited that Todd was real, he was in fact the fabrication of Edward Lloyd, a publisher of 'penny dreadfuls' – sensational serialised stories, which were churned out cheaply and aimed primarily at the working class. Though published in the 1830s, the story of the murderous barber was set in 1785 and it seems likely that the reason for planting the story in the past was so that the publisher could create hype by maintaining that Todd really existed. Certainly, the familiar elements of this legendary character were there in the original story, published under the title *The String of Pearls*: it included a barber's shop, the chair that propelled victims into the cellar and even cannibalistic cook Mrs Lovett, who disposes of Todd's victims in her practical and nutritious way. Since the story was first published, it has appeared in various forms, including plays and even a silent film. Arguably the most famous interpretation of the story, however, was Stephen Sondheim's 1979 Broadway musical (itself based on a 1973 play written by Christopher Bond). In 2007, Sondheim's musical version of the tale transferred to the big screen in a film directed by Tim Burton and starring Johnny Depp in the title role.

Before Burton and Depp got a chance to air their take on the murderous barber, it was explored in this television production. The main character was to be played by British acting institution Ray Winstone with a supporting cast of Essie Davis as Mrs Lovett, David Warner as Todd's father and Tom Hardy as Matthew Payne, a Bow Street runner (one of the first kinds of police officers in London). It was, in fact, Winstone's own production company, Size 9, that was behind the making of the drama, in conjunction with Box TV. The actor had formed the production company in 2001 with Joshua St Johnston and Michael Wiggs, its objective being to develop quality television drama. Prior to *Sweeney Todd*, it had scored a success with *She's Gone*.

With a screenplay written by St Johnston, and with Gub Neal producing, *Sweeney Todd* began shooting in August

2005. The murky streets of 18th-century London, however, were recreated not on British soil but in Eastern Europe; cost implications dictated that the filming take place somewhere where it would be cheaper to shoot than Britain. The chosen location was Romania and Winstone, ever the proud Brit, made no secret of his displeasure at having to decamp abroad. 'It's ironic, but the state of the British film industry means I can't afford to make it in England, so the streets of London are being recreated in Romania. It's stupid. It means that 300 people who would have got jobs on the film and paid their taxes in this country have missed out. It really kills me.'

The drama focussed on the damaging effect that Todd's past has on him, his disengagement from the world around him and his role as a moral avenger. Gub Neal likened their Todd to 'a kind of 18th-century *Taxi Driver*. He is a man who, to some extent, feels abused by society, then rises to respectability and security, but is sickened by the violence of the world and starts to take his revenge on it,' he said to the *Sunday Times* when the programme was first broadcast.

The character Neal describes sounds remarkably similar to some of the complex and disturbed ones Tom would inhabit for the screen a few years hence. In this production, however, his job was to play an upstanding and brave law enforcement officer, a small beacon of integrity amid the gloom and misdeeds of the rest of the drama. But Tom was quick to observe that being a policeman in 18th century London would have required a certain kind of mettle from a man. 'The police force was new and methods were rough and ready – a good beating was often meted out to wrongdoers. I see him as a scrapper, a guy who likes a good fight but equally has a burning zeal to do right.' Once again, Tom was completely committing to the role by trying to find the essence of his character and establish where contradictions might exist to give his performance the depth he always sought.

Matthew Payne is introduced to the story when Todd operates on him to remove a bullet from his shoulder – a sickeningly painful, anaesthetic-free procedure in those days. The debt of gratitude Payne feels to Todd for saving his life ultimately clouds his judgement as to what Todd could be – and is – capable of. When he does finally confront the barber about some of the discrepancies in his stories about folk who have mysteriously disappeared after coming to his shop, he is shocked to discover that the man who enabled him to live is responsible for ending the lives of others.

It was exciting for Tom to be appearing alongside Ray Winstone and he appreciated that it would benefit his own work to observe an actor of Winstone's calibre in action. 'It doesn't get any better than Ray Winstone,' he enthused. 'He's one of the most generous actors in the business and brilliant to watch in action – even when he's scary.'

Scary he certainly was when it came to *Sweeney Todd*, though his character was fortunately no pantomime villain. David Bradley, who played Sweeney Todd's father in the drama, described the production as a 'graphic and violent take on the story' which, though stomach-churning, went down well with television critics who liked its unflinching storytelling. Winstone's complex presentation of the main character was also appreciated. 'Winstone is in his element here and gives it far more than the usual two-dimensional cartoon characterisation often seen with the role,' commented the *Mirror*. The members of the supporting cast were also praised for their contribution to the re-telling of one of London's most macabre mythological creations.

Leaving behind the tricorne hats and powdered wigs of the 18th century (though not forever), Tom took a step further back in the nation's history to 16th century Elizabethan England. His next turn as the BBC's character actor of choice was playing Robert Dudley, Earl of Leicester, confidant of Queen Elizabeth I, in their £9 million drama, *The Virgin Queen*. Originally, the BBC had intended to broadcast the drama in September 2005, but this would have meant airing it at the same time as Channel 4's *Elizabeth I* starring Helen Mirren – so the decision was made to delay it until January 2006. The programme was a four-parter and, because it was broadcast just one month after *Sweeney Todd*, helped to establish Tom's presence as a burgeoning small-screen actor. The part of Dudley suited his looks and demeanour down to the ground and gave him a chance to shine in a more substantial role. Tom's fellow Drama Centre alumna Anne-Marie Duff was to be Elizabeth to his Dudley. Duff had already received critical acclaim for her stage work and, more recently, had been brought to television viewers' attention for her portrayal of Fiona in Channel 4's *Shameless*. Alongside them in the drama was a host of fine British acting talent including Dexter Fletcher, Ian Hart, Emilia Fox and Robert Pugh.

The narrative spans Elizabeth's life from the point at which she was incarcerated by her sister Mary I, through to her old age and finally her death in 1603. As the title suggests, the series uses as its premise the theory that Elizabeth died a virgin, dedicating her life to the ruling of her country. At the heart of *The Virgin Queen*, though, lies the ambivalent relationship between Elizabeth and her trusted childhood friend, Dudley. Events as portrayed in *The Virgin Queen* show Elizabeth clearly in love with Dudley and, when the story first picks up, she is piqued that he has married (as Dudley would have it) according to his father's wishes. As the drama progresses, there are sexually charged scenes between them but their relationship is never consummated. Elizabeth desires Dudley and longs to be close to him but is constantly turning away from her more innate impulses. This version of events posits that her reluctance to be intimate with Dudley (or any other man for that matter) is rooted in the psychological effect of the death of her mother, Anne Boleyn, at the hands of her father, Henry VIII.

Prior dramas about Gloriana had chosen to build themselves around the contradictory viewpoint, that the virgin queen persona was purely a political tool. In both Channel 4's drama starring Helen Mirren and the film *Elizabeth* starring Cate Blanchett, Dudley and Elizabeth were depicted as lovers but *The Virgin Queen* chose to stick with the more literal interpretation of her moniker. 'We are convinced on the basis of the available historical evidence that she died a virgin,' producer Paul Rutman told the *Sunday Telegraph*. 'We portray her as a passionate woman, but a woman who knew there was a line she could not cross.'

Unlike *Sweeney Todd*, this BBC drama was shot on home soil. Although it would have been more economical to move the production to Eastern Europe, it was felt the authenticity of the period piece would be compromised if not filmed in

England's green and pleasant land. Many interior scenes were filmed at a specially constructed set at Shepperton studios and the exterior scenes were filmed at a variety of historic locations including Baddesley Clinton in Warwickshire (Robert Dudley's home), Chillingham Castle in the north east of England (used as Fotheringay, where Mary Queen of Scots was held prisoner), New College Oxford (used as Whitehall Cloisters) and Alnwick Castle in Northumberland, which has starred in many films including the *Harry Potter* series.

Each of the four parts of the series was a self-contained story, and director Coky Giedroyc had a clear idea of the look and feel she wanted to achieve for each segment of the Queen's life. Part one covers the period before Elizabeth accedes the throne, including her imprisonment at the hands of Mary. To reflect the bleakness of this part of Elizabeth's life a cool colour palette and plain, pared-down costumes were employed. The second part of the drama tells the story of the early years of Elizabeth's reign and her passionate relationship with Dudley is heightened by the use of warm reds and golds in the costumes and lighting. The idea behind part three was to create a thriller including the Babington plot, the execution of Mary Queen of Scots and the arrival of the Spanish Armada; the mood for this period is set using earthy tones of brown and green. The final part covers Elizabeth's later years, her relationship with the Earl of Essex (suggested by this interpretation to be the son of Dudley, not simply his stepson) and her death, so the hues are soft and faded.

Thanks to the drama focussing on the human angle of Elizabeth I, much attention is paid to her relationship with

Dudley, which at times consumed her and always confounded her. When Dudley's first wife dies in dubious circumstances, the finger of suspicion is, possibly unfairly, pointed at Dudley and even Elizabeth herself. Because of the scandal surrounding the events, Elizabeth is unable to accept Dudley's proposal of marriage but she keeps him close to her at court.

Of course, the most crucial casting decision for the makers of *The Virgin Queen* was whom to cast as Elizabeth. Around 70 actresses auditioned for the part but it was Anne-Marie Duff who made an immediate impression on the casting directors and towards whom they were instinctively drawn. Their intuitions were justified. The role was challenging, to say the least, as it required portraying Elizabeth from teenager through to her dying breath aged 69. Although costumes, prosthetics and make up (and Duff shaving her hairline!) all played their part in the gradual transformation, it was the actress's extraordinary talent that really made the movement through time believable. As Baz Bamigboye stated in the *Daily Mail*: 'With an actress of Anne-Marie's stature, you're not getting an impersonation. Rather, it's a rigorously grounded performance, with razor-sharp insight into what made this sharpest of monarchs tick.'

Playing Dudley at last allowed Tom to dazzle with his roguish charm and it is testament to the skill of the two actors that there is a tangible chemistry between them – in fact, it is at times heartbreaking to watch the ebb and flow of their emotional turmoil. Needless to say, Tom undertook his role with maximum dedication. He has paid tribute to the research that went into the production and the strength of the script – the quality of both made his job easier, leaving him to get on with developing his character. 'My job is to look at how I can create dramatic licence and create a character from what I've been given and keep it historically accurate,' he commented during the filming of *The Virgin Queen*.

Indeed, Tom admitted that his research for the part hadn't exactly been exhaustive. 'I dug holes around the neighbourhood of the time,' he told the *Sunday Times* in 2006. 'The areas that interested me were more around that period than specifically Dudley's family tree. He's a fairly stock character in the thing. If it had been Robert Dudley: Inside the Mind of a Serial Killer, that would have been a different type of research.'

Joking aside, it was simply not Tom's way to turn in anything other than a pitch-perfect, refined performance. Stock character Dudley may have been – and a far cry from the tortured, disturbed characters that Tom had inhabited for the stage – but, as always, the actor looked for the subtleties in the part he was playing. His skill at doing this was something that the writer of *The Virgin Queen*, Paula Milne, was all too aware of, and it was one of the reasons why she picked Tom for the role. 'I was tenacious about holding on to Dudley's ambivalence, and Tom really did get that. Often an actor will need to know the neat solution to a character, is he good or is he bad? But Tom was happy to take on that moral ambivalence.'

Speaking to the BBC about his take on Dudley, Tom explained he felt the closeness between him and Elizabeth came about because of their shared history. Her affection for him, according to Tom, was born of the draw of their long-standing friendship and similar backgrounds but also in the physical attraction to Dudley. 'He is a dashing, doublet-wearing chancer in many ways,' observed Tom. 'He is roguish – but also of good blood and there's a definite passionate thing going on between them.'

Tom also seemed grateful for the chance to get away from his usual kind of role, claiming: 'I'm not normally cast as that sort of character, dashing and British. I've been pining for my doublet and breeches since a part in a Christopher Marlowe play fell through about 18 months ago, and so it was such a pleasure to get them on and get a sword.'

While the prime-time television exposure would do Tom's career no harm, it was hardly a pivotal moment in his acting career. On the personal front, though, *The Virgin Queen* would turn out to be a life-changer. The assistant director on the production was Rachael Speed and romance blossomed between her and Tom on the set in 2005. In interviews given during their relationship, Rachael is credited as a steadying force in Tom's life, an element of the calm after the storm of his addiction and rehabilitation.

In interviews, Tom has retrospectively described their relationship as 'on and off' but, in April 2008, Tom's life would change forever when Rachael gave birth to their son, Louis. Speaking to *Arena Homme* in 2008, after Louis had arrived, Tom still referred to Rachael as his girlfriend but stated that they had 'just split up when she got pregnant.' It's fair to assume that they were reconciled for the pregnancy and birth of their child, but by 2009 had separated for good. Speaking to *Men's Health* magazine in August 2010, Tom admitted that splitting up with Rachael after Louis was born was one of the toughest decisions he's had to make. 'I had a child with my ex. We weren't right together. In my head it was a lot to do with: I must be in a family. Being brave and saying, "actually I don't think I'm in the right relationship here" terrified me.'

Meanwhile, in 2006, the BBC's poster boy continued his run of drama appearances. Hot on the heels of *The Virgin Queen* came acclaimed writer Stephen Poliakoff's one-off drama, *Gideon's Daughter*. The play is set during the closing years of the 20th century and the story begins in 1997, the year in which both New Labour swept to power and the death of Princess Diana heralded an unprecedented outpouring of collective national grief. *Gideon's Daughter* starred Bill Nighy as successful but troubled PR guru Gideon Warner, whose relationship with his daughter (Emily Blunt) is foundering and who starts an affair with a grieving mother, played by Miranda Richardson. Tom played the part of Gideon's assistant, Andrew, a young alpha male whom Tom described as 'very astute, but not too fussy about the ethics of his business. He operates in a pretty amoral way.'

As Gideon's personal crises take hold, he starts to become disillusioned with his work and, even though he is regarded as the master of his game, he finds himself questioning his role in the vacuous world of PR. Andrew, meanwhile, is excited by the changes going on in Britain. He represents the new guard of PR, he is someone who is attracted to power, an adept schmoozer who is determined to get to the top of his game. His path starts to go in a different direction from Gideon's, who is tiring of moving in a world increasingly obsessed with pointless celebrity and spin.

Though the role of Andrew was not a huge part in terms of screen time for Tom, he referred to it as 'a really lovely character role' and was fulsome in expressing his gratitude at having been given the chance to be part of a Stephen Poliakoff project. In an interview with the BBC he said: 'Stephen is a class act. He has his own vision and he brings it to fruition without any interference from anyone. He has complete control over every syllable. In this day and age, that's incredibly rare. It was a privilege to work with him.'

Tom was also delighted – and slightly awed – to have the opportunity to work alongside such incredible talent as Bill Nighy and Miranda Richardson, both of whom he has described as 'top tier'. Here was a chance for him to observe and absorb the craft from more experienced performers and he has described how he loved watching Nighy work, calling him 'an actor's actor'. He recognised, though, that as a less experienced actor he really had to sharpen his focus when working alongside the likes of Nighy. 'Sometimes I get a little frightened because he is so good… as a younger actor I have to be on my game very tightly with him,' he admitted while making the drama.

The last time Tom had ventured into the world of science fiction had been prior to his breakdown, but he was to revisit the genre for his next BBC outing. *A for Andromeda* was aired in March 2006 on BBC4 and was a remake of a 1961 BBC serial drama. Two interesting facts about the original series are: that it provided a screen debut for actress Julie Christie and, mysteriously, only one complete episode of the first outing has survived.

The original series was co-written by British scientist Sir Fred Hoyle and author/television producer John Elliot. While Hoyle was an accomplished science fiction author, he was a controversial, if influential, figure in the world of astronomy and maths. He was a proponent of the theory that the universe had existed for an infinite time in the past and would continue to exist for an infinite time into the future – a hypothesis that stood in direct opposition to the big bang theory. *A for Andromeda* proved a TV hit and was watched by 12.9 million viewers – no mean feat in 1961, in spite of the fact that at that time there were only two television channels to choose from.

The 2006 drama was significant to BBC scheduling as it formed part of the channel's return to classic science fiction drama. In 2005, *Dr Who* had been revived to fans' delight and to huge critical acclaim, plus in the same year, Richard Fell (the writer behind the 2006 *A for Andromeda* adaptation), had also revived a sci-fi TV classic from the fifties, *The Quatermass Experiment*. There were some changes made to this *A for Andromeda* adaptation. For one thing, the original had been a serial, whereas the newer version was a stand-alone drama and therefore required abridgement, but the essentials of the plot remained the same.

The story centres around Dr John Fleming (Tom Hardy) and a group of scientists working at a remote monitoring station in the north of England. They are shocked when they receive a message from the Andromeda galaxy which, when deciphered, gives them instructions to build a super-computer. Once the computer is built, one of the group, Professor Dawnay (played in this adaptation by Jane Asher) takes it upon herself to use the computer to build a human life form. The computer creates a being in the physical likeness of Dawnay's assistant – and Fleming's lover – Christine (Kelly

Reilly). Named Andromeda, the humanoid is deemed to be a threat to the human race.

Originally, Tom had auditioned for the part of one of the other characters, scientist Dennis Bridger, who would ultimately be played by Charlie Cox. Once again, though, there was something about Tom that set him apart from other actors and the producers of the show realised that he could bring an extra dimension to the lead character if he was cast as Fleming. His performances to date had been standout thanks to their emotional depth – something producer Alison Willett had noticed even before the audition process got underway, having been mesmerised by Tom's performance in *Festen*. 'He has an absolute intensity to him. He came in and read for us beautifully, absolutely brilliantly, but we were all so impressed that we thought we could do something here for Fleming and make him less of a conventional hero, bring some of that angst and intensity to our lead.' Congratulations, Tom – upgraded to the lead role in the drama!

Once cast, Tom had his own ideas about how he wanted to cultivate the character of John Fleming. He knew that he wanted him to be credible and likeable and achieving this came down in part to simple things such as his appearance. Originally, the wardrobe of the character had been envisaged as rather clinical and high-tech, but Tom soon put paid to this as he felt it would detract from Fleming's relatability. 'Initially they wanted to put me in this all-white cool suit, slightly funky doctor type and I was, like, no, it's got to be leather patches on tweed jacket, and cardigan and barber shirt – very important to have a barber shirt, which is old, really old, and ink-stained... and corduroy trousers and brogues with holes in – this standard uniform.'

There is a trait that often exists in those engaged in in-depth academic pursuit: a difficulty in relating to those around them and, while being able to perform hugely complex mental exercises in their area of expertise, struggling to carry out the most basic of everyday tasks, such as making a cup of tea. Tom was keen to highlight this characteristic in Fleming and in his character's relationship with Christine – in both her forms – we see him forced to come to terms with an emotional part of his make-up probably not too often accessed.

The production schedule was demanding and the stops were well and truly pulled out to make sure filming was completed on time. The cast assembled to read through the script just three days before shooting began, and there was the added stress of the script being refined as they went through it. Plus, just 24 hours before the first day of the shoot, Tom Hardy and Charlie Cox had time to squeeze in just one hour's practice on a climbing wall in London before they found themselves transported to the Brecon Beacons to film the rock-climbing scene at the start of the drama.

A for Andromeda was shot between 2 February and 21 February 2006 – an astonishingly quick turnaround. Tight it might have been. but director John Strickland was, according to Tom, instrumental in holding the whole production together during these tense times. Such was Tom's admiration for Strickland's unflappable nature, he went so far as to say: 'I would go through hell with John on another script.'

There were a few locations for filming the sci-fi drama. For exterior scenes, the cast had to brave the often inhospitable weather conditions in Wales, while the locations used for the interior scenes were a former nuclear bunker at an RAF base in Stanmore and an MOD base in Chertsey, Surrey. None of these were too favourable and the cast found that the Surrey MOD complex was distinctly chilly, especially poor Kelly Reilly who, for her scenes as Andromeda went barefoot: 'We were in these freezing cold warehouses. It was a case of shoot and then get by a heater!' she recalled.

In spite of the pressure on all involved to get the drama in the can, the cast bonded well. Tom and Jane Asher already knew each other from having acted in *Festen* together and Tom couldn't speak highly enough of his co-star Kelly Reilly. 'When you work with someone who is absolutely there for you as an artist and as a person then you feel incredibly safe, and there's a possibility to do some really good work and take things a lot further off the page. Kelly's the full ticket. I think she'll be hugely successful in time.'

When the drama was broadcast it provoked a mixed bag of comments from the critics. The *Guardian*'s comment was relatively positive and declared that the show 'does what good TV sci-fi should: it makes you believe that two people in lab coats arguing in an empty room could result in the end of life as we know it.' And Hermione Eyre wrote in the *Independent on Sunday*: 'I really liked it, even though I knew I shouldn't.' The *Mirror*, on the other hand, complained: 'A remake is long overdue, but this BBC version is too long on E for Exposition and too short on B for Budget to do it justice.' You can't please all of the people all of the time.

For Tom, though, the experience proved positive in ways that exceeded his expectations. In developing Fleming, he really felt he had a good piece of character work to use as a building block for the future. In an interview about the show, he mused: 'John Fleming is one of my favourite characters I've ever played. I'm gonna use him as a foundation for other character work that I'll be doing in the future. I was really pleased with him, actually, and I'm not easily pleased with anything at all, but I really really liked him, and that was an achievement as I didn't see how I was going to make it work whatsoever.'

The film *Minotaur* had a difficult birth. After two false starts and a year in development, shooting finally started in early 2005. As the title suggests, it is a retelling of the Greek myth of Theseus and the Minotaur. Tony Todd, of *Candyman* fame, had already been attached to star in the project but, along with new financial backing, came class act Rutger Hauer and rising star Tom – an attractive prospect all round. The difficulties in getting the film off the ground should perhaps have been heeded as an omen regarding its eventual fate: lack of commercial success and scant critical acclaim led to it sinking without trace.

Shot in Luxembourg, the film tells the story of an Iron Age village that, every five years, must sacrifice eight young people to a bloodthirsty Minotaur – which, unsurprisingly, inhabits a labyrinth below the king's palace. A young man from the village, Theo (Tom Hardy), is lamenting the loss of his girlfriend in the previous sweep of offerings to the beast so when he discovers that there is a chance she might still be alive he decides to accompany the next batch of lambs to the slaughter.

The project was a disappointment in many ways: the characters were poorly developed and the script left a lot to be desired. Add to that a flimsy plot and a disappointingly unscary monster and you've got a pretty below par viewing experience. It was billed as a horror but it did little to raise hairs. The film only managed to secure a limited release, in the US, Russia and Germany – and the UK was fortunate enough only to have to endure it in DVD format.

But don't just rely on this particular viewer's opinion – instead take it from the horse's mouth. In February 2012, Tom appeared on ITV's *The Jonathan Ross Show*. This particular instalment of Ross's programme had attracted a great deal of advance publicity, thanks to an audience member apparently reporting to the media that relations between the two men had soured during the course of the interview. Though Tom had been reticent when quizzed about the *Dark Knight Rises* film (with good reason, not wanting to spoil the surprise for film fans), things allegedly took a turn for the worse when Ross unearthed a clip from Tom's 'Find Me a Model' win. Tom admitted the clip was 'awful' but the banter that followed was all a good-humoured wind up, as both parties were at pains to point out subsequently. Tom later remarked: 'It was funny as hell and embarrassing, yes, but I was in on the gag and winding Jonathan up to put him in an awkward seat for a laugh.' Tom then didn't mince his words when suggesting which clip of his work should have been shown had the goal been to show him up, saying: 'If people want a good laugh at me desperately trying to get up the ladder, tell 'em to watch *Minotaur*. That's a pile of sh*t.'

Similarly strident opinions were in evidence when it came to analysis of the next motion picture in which Tom had a role – particularly if you chose to canvas opinion from the French.

Marie Antoinette was the third directorial offering from Sofia Coppola, daughter of *The Godfather* and *Apocalypse Now* director, Francis Ford Coppola. Prior to making *Marie Antoinette*, she had scored a commercial and critical hit with *Lost in Translation*, the film that made a star of Scarlett Johansson. *Marie Antoinette* saw the director reunited with Kirsten Dunst, an actress with whom she worked on *The Virgin Suicides* and who has sometimes been cited as her muse. Following *The Virgin Suicides*, the pair had expressed a desire to collaborate again and *Marie Antoinette* presented them with the perfect vehicle to do so.

The film was based on the book *Marie Antoinette – The Journey* by Lady Antonia Fraser. Marie Antoinette is often portrayed by historians as a shallow and frivolous woman – and by some, even as being the cause of the French Revolution. The book and therefore the film on which it was based are rather less critical of her and present her instead as a young woman struggling to come to terms with being uprooted from Austria and used to make a political alliance between Austria and France through her marriage to the Dauphin. Forced to deal with the protocol of life at Versailles and a husband who has little interest in her sexually, she seeks solace in expensive clothes, fine food and frivolity.

Probably largely thanks to her success with *Lost in Translation*, Coppola secured backing for her £21 million venture from Colombia Pictures. The film was clearly made to reach out to a young female audience and, as such, was laced with modern twists – there was, for example, a distinctive and incongruous soundtrack with music from the likes of The Strokes and Siouxsie and the Banshees and a lot of screen time was devoted to showing off sumptuous dresses and fabulous shoes.

Tom's role in the film was a small one and he only appears in a couple of scenes. He plays a character called Raumont who first makes an appearance on screen during the period of time when Marie Antoinette is occupying Le Petit Trianon, her nature retreat within the grounds of Versailles. He is one of her circle of friends at court whose main occupations seem to be gambling, dining and partying. There is a suggestion, too, that he is a little jealous of the queen's obvious attraction to Count Axel Fersen.

The film premiered at Cannes in May 2006 and, perhaps expectedly, got a poor response from French filmgoers who angrily hailed it as revisionist fantasy. Not everyone agreed, though, particularly on this side of the Channel. Many critics felt that it was technically a good film but that it lacked credibility as a historical piece. Writing in the *Observer*, Jason Solomons defended the film, saying: 'This is a funny, beautiful and, yes, cool film, blending fashion and pop with subtle comments on celebrity, emptiness and excess.' He did, however, go on to say that 'Coppola's poor little rich girl schtick can be annoying'.

From the lush grounds of Versailles in the 18th century to the urban stickiness of a summer's day on Hampstead Heath – and a very different kind of character for Tom to get his teeth into. Looking over Tom Hardy's cannon of work, it's a rare occurrence to see him turn in a comic performance – which is a shame because, when watching him in interviews and reading his comments in the press, it is clear that he is witty and has a keen sense of humour. In *Scenes of a Sexual*

Nature, Tom showed he was every bit as capable of delivering comedy as he was intense, serious drama.

As an exercise in making a film from scratch, *Scenes of a Sexual Nature* is a standout example. It was made on a shoestring budget of £500,000 and was shot in less than three weeks – and just to make the whole process even more fraught, the script was completed just two weeks before shooting started. For producer/director Ed Blum it was a baptism of fire as, although he'd directed for television and made a short film, this was his first foray into a full-length feature.

The idea for the film was the brainchild of Blum and his friend, television writer Aschlin Ditta. Originally, Blum had wanted to write seven short story pieces but, between the two of them, they realised that if they made the stories about 10 or 12 minutes each, they could weave them together into a feature-length film. What he was certain about at this stage was that he wanted the action of the film to take place outdoors and that it was to be filmed in a simple and uncluttered way.

It is credit to Blum and Ditta that they succeeded in recruiting a stellar British cast for their film. Considering they were pitching to actors' agents with an unfinanced script and a new director, this was a huge accomplishment. There were several factors that drew actors to the project, the primary one being the strength of the script – most loved the simplicity of the idea and the honesty of the writing. Blum observed: 'To attract really good actors you need really good parts and material and the individual stories really appealed to them.' And one of the stars of the film, Adrian Lester, agreed, noting that in the script, 'Nothing happens, but everything happens.'

Once a couple of big names had attached themselves to the film, interest snowballed and other actors were soon volunteering their services. Hugh Bonneville was amongst the first to come on board and, because Gina McKee had expressed a desire to work with him again, it wasn't long before she agreed to appear as well. With two actors of their stature involved, more impressive names were soon added to the call sheet including one of the hottest properties at the time, Ewan McGregor. Other stars included Andrew Lincoln, Mark Strong, Catherine Tate and, of course, Tom Hardy. For Tom, one of the big draws was that, for his scenes, he would be predominantly working with Oscar-nominated Sophie Okonedo (with whom he would also be paired in the BBC's *Oliver Twist*). Although the actors were paid Equity minimum for their work, on the upside the structure of the film meant they were only required for two or three days' shooting in total, so could fit the project in around their other work commitments.

Although the title of the film suggests the content might be near the knuckle, it's far from it. The ensemble piece covers the stories of seven unconnected couples over the course of one sunny summer afternoon on Hampstead Heath. The strands that make up the narrative paint pictures of people of varying ages and backgrounds, all at different points in their relationships. It's a slightly contrived set up and the range of characters has an 'all-inclusive' feel to it: we are offered a glimpse of, for example, a gay couple, a happily divorced couple, a young married couple and a pair on a blind date.

Tom's character is a young man called Noel who happens upon Anna (Sophie Okonedo) just as she has been dumped by her boyfriend Ludo (or Monopoly as Noel calls him during the course of their conversation). Noel is a lecherous but essentially harmless desperado in search of sex. He and Anna engage in a tit-for-tat conversation with Anna discharging barbed comments at this hapless character who has stepped into her line of fire. Ultimately, the confused and emotionally vulnerable Anna demands sex from Noel right then and there, on the heath, to which he at first nervously, but then enthusiastically, consents... only to have Anna reject him and walk off, leaving him with trousers around ankles and (to the delight of Hardy fans once again) bare bottom on display. This is the principal scene for Noel but we encounter him again as he loafs around the Heath seeking a woman who is as desperate as he is, only to be spurned each time.

Tom appreciated the chance to work alongside British acting royalty: 'It was exciting because I knew that the standards were going to be high,' he said. Perhaps because of the people he would be working alongside, he admitted he was nervous before he had to film his scenes, but that ultimately this was a positive thing as he can produce his best work when he is scared of the situation before him.

Whilst some of those who wrote about the film found the piece as a whole to be superficial and laboured, most picked out redeeming features from the individual performances. The luckless nature of Tom's character and the humour to be found in his impetuosity make his scenes amongst the most memorable in the film. Tom was singled out for praise on more than one occasion, with the *Evening Standard* commenting that he was 'pure comic relief.' Toby Clements in the *Telegraph* stated: 'Tom Hardy as the demented sexual predator is a delight.'

Light-hearted roles weren't something readily associated with Tom Hardy, but in *Scenes* he proved that he could more than deliver – though Noel does have a slightly deranged aspect to him that we might more easily associate with a Tom Hardy character. In years to come, Tom would revisit comedy on a much grander Hollywood scale – but sadly to a less favourable reception than he got for this low-budget British flick.

The miniscule budget of *Scenes* stands in stark contrast to the £16 million budget of the next job that came Tom's way. In 2007, the disaster movie *Flood* dramatised what would happen if the Thames Barrier were to be breached by a huge surge of water. *Flood* was based on a book written by Richard Doyle, who believed that the rising water levels caused by global warming were a serious threat to the capital. He wrote the book in 2003, having spent two-and-a-half years studying issues of climate change and its effect on weather patterns.

The film was made by UK production company Power, in association with both South African and Canadian production companies. It was shot over 11 weeks in South Africa and on location in London. The big names attached to it were Robert Carlyle, who plays a marine engineer, Tom Courtney who takes on the role of his estranged meteorologist father and David Suchet who plays the deputy prime minister.

Tom plays Zack, one of a pair of London Underground workers caught up in the mayhem. His part in the film consists mostly of chasing around dark tunnels underneath the city whilst pursued by furious surges of water – or being semi submerged in the water once it has caught up with him. As the characters are a pair, the action is nicely set up for one of them to come to a watery end while the other tries in vain to rescue him – but which one will it be?

In an effort to arouse interest in the film, publicity shots were released showing familiar London landmarks partially below water. The distributors refused to show the film to the press before it opened to the public in August 2007 – it had been rushed out to cinemas to take advantage of the fact that Britain was suffering an incredibly wet summer. This was a rather illogical move and, as the *Daily Record* pointed out: 'Why would we want to subject ourselves to more torrential rain in the name of entertainment?'

The film had its television debut on ITV1 in May 2008. TV reviewer Nancy Banks-Smith opened her critique with: 'When you feel lazy, there's a lot to be said for tosh, and tosh is available by the bucketful in *Flood*.'

Oh well, Tom, you can't win them all! Aquatic disaster films have a habit of sinking without trace. *Waterworld*, anyone?

Though *Scenes of a Sexual Nature* had been a masterclass in how to turn around a film on a sixpence, the Old Vic's 24-hour gala was more akin to the 'shotgun' theatre that Tom had been involved in with his own company. Since 2004, actor Kevin Spacey had been in place as the artistic director of the Old Vic theatre in London. The idea for the 24 Hour Plays Celebrity Gala had evolved there under his guardianship to become an annual event. Its purpose was to raise money for the theatre's Old Vic New Voices development programme, which showcased new writing.

The line-up of household names was announced the month prior to the gala and, as well as Tom, included the likes of Tamzin Outhwaite, Dominic West, Patricia Hodge and Hollywood star Vince Vaughan. The object of the exercise was for the cast to perform six plays, written from scratch at the theatre in the space of 24 hours – not too much to ask, then!

The proceedings began at 10pm on Saturday, 7 October 2006, when the actors involved came together to develop six short plays – which would then be penned overnight by writers such as Colin Teevan and Snoo Wilson, amongst others. The plays were then rehearsed by the assembled actors from 8am on the Sunday morning – and finally performed in front of an audience of about 1,000. Talking to the *Evening Standard* about the event, Kevin Spacey said: 'The 24 Hour Plays is one of the most thrilling and terrifying experiences an actor can have in a theatre. It's an adrenaline rush like no other and a great event for the audience.'

The fundraiser was a huge success and raised £110,000, as well as allowing the actors involved to experience a whole new way of performing – and have a lot of fun into the bargain. Once they had done their bit for charity, the thespians repaired to the Riverbank Plaza Hotel for a celebratory party.

The charity gala wasn't Tom's only performance in front of a live audience at this point in his career. In January 2007, Nicholas Hytner staged his modern interpretation of George Etherege's Restoration comedy, *The Man of Mode*, at the National Theatre. The central character of the play is a rake called Dorimant who, it is believed, Etherege based on the second Earl of Rochester, John Wilmot, a libertine and writer of bawdy poetry. Tom was to play Dorimant, who spends the play juggling the women in his life, and alongside him in the cast were Rory Kinnear as Sir Fopling Flutter and Hayley Atwell as Belinda.

In modernising the 17th century play, the action was transported to a present-day London. Language and references were brought up to date: instead of letters arriving by hand, they came via email; instead of characters taking carriage rides, they took taxis. Costumes too were contemporary; in an online promotional film for the production (perhaps designed to reach out to theatregoers who might have felt that Restoration Comedy would ordinarily not be for them), Tom can be seen looking sultry in a slick, dark suit while other members of the cast strut their stuff in either glamorous, sexy attire, or not much attire at all.

Modern reworkings of plays from bygone centuries are often well received. For example, Carlo Goldoni's 1743 play *The Servant of Two Masters* was adapted by Richard Bean to become *One Man Two Guv'nors*. Bean replaced the period Italian setting with Brighton in 1963 and the play enjoyed a successful West End run in 2012, with James Corden in the starring role. Would the new staging of *The Man of Mode* be a hit?

Prior to opening, *The Man of Mode* was singled out as a highlight of forthcoming cultural attractions in the press, with the prospect of Tom playing a sexy cad generating quite a bit of excitement in theatreland. Paul Taylor stated in the *Arts and Book Review* that he was 'salivating' at the thought of Tom, 'an actor who oozes sex and cockiness' taking the lead role in Hytner's production. Patricia Nicol in the *Sunday Times* concurred, proclaiming: 'At the National, a draw for all right-thinking women will be the dangerously charismatic Tom Hardy as Etherege's *Man of Mode*.'

However, when the play did open, it was greeted with varying degrees of enthusiasm. Many felt that the modern trappings were overdone, and that the abundant humour to be found in the script had been underplayed; it was 'long on cool but short on comedy,' The *Express* declared. Meanwhile, on the flipside, Quentin Letts of the *Daily Mail* deemed the modern slant 'strikingly successful'.

For once, it was not Tom who was lavished with the praise of the critics but Rory Kinnear. Opinions on Tom's performance were divided and it seemed that – unthinkable though this may seem – some who saw the play found the sight of Tom's toned and decorated torso a distraction rather than an attraction. Most of the critics agreed that Kinnear stole the show, which was unfortunate as Dorimant was the central role and all eyes should have been on him. Christopher Hart in the *Sunday Times* lamented that, alongside Kinnear's performance '...poor Tom Hardy, as Dorimant, seems to shrink into insignificance as the play progresses', while Nicholas de Jongh felt that Tom's performance fell short of a completely faithful portrayal of the character: 'He catches Dorimant's narcissism but none of his exploitative nastiness.'

In fairness, Tom had made no secret of how challenging he had found the role. It was obvious why he had been cast: in looks and demeanour he was a perfect fit for a charming seducer. He admitted, though, that he struggled with trying to find a way into the text. Having never had to get to grips with the language of a restoration drama before, he'd really had his work cut out. Ordinarily more at home with scripts that required him to have a brooding, edgy presence he now had to tackle more complex and florid dialogue. At the time the play was written, 'people knew how to speak a sentence as if they were writing, and they talked at high speed. I'm more of the grunting and nodding type so I've had a really big mountain to climb,' he explained to the *Daily Telegraph* in February 2007. 'At first, I found Etherege absolutely impenetrable. His wit is as difficult to understand as Latin.'

Mediocre reviews from theatre critics are one thing, but Tom's performance in *The Man of Mode* was on the receiving end of some rather more personal criticism. It came in the form of a letter from one of his teachers from Drama Centre. The letter was critical of the production of *The Man of Mode* as a whole and maintained that the play had not been interpreted as he felt it should be. Furthermore, according to Tom, the letter went on to state 'you are not a star'. Speaking to the *Telegraph*, Tom was understandably defensive. 'I decided against contacting my teacher because it was enough to know that I had worked at the National and he never f*****g would.'

With the benefit of hindsight, the statement 'you are not a star' was an ill-judged one. Though he had thus far only achieved a fraction of what he was capable of, the momentum behind Tom was building steadily. He had been given opportunities to learn from a host of experienced actors alongside whom he had been lucky enough to work, and he now had a good solid body of television work behind him. He'd taken on interesting character roles and shown he could turn his hand to comedy. But he was just about to find the characters with whom he could really make his mark. Bring on the bad boys.

CHAPTER SIX

TOUGH GUY

'I've cornered the market on the old psychos and weirdos,' Tom observed in conversation with Alan Carr on his Channel 4 chat show at the start of 2011, and there's certainly no arguing with that! Since 2007, Tom had played a host of villains, madmen and sociopaths, from Bill Sikes to Charles Bronson. Prior to that, he'd been working solidly and accumulating varied but unremarkable character roles for his CV. The point at which people started to remember his name, though, was when he showed just how well he could play bad. As he put it: 'No one's ever sat up when I've played someone nice or easy to watch.' In years gone by he'd brought his brand of intense and brooding menace to a relatively small arena on the London stage; he now stood poised to expose his dark side to the wider world of film and television audiences. Tom had been biding his time and was about to show what he was really capable of.

His first excursion into the darkness came with a role in a grisly horror film, *Waz*. In fact, the real title of the film was actually *W Delta Z*, but the use of the Greek letter to symbolise delta ($\triangle$) led to the film commonly being referred to as *Waz*. The significance of the title is made clear once the film gets underway: the equation is carved onto the skins of the victims of a recent spate of serial killings in New York, where the action takes place. The formula, it transpires, is in fact the Price Equation, a mathematical translation of the theory of natural selection. When used in the framework of the film's narrative, it refers specifically to the choice of either killing a loved one or being killed yourself. So far, so horrific.

Though set in New York, the film was mostly shot in Belfast and boasted a bizarre mixture of acting talent in its cast. Weary cop Eddie Argo is played by Stellan Skarsgard (usually the actor of choice for director Lars von Trier), and his rookie sidekick, Helen, by former Australian soap actress Melissa George. The only concession to a big Hollywood name comes in the form of actress Selma Blair who is, as ever, utterly convincing as the victim of an attack by brutal gang and who exacts her revenge on them one by one. The gang of hoods is headed up by Pierre Jackson (Tom Hardy) and also includes former So Solid Crew member Ashley Walters, who plays Daniel. Rounding off the eclectic cast is quirky actor and comedian Paul Kaye, who plays the scientist proponent of a gene theory derived from W Delta Z.

One of the themes explored in the film is the blurring of the boundary between good and evil. Most of the characters are shown to be capable of both: Eddie is driven by the desire to catch the bad guys but we question his grasp of right and wrong as the film explores some of his actions and the motives behind them. Gang member Daniel is morally ambiguous too: he is essentially a good person but is caught up on the fringes of the gang's despicable deeds. Though we would like to think there is nothing redeeming about violent gang leader Pierre, even he is given a chance to show his human side via his relationship with his grandmother. In one scene, he is seen on the phone to her, saying he loves her, just seconds before carrying out what he believes to be a revenge shooting.

Tom's looks, his swagger and his dominant presence on screen all made him credible as this nasty piece of work. The teeth that had once been his downfall were now just part of the appeal. Always wanting to do his job to the best of his ability, Tom was able to draw on the well of darkness he seemed to be able to divine when he needed to. He did, however, recognise that digging so deep for a part had its pitfalls. 'Once I start work, I'm a bit of a dick in this character. It's very hard to pull him back... he's a nutter.'

Directed by first-time feature director Tom Shankland, the film fell somewhere between the psychological thriller *Se7en* and the more gratuitous torture fest of the *Saw* franchise movies. It didn't make much of an impact on its release; it had a lukewarm reception in the UK, with most reviewers regarding the film as unconvincing and a touch tedious.

Landing the role in *Waz* did, however, turn out to be a pivotal point in Tom's life and career. It was on the set of this film that he met former US Marine turned personal trainer Patrick Monroe – otherwise known as Pnut. Having cemented their friendship, the pair began to work together regularly and it is Pnut whom Tom credits for helping him achieve the remarkable physical transformations in evidence in many of his films. Tom's respect for his friend shines through whenever he talks about him. 'He's everything I ever wanted to be. He's done so much and he's potentially a truly dangerous, fierce man. But he's the softest guy I've ever met. Full of humanity. And humour. And tolerance. Everything that I really want to be,' he told *Men's Health* magazine.

It's not just his physical form that Tom entrusts to Pnut, it's also his mental wellbeing. 'Counsel… I can't keep counsel with myself because I always tell myself the wrong thing. I have to keep people nearby from whom I can learn.'

It would be fair to say that Pnut's presence has been a driving force in Tom's upward trajectory. The pair met just as Tom was starting to sink his teeth into meatier roles, ones that demanded physical change as well as the ability to shift mentally. It was Pnut who made sure Tom went about changing from emaciated Stuart Shorter in *Stuart: A Life Backwards* to bulked-up Charles Bronson in the correct way. More recently, Pnut has had his work cut out as Tom has had to pack on even more muscle for the roles of Tommy Conlon in *Warrior* and Bane in *The Dark Knight Rises*.

Jack Donnelly from Channel Four's series *Cape Wrath* has become something of a legendary character in TV history, thanks to Tom's deeply sinister portrayal of him. With Jack, Tom showed just how far he could take it when inhabiting menacing and unstable characters. The role was a great opportunity for him to venture even further into the recesses of his psyche and, because the character of Jack had committed a violent crime in his teens, Tom sought to get under his skin by researching the boys who had killed James Bulger. Duane Clark, the director of *Cape Wrath* was unequivocal about why he chose Tom to play Jack. 'The minute he walked into the audition, I knew he was what we needed,' he explained to the *Telegraph*. 'When his name came up, the producers said he was too posh. But anyone who meets Tom knows he is a nice middle-class boy from East Sheen with a very dark underbelly.'

It was in 2007 that Channel Four cast a dark shadow over the summer months with its new, much-hyped series. The show kicks off with the Brogan family (Danny and Evelyn and their teenage twins Mark and Zoe) arriving, blindfolded, at an isolated settlement called Meadowlands. The reason for the secrecy is because they are part of a witness protection programme, but viewers aren't let in on this secret immediately. With its uniform houses in brightly coloured cladding, Meadowlands looks idyllic – but on closer inspection is a spooky and disconcerting place. The Brogans feel even more ill at ease when it transpires the residents of the town have already been informed of their arrival and even their (assumed) names.

At first, only Danny knows the truth about Meadowlands: that, in fact, all of its residents have been relocated there by the authorities, so have either transgressed or been the victim of a crime. Whatever their story, they are all there for a reason and they all have murky secrets to hide. The very fact that they live in Meadowlands at all means they have a past they must forget and a present they are forced to embrace. As the creepy local cop Bernard Wintersgill mutters to Danny: 'The past is not just another country – it's another planet.' The town is closely monitored and only those with permission arrive – though no one ever seems to leave.

The most unsettling – and memorable – character we meet in Episode One is handyman Jack Donnelly – or as his scrappy business card would have it, Jack 'of all trades'. Jack is a baseball-hat-wearing psychopathic sex offender whose presence is described by another Meadowlands resident as 'looming'. He is by turns intimidating and angry, and the violence within him is roused if those he is threatening show fear.

From his first scene it is clear that Jack is both a disturbed and disturbing man. He creeps up behind Zoe, sniffing her hair and standing invasively close. Zoe's reaction, however, is not quite what he expects – she shows no fear of him and instead acts suggestively, encouraging him to come and see her at home on the flimsy proviso of fixing a light. At no point is Zoe scared of Jack – rather, she is convinced that she alone can cure him of his deviance and goes so far as to say that she is his 'last hope'. His relationship with her, while deeply dysfunctional, is different from those he has with other women. For example, Jack is also getting his kicks from an abusive relationship with doctor's wife Abigail. With her husband all but ignoring her at home, Abigail indulges in the unbalanced relationship with Jack because attention from him, she feels, is preferable to no attention at all.

Given his behaviour and how much of a threat Danny sees him as being to his daughter, it's no surprise that Jack comes to a violent end as the first episode draws to a close – though he does return as a ghost to offer advice to Sergeant Wintersgill, who is determined to find out the truth about what happened to him. Ironic, considering it is Wintersgill who beats Donnelly to within an inch of his life on the football pitch after Danny expresses his concern for Zoe's safety around the handyman. Such is the twisted justice meted out in Meadowlands.

While the series looked promising when it was first broadcast, it didn't become the cult hit it was supposed to be. The intention was for it to fall somewhere between the mystery of *Lost* and the veiled suburban menace of *Desperate Housewives*, but it somehow failed to hit the mark. As Jaci Stephen commented: 'In trying to take its lead from such shows, it ends up being a weak carbon copy.' The mystery was at times overplayed to the point of becoming confusing, and the goings-on were perhaps just a little too odd for viewers to be able to realistically buy in to them. Ratings for *Cape Wrath* fell below expectations and the planned second series was never commissioned.

The show wasn't without its redeeming features, though. The central performance from David Morrissey was strong and convincing, as was the insidious Sergeant Wintersgill played by Ralph Brown. For all its weirdness, many viewers felt that Tom's performance as Jack was one of the best – if not the best – things about *Cape Wrath* and that the series lost one of its biggest draws when he was killed off. The *Observer* columnist Kathryn Flett, for one, raved about his presence in the show: 'Tom Hardy, as the terrifying Jack Donnelly, was very dangerously, positively murderously, dark and twisted... and as sexy as hell with it.'

Evil, it seemed, was the order of the day and for those who love to see Tom at his villainous best, it was exciting to hear that he was to play Bill Sikes in a forthcoming BBC adaptation of *Oliver Twist*. For Tom, it would have been hard to pass up this gig. As well as being excited about working with *EastEnders* writer Sarah Phelps, the show would see him reunited with *The Virgin Queen* director Coky Giedroyc. To complete a triumvirate that he's referred to as 'magic' was casting director Maggie Lunn. If that wasn't enough, the Nancy to his Bill Sikes would be played by Sophie Okonedo, with whom he'd loved working on *Scenes of a Sexual Nature*.

Over the years, there have been numerous retellings of the Charles Dickens classic, so the challenge for any reworking is always how to breathe new life into the material. Amongst the most memorable adaptations are David Lean's 1948 film starring Alec Guinness as Fagin, Carol Reed's film version of Lionel Bart's musical, *Oliver!* and Roman Polanski's 2005 film which saw Ben Kingsley take on the role of Fagin, with Jamie Foreman as Bill Sikes. How would this series go about offering a fresh perspective on the story we think we all know inside out?

For one thing, the structure of this *Oliver Twist* would be different from other classic adaptations that had gone before it: the first instalment was an hour-long episode and was followed by half-hour segments, which were to be aired on consecutive nights. This approach had been tried out for the BBC adaptation of *Bleak House* in 2005 and could be construed as going back to basics with Dickens' material. His novels were originally written with the intention of feeding them to the public in serial form, so his skill was in constructing a story to which readers would want to return for more (no pun intended) week after week. This kind of rolling drama with a cliffhanger at the end of each episode is of course exactly how *EastEnders* is formatted for television, so was familiar territory for Phelps. 'Dickens wrote for an immediate response from an audience that just wants to be told a story. *EastEnders*, at its best, has that,' she commented to *Time Out*. What she really wanted to do was to create 'an *Oliver Twist* for our times'.

Tom had his own theory about why a new exploration of *Oliver Twist* would stand up in its own right. To him, it was the same as when approaching any classic like Dickens or Shakespeare – the material has been reinvented time and again but each time, the group of people working on the project can mould it into a new form. 'Everybody's got a perspective and [when] you get a team together, the alchemy on each project will be different from the last.'

Phelps's refreshing and accomplished script was responsible for attracting a superior British cast to the production. In the spirit of bringing a new slant to the story, some of the actors appointed were ones you might not readily think of as being a conventional fit for these established Dickens characters. Traditionally, actors who have played Fagin have been thin and stooped but, in a genius move, Timothy Spall was cast to play him. Phelps knew she wanted the actor who played Fagin to be 'somebody more expansive' than in the past and, with Spall, they created a Fagin who was more colourful and complex than previous incarnations. He is charming but beneath the charm lies a steely desire for self-preservation. 'He manages to use his warmth as a channel for his deviousness,' observed Spall of his character.

Julian Rhind-Tutt, better known for his role in cult comedy *Green Wing* was cast as the sinister Monks, Oliver's nemesis;

and Sarah Lancashire (previously the bubbly Raquel in *Coronation Street*) was to be the conniving, grasping Mrs Corney. Rob Brydon, better known for his comedy acting, was to play the unyielding judge, Mr Fang. Unconventional choices, but they all brought something new and surprising to their characters.

The casting decisions for *Oliver Twist* were vital in giving it more resonance with the 21st century. There has traditionally been a tendency to portray Oliver as an angelic, naïve, slightly wet lad – and the actors who have played him have often had accents which sound more like Surrey schoolboy than workhouse orphan. When writing her Oliver, Sarah Phelps had a clear idea of what she wanted from her protagonist. Oliver is an orphan who has been passed from baby farm to the grim confines of the workhouse. He's been hungry his whole life, mistreated, but has had enough nerve to challenge the figures of authority around him. Phelps's Oliver would be no angel: he would be a tough child, albeit with a good, kind soul.

Having auditioned 750 boys, Maggie Lunn then happened to ask a friend if she knew any young actors who would be suitable for the role. This friend knew the mother of William Miller and he was put forward for the part. He was ideal in looks and in personality: he had brown hair, startling, honest eyes and he radiated confidence. 'He looks beautiful but he's a little fighter and he looks people in the eye, which is what I wanted with my Oliver – that he looks Bill Sikes in the eye.'

Her decision was spot on – Miller nailed completely what she had wanted to achieve with the character. There is a scene which captures the essence of this Oliver perfectly. It is one in which he looks Sikes straight in the eye and tells him that he's not scared of him because he's already seen worse in his life, and it is one of the most powerful and affecting in the drama. The *Independent* was effusive in its praise for Miller in the lead role, saying: 'The real casting coup is 11-year-old William Miller as an Oliver far removed from the wan child actor who usually inhabits the role. Miller is also probably a far cry from the somewhat soupy Oliver that Dickens created, but the story is better for it.'

Casting Sophie Okonedo as Nancy was also an inspired choice. Phelps admitted that she was fed up with period dramas set in London always being dominated by white faces and was determined that her Nancy would be black or mixed race. In reality, the London of Dickens' time was ethnically diverse – it was home to Jewish and Irish immigrants and by the mid-19th century there were already second and third generation black Africans living in the capital. Okonedo brought to Nancy a balance of fearlessness and tenderness.

The relationship between Bill Sikes and Nancy is another part of *Oliver Twist* we might assume we already know inside out. But this new script and the pairing of Sophie Okonedo with Tom Hardy meant that the focus was not solely on the abusive nature of their relationship. Instead it sought to show that affection and a chemistry of sorts was present between them. In this drama, the killing of Nancy is as violent as ever but we subsequently see Sikes unable to come to terms with the reality that his blows have killed her. He deludes himself into thinking that he's given her a punishment beating and implores her to get up, struggling to let his eyes rest on what he has done. When Bill goes on the run with Oliver, his guilt is in evidence as he is haunted by visions of Nancy (which is referred to in Dickens' book but which is often left out of dramatisations).

Bill Sikes is unquestionably a bully who maintains his status through intimidation and violence, but to have played him as a larger-than-life aggressor was neither what this new take on the story required, nor was it how Tom wanted to develop the character. In the 1968 film of *Oliver!* Oliver Reed had put in a masterful and memorable performance as Sikes. It was impossible for Tom to ignore Reed's portrayal but he was confident in his own interpretation of the man. 'I could never go up against a performance as classic as that. Oliver Reed played Bill as this horrible, booming, alcoholic brawler. I play him softer, a bit sensual and maybe a bit more pathetic,' Tom told *The New Review* magazine.

In making this an *Oliver Twist* relevant to today's society, Bill was presented as a threatening presence but also as a man who displays certain vulnerabilities. This was familiar territory to Tom who, rather than play these kinds of baddies at full throttle, always pulled back and sought out their weaknesses to create more convincing and shaded characters. He did his homework on developing a 360-degree Sikes, saying, 'What's interesting for me to explore is where the vulnerability is going to be with a character like Bill,' he said. 'This manifests itself in relationships with Nancy and Bullseye – and gin... he's trying to fill something with the companionship of a good woman, with the dog and with getting out of his head, which to me immediately ring [sic] alarm bells of somebody who needs a cuddle.'

He also admitted that the character research and development he had been putting into prisoner Charles Bronson would be coming in useful for Bill Sikes. The filming of *Bronson* had been delayed by a year, so 'I put a lot of the work I did on him into Bill'.

Tom's portrayal of Bill Sikes is mesmerising. Every scene in which he appears is infused with knife-edge tension and he is like a coiled spring, waiting to be triggered. This character doesn't show his brutal side by being ostentatiously belligerent but succeeds in being terrifying by his stillness – the softly spoken words and penetrating stares are enough to make the blood run cold. Writing in the *Sunday Telegraph*, John Preston summed up Tom's performance perfectly, saying: 'This was by far the most sinister Sikes I've ever seen – this was a man seething with aggression, his eyes forever roaming round seeking someone to bottle or bash.'

The fact that the drama was filmed in London added to its air of authenticity. As previously mentioned, budget restraints have forced the making of many dramas out of the UK and into Eastern Europe. In fact, Roman Polanksi's feature-length adaptation of *Oliver Twist* was filmed in the Czech Republic. For this *Oliver*, though, director Coky Giedroyc and production designer Grenville Horner devoted time to scouring London for appropriate locations for filming and then decided how they would fit those locations into the story. Horner knew that he didn't want to just copy how other period dramas had tried to depict London and instead went back to some illustrative source material from Dickens' time for his references.

Each part of the drama has a unique look to capture the changing mood depending on where Oliver is on his journey.

The workhouse is filmed in grey tones (to match the gruel, which was in fact Ready Brek made with water, with a dash of black food colouring thrown in); London, by contrast, is full of bustle and noise; Fagin's den is intriguing and colourful while the sanctuary represented by Brownlow's house is all cool colours and clean lines.

The hard work and careful thought that had gone into ensuring that this production held its own as an interpretation of the Dickens story paid off. 8 million viewers tuned in to watch the first episode, which was aired on 18 December 2007. Most critics, too, seemed to appreciate *Oliver Twist* and agreed that it was a dark and brooding piece with a magnificent cast. The *Sunday Telegraph* even stated that, had five stars not been their highest rating for a show, they would have given *Oliver Twist* six stars. Praise indeed!

As for Tom, he'd had a ball. He'd admitted that he'd loved the rollercoaster nature of Dickens stories and likened them to oscillating between the mood of *Taxi Driver* one minute, and Disneyworld the next. '*Oliver Twist* is a great thing to be a part of – and I'm in it!' he enthused.

Other actors on set had been delighted to work with Tom. Young William Miller commented: 'The crew is nice, the actors are nice, especially Tom Hardy, he's really cool.' And Rob Brydon had nothing but praise for him, saying: 'Tom is an extraordinary talent and an impressive individual.'

'I'm an actor, for f***k's sake. I'm an artist. I've played with anything and anyone.'

Tom Hardy is known for his honesty when being interviewed. He is forthcoming, entertaining and rapid-fire.

Just occasionally, though, his unchecked truthfulness can create an undesired media storm. The above quote, for example, was Tom's response to a question asked of him during an interview with *Attitude* magazine in 2008. The question was 'Have you ever had sexual relations with men?' and had been asked because Tom's latest character, Handsome Bob in Guy Ritchie's film *RocknRolla* had come out as gay during the course of the film.

The press, of course, went into overdrive and the quote was re-quoted, written about and pulled apart for days afterwards. Subsequently – and probably growing increasingly tired of having the statement thrown back at him – Tom explained that he was referring to the work he had done as an actor, not about his personal life. In 2011, he clarified matters further in an interview with *Marie Claire* magazine, still annoyed that his words had been misconstrued: 'I have never put my penis in a man,' he declared starkly. 'If that's what you like, cool. But it doesn't do it for me.' Sorted.

Guy Ritchie had made a name for himself as a director with *Lock, Stock and Two Smoking* Barrels in 1998. It was a stylised, punchy criminal caper and was credited as being the film that revived the gangster genre for the modern era. He followed it up in 2000 with *Snatch*, which was in a similar vein and also well received. Unfortunately for Ritchie, he then turned out two commercial flops in the form of the much-ridiculed *Swept Away* (made with his then-wife Madonna) and *Revolver*, which was given a hearty thumbs down by reviewers who criticised it for having an overly complicated, pretentious plot. *RocknRolla* was being touted as Ritchie's return to form as he revisited the familiar territory of a pacy gangland tale – albeit a more cuddly one than conventional underworld films. 'I just like the underworld because it is an efficient polarisation of humans. My protagonists flirt with the law and have probably done a few naughty things but are actually good guys,' he stated when asked about the nature of the films he made.

The plot was, unsurprisingly, formulaic. It seemed that Ritchie's earlier triumphs were a blend of certain ingredients which had equalled success and he was sticking to his recipe. The film weaves itself around a story involving a property scam and a bunch of shady characters including a rather obviously named Russian billionaire Omovich (who just happens to have a stake in a London football club – wink, wink); gangland boss Lenny, played by Tom Wilkinson; underworld minnow One Two (Gerard Butler) and his two sidekicks Mumbles (Idris Elba) and the aptly-named Handsome Bob (Tom Hardy). Also roaming around in the action are junkie pop star Johnny Quid (Toby Kebbell), a crooked accountant played by Thandie Newton and Mark Strong as Lenny's right-hand man. As usual, there's a spider's web of relationships between the characters, each of them owing money to another higher up the food chain or being in possession of valuables that belong to someone else.

Handsome Bob is the getaway driver for the rag-tag gang of hoodlums headed up by One Two – ironic considering at this point Tom had not yet learned to drive! Bob also turns out to be the lynchpin of the surprising sub-plot. In this testosterone-fuelled, macho film, Ritchie throws the audience a curveball by having Handsome Bob reveal that he is gay. This narrative strand marked out *RocknRolla* as being different from his other films and perhaps, as it came out 10 years after *Lock Stock*, the storyline was a gesture at giving the film a more up-to-date feel.

The pivotal scene for Tom's character comes the night before he is about to be sent to prison. One Two has organised what he thinks will be a send-off to remember for his friend, involving strippers and excess. Handsome Bob, though, is not cheered by the prospect and, while in the car with One Two, admits to him that he is gay and that it is One Two who is the object of his desire. There follows a scene that brings a smile to the face in which Bob and One Two dance, awkwardly, in a clinch in a salsa club. This touching moment was, according to Tom, his favourite part of filming.

Handsome Bob was based on a real-life gangster who had apparently come out to one of the writers of the film. 'But the real guy sounded a lot tougher than Handsome Bob,' admitted Tom to *Out* magazine. He went on to make it clear that he was pleased that his character had been taken in this direction by Ritchie, that it felt good to shake up perceptions in a film that would generally be considered fodder for alpha males : 'Playing a gay man in a Guy Ritchie movie is a finger up to that whole attitude of men talking about men doing men's thing, which is so f*****g narrow-minded. Handsome Bob is what a man should be – except for the part of him taking a crowbar to the back of someone's head.'

When recalling the making of *RocknRolla*, Tom confessed that there had been a great atmosphere on set and a lot of 'schoolboy humour'. Although the cast was almost entirely male, the presence of females on set prevented things from becoming too laddish. He got a shock, though, when a very notable female appeared on set one day. Just as Tom was sitting in Bob's Land Rover, preparing for his big confessional scene with Gerard Butler, who should appear in the back of the car but Madonna herself! So in awe was Tom that he admits he can't recall the conversation they shared.

One thing he can remember, though, is what happened next. Gerard Butler had apparently been feeling under the weather that day and Madonna insisted that he have a Vitamin B12 jab. But not in the arm... 'Then she gave Gerard Butler a shot of Vitamin B in the arse in the back of the f*****g Range Rover! Gerard Butler's flabby arse came through the window and she shot it with a jab of B12. Right in his arse! As attractive as he is, his arse just has no appeal to me. It's a distraction when I'm trying to learn my lines!' he told *Attitude* magazine in 2008.

A lot of filming took place in London, which has a strong presence in the film. Shooting was also a swift affair, according to the stars: Ritchie was efficient with structuring his work, always knowing what he was setting out to achieve. Unlike a director such as Ridley Scott who shoots as he wants to edit, Ritchie would tinker with the look, feel and structure of his story at editing stage. 'There's the film that we all read on the script and then the film that's in Guy's head and sometimes you're not going to know what that is... until I saw [sic] the final edit,' remarked Tom.

Unfortunately, the film contained several out-of-date references which jarred and gave the impression that it was too much of a hark back to the Ritchie films of the nineties. In *RocknRolla*, Tony Blair is still the Prime Minister and we are told in the opening sequence that London property prices are on the rise (which was far from the truth towards the end of 2008). Some enjoyed the film not for its plot but for its atmosphere and sense of fun, but most were unimpressed. Christopher Tookey writing for the *Daily Mail* thought it was an 'embarrassing piece of self-parody'.

Tom, though, had wanted to work with Guy Ritchie for a long time and was delighted to have been able to do so. 'He's my boy,' he once said of the director. At the end of the movie, there had been an indication that sequels were in the offing, but it's not particularly astonishing that none has been forthcoming. Besides, Ritchie has since had his renaissance with the *Sherlock Holmes* films starring Robert Downey Jr and Jude Law. When Tom was asked in an interview what would become of his character if a sequel were to be made, he replied cheerily that he would get to wear 'sparkly boots and better clothes'.

Ritchie could perhaps have taken a lesson about pared-down, less ostentatious film-making from a young man called Charlie Belleville. At just 23 years old, Belleville directed his first full-length movie. It was shot in 11 days on a budget of just £5,000 – shame on you, Hollywood blockbusters. *The Inheritance* was written by Edinburgh-born producer Tim Barrow and told the story of two estranged brothers who travel from Edinburgh to the Isle of Skye to claim the legacy left to them by their father. By day, Belleville worked in PR but had fitted in the directing project around his nine-to-five job.

Belleville knew Tom Hardy through friends and, with a stroke of luck, he managed to get him – as well as the other actors who appeared – to star in the film for free. The cast was small, with Tim Barrow and Fraser Sivewright playing the brothers, Tom Hardy playing their father and Imogen Toner as Tara, a hitchhiker the brothers pick up on their road trip. Shooting took place entirely in Scotland and only in natural light, so the filming schedule was compact to say the least. The scenes with Tom were used as flashbacks in the film and shot in London.

Charlie Belleville expressed huge gratitude to Tom for giving up his time when he was just fresh off the set from *RocknRolla*. He was also very impressed with Tom's grasp of a Scottish accent for the film, which sounded totally authentic.

The Inheritance premiered at London's Raindance Film Festival in the autumn of 2007 and was shortlisted with four other films in the Best UK Feature category in the Raindance awards. 'We were so lucky to get Tom Hardy,' Charlie enthused to Edinburgh's *Evening News*. 'He is such an accomplished actor and it has given the film a terrific sense of legitimacy when we are competing against so many other low-budget films.'

Although the film missed out on the prize at the festival, it was then nominated – and won – the Raindance Award at the British Independent Film Awards later that year. On top of that, it was nominated for Best First Time Director and Best First Time Producer at BAFTA Scotland's 2007 New Talent Awards. It also boasted a wealth of positive reviews, with *Time Out* referring to Belleville as 'a talent to watch'.

Tom said that when he saw the final cut of the film at the festival, he was thrilled with what had been achieved. 'Everything that was stacked against *The Inheritance*... it's incredible that the piece actually made it to the screen, for starters – and then I think the bonus of it is that it's an award-winning film.' He also pointed out that it was a spectacular achievement, given that it was made with scant finance.

It's perhaps ironic that just as Tom was carving a name for himself as the go-to man for tough guy roles, something happened in his life that brought the nurturing, softer side of the actor to the fore – he became a father. On 8 April 2008, Louis was born to Tom and Rachael Speed.

Becoming a parent means that priorities in life change and everything centres around the new life that has been brought into the world. For Tom, having a son was undoubtedly a grounding experience and one which drew a line under the life he'd previously lived. 'Having my son stripped away so much unnecessary baggage,' he reflected a few years after Louis was born.

During the filming of *RocknRolla*, Tom had noted the irony of being cast as the getaway driver even though he was not able to drive. That changed, however, when he realised that he needed to be able to drive Rachael to and from hospital during the pregnancy. By this time Tom was 30 and it was probably high time he got his licence – the fact that he hadn't done so until this point was a hangover from his wayward youth. In an interview with the *Observer*, he said: 'I couldn't be trusted with a car when I was younger, so I got used to travelling by tube... I love it because it's new to me. I've got years of driving to catch up on.'

The fact he can now drive has brought additional benefits for Tom. Car manufacturer Audi saw something in the actor they liked and he currently has a promotional deal with them so is now only to be seen behind the wheel of an Audi motor.

'People ask me about cars and I am all about the Audis. All I ever drive.' No surprise there – these deals are lucrative and the manufacturer will always want to guarantee exclusivity for the relationship between the product and its celebrity endorser. You'll never see Roger Federer holding anything other than a Wilson tennis racket, for example.

Tom makes no secret of how proud a father he is, often taking photos of his son to show journalists when he pitches up for an interview. A burgeoning career and supportive family have played their parts in helping Tom on the path to rehabilitation but Louis is a very real reminder as to why he can never go back to his old ways. 'There are two things that are great in my life,' he told *Marie Claire* magazine in 2011, 'One is my family and the other is my work, and I will protect both to the death.'

He has also mused about the contrast between the disturbed, psychotic screen characters he has become so synonymous with and the doting father that he really is. 'It's funny, isn't it? The characters I've played have been mostly violent, and I'm so far from being violent or aggressive. I spend a lot of time watching *Fireman Sam* with my three-year-old son Louis,' he reflected when speaking to the *Daily Telegraph* in 2011. There's an image that's sure to make women's hearts melt – hard man Tom snuggled up on the sofa with his little boy watching children's TV.

As Tom's career grows and he becomes an international star, inevitably he will have to endure long periods of time away from the UK – and from his son. He has spoken of his concerns about being a long-distance father but is aware that if he suffers a little bit for it now, hopefully in the future he might be able to pick and choose his commitments a bit more freely, just as Brad Pitt and Angelina Jolie now do in order to look after their sizeable brood. Plus, of course, he wants to keep working so that he can make sure Louis has everything he needs as he is growing up. 'I am very much aware of being a Skype father, which is really sad sometimes,' he told *Hello* magazine in 2012 as he prepared to up sticks in order to start filming *Mad Max*. 'But one reason I'm away so often is to secure enough finances, so that in the future I can choose to go away for shorter periods and command enough money to bring my family with me. At the moment I'm just doing what I have to do.'

Whilst he obviously doesn't like being apart from Louis, he is able to rest safe in the knowledge that when he's not in the UK, his son is looked after by Rachael and her husband – and he also told *Hello* that Rachael is now pregnant again, so Louis will have a half-sibling to keep him company.

It was good fortune that just as Tom took on the responsibility of being a father, so his career started on a steep upward trajectory. He was chosen to portray two very different but equally challenging real-life characters in dramatisations of their lives. The two performances would be the start of establishing Tom's reputation as one of the finest actors of our time.

CHAPTER SEVEN

TOM: A CAREER TRANSFORMED

Tom is a shape shifter. His best work is done when he is entering into a character that isn't himself.' These words were spoken by Tom's friend, the director Robert Delamere, and never was the actor's transformative ability more in evidence than when he took on first the role of Stuart Shorter in *Stuart: A Life Backwards* and then Charles Bronson, Britain's most notorious prisoner, in *Bronson*. These two utterly contrasting roles were pivotal in shifting Tom's career up a gear and marked the beginning of his metamorphosis from jobbing actor to big star.

Stuart: A Life Backwards by Alexander Masters was published in 2005 and went on to become an unlikely bestseller. It was an unconventional book in many ways. Its hero was, at first glance, something of an anti-hero – a homeless man with multiple drug addictions; an alcoholic with a disturbed mind who was prone to unpredictable bouts of rage. The book also fell somewhere between biography and memoir – plus, as its title suggests, it tells the story of a life in reverse chronological order.

Masters first encountered Stuart in 1998 in Cambridge, where they both lived – albeit in very different circumstances. Masters was a writer who worked part-time as a fundraiser for Wintercomfort, a day shelter for rough sleepers in the city. When the two people who ran the shelter were wrongfully arrested and imprisoned over drug-dealing allegations at Wintercomfort (it was in fact some of the homeless people who used the centre who were dealing drugs on the premises, unbeknown to the managers), Alexander was, rightly, incensed at what had happened and launched a campaign to Free the Cambridge Two. It was at one of the meetings about the appeal that he met Stuart and the two became unlikely friends.

At the start of the book, Masters describes Stuart as a 'thief, hostage taker, psycho and sociopathic street raconteur, my spy on how the British chaotic underclass spend their troubled days at the beginning of the 21st century'. He was at first fascinated by Stuart but, as he came to spend more time with him, a genuine friendship evolved between them. Masters was intrigued by Stuart's life and what had made him the man he became, so persuaded Stuart to let him write his life story. The first draft took two years to complete but was rejected by its subject. Stuart felt that the structure of the story was boring and that it should be more like a murder mystery, where the plot builds towards the revelation. As he put it, he wanted the reader to discover 'what murdered the boy I was…'.

Although the subject matter is not the usual sort of fodder

for a biography/memoir, the book was a hit and went on to win awards, including the *Guardian* First Book Award in 2005. The critical acclaim and healthy sales were thoroughly deserved: the book's structure was unique and captivating, and the author's depiction of Stuart inspired tears, laughter and frustration – we see Stuart through Alexander's eyes and we feel for him as the author does. It was an important book to have written because it was a story that needed to be told – people like Stuart are rarely given a voice, especially one as eloquent as Masters'.

Literary critics were united in their praise for *Stuart*. Minette Martin in the *Sunday Times* described it as: 'One of the most remarkable and touching biographies I've ever read. It also raises more urgent, contemporary questions about the human condition than any other biography I can think of.' Anne Chisholm, writing in the *Sunday Telegraph*, said the book was 'humane, instructive and entirely original'.

When a book catches readers' imaginations as *Stuart* did, hearts sink slightly at the prospect of the story being made into a film, be it for television or the big screen. Readers often feel a sense of ownership towards a book they love and worry that changes might be made during dramatisation. So it would have been a relief for fans to learn that the author of the book was to turn screenwriter for the TV film – at least Stuart and Masters' story would remain in the hands of its originator. Production company Neal Street was to make *Stuart: A Life Backwards*, with David Attwood directing and Pippa Harris producing. The executive producers would be Oscar-winning Sam Mendes along with Tara Cook.

While Masters was in charge of adapting his book, he was

of course justified in having concerns about who would take on the two lead roles. According to Pippa Harris, when he initially went to see Neal Street, he spent a long time asking them questions about how they would approach the film and who might star in it. One actor would have to do justice to his complicated, many-faceted friend, Stuart and the other would have to, well, be an accurate representation of himself. He needn't have worried. There were, apparently, only ever two actors on the wish list for the roles.

Benedict Cumberbatch's reputation as a talented new face was steadily growing and he had a healthy body of work behind him. He'd not yet reached the heady heights of fame and adulation that *Sherlock* would bring him, but it was clear he was an intelligent, gifted man who had the potential to become a star. His turn in the film adaptation of David Nicholls' book *Starter for Ten* (on which, coincidentally, he'd worked with Pippa Harris) had been one of the most memorable performances in the movie. He had also previously worked with David Attwood on another BBC drama, *To The Ends of the Earth*. Cumberbatch's attachment to *Stuart: A Life Backwards* started with an introduction to Alexander Masters who had come to see a play he was in at the Almeida with Harris and Attwood. Cumberbatch had heard good things about the book and had listened to the Radio Four adaptation, so was familiar with the story. It was later, while he was filming *Atonement,* that he got the call about the part of Masters – he read the script, loved it and was on board.

The only actor ever on the cards to play Stuart was Tom. In fact, Pippa Harris has subsequently said that both she and David Attwood knew that he was born to play the part. When speaking to the *Daily Telegraph*, Attwood said: 'In many ways Tom is very similar to Stuart. He is an addict. He is slightly crazy. He is damaged and wounded. But, unlike Stuart, he has come out the other side.' Tom found it amusing that he was considered the ideal actor for this alcoholic, drug-addicted street-dweller. But he shared the opinion and made no secret of how badly he wanted the part. 'I fell in love with the piece. I could hear the music of it,' he later commented.

Tom is a stickler for getting his performances technically perfect so that they look and feel authentic and he had a lot of preparation to do for *Stuart* before he even appeared on set. He recognised that Stuart had multiple issues that he as an actor had to learn how to represent. There were certain points of reference that Tom already had, due to the life he had once lived: with alcoholism, drug addiction, brushes with the police and, to an extent street living, he had his own catalogue of experiences he could refer back to. More complex and challenging would be getting to grips with areas of Stuart's life of which he had no personal experience, such as living in care, childhood sexual abuse and having to live with muscular dystrophy (a debilitating condition which gradually weakens muscle cells in the body). Tom felt that the key to successfully capturing Stuart would be not to focus on one element of his personality or circumstances but to portray him in a complete way. He described Stuart as 'a very ordinary guy with an incredible amount of baggage, trying to break out of all the baggage, constantly'.

These days, Tom's ability to physically transform for a role has become something of a trademark. As well as preparing the mental groundwork for Stuart, he also had to consider how his body would need to appear for him to look the part. Stuart was, after all, an alcoholic ex-junkie and his frame was much slighter than the average man. Prior to landing Stuart, Tom had been packing on muscle in preparation for playing Charles Bronson, which was then put on hold because of financial problems. Then *Stuart* came along and he needed to reverse what he'd been doing to his physique. To ensure he did this sensibly, he employed nutritionist Lisa Jeans who made him run five to seven miles a day and put him on a diet consisting of blueberries, boiled eggs, apples, salad and tuna. It worked and he shed over two stone in just five weeks. 'Lisa was brilliant, and I need all the help I can get,' said Tom to the *Evening Standard*. He didn't fancy embarking on a Christian Bale-style starvation programme to lose his weight, noting 'I'm not as wired as he is.' He also recognised that he needed his brain to be working properly in order to meet the challenge of this demanding role and for that to happen, he needed to feed it the right ingredients.

Tom also had to take on board the physical effects that Stuart's illness would have had on how he moved his body. 'When I was filming, I attached 5kg weights to both of my ankles and an elastic band around my upper body so I couldn't lift my arms,' he admitted to the *Daily Telegraph*.

They say you reap what you sow and in this case, Tom's detailed, exacting character preparation for Stuart paid huge dividends. Alexander Masters has recounted in a piece written for the *Evening Standard* how Tom had asked him if he was like Stuart, to which the writer had replied: 'Well, you talk the ear off your listener just as much.' He had then expressed concern as to whether Tom could have understood 'the sheer pain in his life.' However, he went on, 'Later, watching rushes of Tom I had to leave the room,' saying, 'They were too good, too close to memory'.

Masters was stunned by how close he came to the real Stuart. In what was unquestionably a difficult role, he had perfectly captured his character's humour, his insight and of course his pain and anger. Speaking to *The Times* at the time the drama was aired, he again couldn't speak highly enough of Tom: 'It's a stunning performance. Tom seems to have absorbed the character completely. On and off set, he *lived* the character.'

Benedict Cumberbatch was always determined that he wouldn't deliver just an imitation of Alexander Masters. He knew he needed to capture the essence of the man and his relationship with Stuart. He was aware that Alexander needed to be presented as an everyman figure but that he must appeal to the viewer, that they had to like him enough to be taken on the journey through Stuart's life with him. Prior to filming, he met Masters a few times and asked him questions about his parents and the kind of life he'd lived. Masters was always, according to the actor, 'affable and supportive.' Cumberbatch also spent a day as a volunteer at Crisis in London, to experience the atmosphere and the kind of care that the people who work there offer to the homeless.

Crucial to both actors was that, as well as doing justice to their individual characters, they established the nature of the special relationship between the two men. Cumberbatch commented on the stark contrast between them and how the friendship would work on screen: 'What on the face of it could be a very uneasy partnership between a, sort of, nice, middle-class studentish type of guy... and this very worldly-wise, street, ex-psychopath, poly-drug-addicted, homeless fiend of a fireball of humanity. They're quite polar opposites and that's what's charming about it.'

Benedict Cumberbatch was aware of the importance of the synergy between them and observed, 'There's a relationship that we have as actors together off camera which means there's a real intimacy to what we do when the camera starts rolling.' He was also fulsome in his praise of Tom's skill as an actor, commenting that he had 'inhabited Stuart in such a beautiful way'.

The two actors had known of each other before *Stuart*, but they hadn't previously had the opportunity of working together. As their partnership developed, so did a mutual respect which, as well as allowing their individual performances to flourish, ensured the bond they formed carried through into their portrayal of the Stuart/Alexander friendship. Tom said of his co-star: 'He's a very generous, very sensitive, very thoughtful, focussed, disciplined actor... he's got it.'

All credit to the two of them, they perfectly captured the unconventional affinity that had existed between the men. Alexander Masters had always maintained that the most important thing in dramatising his book was that this relationship was right, and the proof that they had succeeded in this was in evidence on one occasion when the author was on set. He was watching a scene being played out on one of the monitors and so moving was it that he had to step away, overcome with emotion.

As he had done in *Black Hawk Down* and *Band of Brothers*, Tom was playing a real person. The responsibility of doing justice to Stuart's character and his life was particularly relevant for Tom, as Stuart had only passed away a few years prior to the book being published and the film being made – he had to be played, as Tom put it 'with taste and integrity'. It was also essential that Stuart's family were happy with how the drama portrayed him. Both Benedict Cumberbatch and Tom spent time with Stuart's family, who were incredibly helpful and answered any questions the actors had about Stuart and his life.

The drama was filmed in both Cambridge and London and homeless people from Cambridge were used as extras. *Stuart: A Life Backwards* was shown on BBC2 on a Sunday night in September 2007 and achieved everything it had set out to do. It remained faithful to the structure and spirit of the original book and the two lead performances were breathtaking. Stuart was a complicated character, but so much love and care had gone into Tom's performance that it radiated out of the television to touch the viewer. The quiet assurance of Benedict Cumberbatch's portrayal of Alexander Masters and the little quirks he brought to the character made him fascinating and sympathetic. The drama was funny, heart-breaking and poignant.

'Tom Hardy… makes a compelling, wounded, shuffling Stuart,' wrote the *Guardian*, stating that the piece was 'a remarkable one-off film.' Rachel Cooke, writing in the *New Statesman*, though, summed it up the most accurately. She said of Cumberbatch that 'he brought Masters alive with the smallest of tics – slow-blinking myopic eyes, the odd wry look – and managed to avoid making him seem like a patronising prig'. She went on to say: 'It was Hardy, though, who broke your heart. I can't remember the last time I saw a performance as convincing as this. Hardy was Stuart, and every time he was on screen – which was most of the time – I was mesmerised.'

Deservedly, Tom was nominated for the 2008 Best Actor British Academy Television Award. He was up against Andrew Garfield for *Boy A*, Matthew Macfadyen for *Secret Life* and Anthony Sher for *Primo*. Sadly, this time, the award went not to Tom but to Andrew Garfield.

Although the recognition that came with the award would have been a positive affirmation, Tom didn't really need it to validate the work he had done on *Stuart*. He recognised that he had put heart and soul into a character he had come to know, understand and love. Those who had seen the film also recognised that, surely, now Tom was going to be the actor everyone wanted to see more of. It almost seemed as if the work he had been doing had been building to this point – the timing was fortuitous and he had been at a stage in his career when he was ready to immerse himself in such a complex part. Reflecting on what he had learned from the experience, Tom stated thoughtfully: 'He's an odd superhero, but that's what he was for me. He made me grow and he made me think about what I want with my career.' He also claimed that Stuart was the best role he'd ever had and was ever likely to have again. 'I could stop now, technically. I'm not going to, because I love the craft.'

The motivation to continue improving his skills meant that Tom was eager to keep pushing forward, ready to test himself with a new challenge. Luckily, a second career-defining role was just around the corner.

'My name's Charles Bronson and all my life I've wanted to be famous.' The opening line of *Bronson*, aside from being controversial, encapsulated what its Danish director, Nicolas Winding Refn, hoped to explore when making his film about the life of the prisoner. What drove Bronson's desire for notoriety? How had he managed to build a mythology around himself? For the director at least, the film was not to be a straightforward biopic but a piece that used Charles Bronson as a means to examine one man's relationship with fame.

Charles Bronson was born Michael Peterson on 6 December 1952. His upbringing in Luton was unremarkable but when the family moved to Merseyside, he apparently fell in with the wrong crowd and his behaviour grew increasingly violent. He was originally sentenced to seven years in prison in 1974 for a bungled post office robbery – the sum total of the loot being just £26.18. The gun he took with him for the job wasn't loaded.

He changed his name to Charles Bronson during a stint as a bare-knuckle fighter, his promoter insisting he needed a more exciting fighting name. In prison, Bronson's violence continued and saw him lashing out at officers, fellow prisoners and prison workers. His charge sheet grew and amongst the offences he racked up were wounding with intent, criminal damage and GBH. It seemed the system didn't know what to do with him, and time and again he was transferred between prisons. He was eventually deemed criminally insane and sent to Broadmoor Hospital where, in 1983, he famously led a rooftop protest.

He was released in 1988, having been declared sane. Free for just 68 days, he was imprisoned again after stealing an engagement ring for his fiancée. He was released in November

1992 and spent only 58 days as a free man before being sentenced for conspiracy to rob. That was, to date, the last time Bronson lived outside prison walls; in 2000, he was sentenced to life for holding a prison teacher hostage.

Bronson has spent much of his prison life in solitary – 33 years of it, in fact. He has very limited contact with the outside world and keeps himself occupied (when permitted) with art. He is a talented artist and has won six Koestler awards for his work. He takes pride in keeping himself fit despite only having four walls to use as gym equipment and has even published a book called *Solitary Fitness*, which describes how to stay in shape in prison. In fact, Bronson's publishing output has been quite phenomenal for someone inside and he has written a host of books including his life story and even a guide to Britain's prisons, *The Good Prison Guide*.

Bronson is an expert in drawing attention to himself – he will never allow himself to be just be a number, lost in the prison system. He makes sure the public know who he is and that he will not be forgotten. As Tom put it: 'His fame keeps him safe.' Winding Refn was clear from the start that the personality of the figure would be key to the film and when he read the first draft of the script, he felt more could be done to infuse it with greater character. Hence we see the varied elements of Bronson's personality through different prisms during the film: he is a narrator telling his story, he is a performer and he is an artist.

The path that led Tom to *Bronson* was not a smooth one. He and Nicolas Winding Refn had initially tried to get the project off the ground together but had not seen eye to eye on certain aspects of it. Later on, after the film had been released, the pair were able to look back at that time and joke that they had 'hated each other'! Having parted company, Winding Refn went off to work on the script for a year and Tom went away and immersed himself in other projects. When they met again, the chemistry needed to make the film was there. According to Winding Refn, Tom had grown as an actor and he could now envisage him as Charles Bronson. Tom agreed with this, saying 'there was a succession of characters that sort of led me there...'

There were also some press stories that circulated at the time, implying that Bronson was unhappy that the film had faltered and that Tom was rumoured not to be in it any more. Bronson himself had seen Tom in *Oliver Twist* and *Stuart: A Life Backwards* and had liked what he'd seen. 'I know he will play the part of me really well,' he said. 'Plus my mum likes him, so he can't be bad, can he?' The ultimate seal of approval.

For Tom to be able to develop his Charles Bronson character – and also so that he could gain his subject's approval on certain elements of the story – he needed to see the man in person. This was no mean feat. Prison authorities had got wind of the fact that a film about Bronson's life was in the offing and were staunchly opposed to it. In fact, when it was announced that the film was to be made, Bronson wasn't permitted to receive correspondence relating to it, nor was he allowed to see visitors connected with it. This of course applied to Tom, who was denied access to him. So incensed was Bronson that he consulted his lawyer and a letter was fired off to the governor of Wakefield prison, where Bronson was at that time incarcerated. His letter stated: 'Tom Hardy is a proposed visitor who has been vetted by police and passed. But he has been stopped by the governor here for no other reason than a "power decision". Give Tom Hardy a pass or let's take it to court and let a judge decide who's right or wrong.' It did the trick and Tom was granted a visiting order.

Bronson is sometimes touted, unfairly, in the media as being Britain's answer to Hannibal Lecter because of the highly secure conditions in which he is kept. So one would imagine that going to see him would be like undertaking Clarice Starling's tortuous walk down the dark, threatening corridor at the end of which is the prisoner, spookily illuminated. Not a bit of it. Tom described going to see Bronson as a much more clinical affair. 'It was more like visiting a patient in a hospital,' he stated.

Others who have been to see Bronson in Wakefield prison report that upon arrival, the visitor is greeted by a sniffer dog to detect if they are carrying any drugs. This is followed by a security process similar to one you might experience at an airport. Visitors are prohibited from taking anything at all in with them, not even so much as a pen. The only concession to this is some small change, so that you can buy Bronson's favourite soft drinks and chocolate from the prison's vending machine. The journey to see him takes you through three or four pairs of double gates which are opened and locked again one at a time. The visitor is shown into a room and Bronson is shown into a cell on the other side of it – there's a barred gap of about two square metres in the wall and Bronson and his visitor converse through the gap, sat on chairs bolted to the floor.

Bronson enjoys having visitors and the session usually lasts a couple of hours. He will sometimes entertain his visitor with a display of his fitness, such as hand-stand press ups. The visit will ordinarily be rounded off with one of Bronson's crushingly strong handshakes.

Understandably, Tom was nervous about meeting Bronson for the first time. He felt a slight unease about his motivation for being there – he was not there in an official capacity, but to draw inspiration from Bronson and to study him. 'I can do an impression of Charles Bronson to a certain extent but then I was face to face with my subject and I'm not any relation to him. I'm not his family, a friend, a doctor or a social worker. I have no official capacity to help him. I'm there to pretend to be him,' he commented, when speaking to the *indieLondon* website. Tom's anxieties were allayed when Bronson greeted him through the wall with: 'Tom Hardy? Bill Sikes? What a part. You was robbed of that BAFTA.'

One thing that did concern Bronson at this first meeting was Tom's physical appearance. Tom was still slight of frame from *Stuart* and Bronson couldn't for the life of him see how he was ever going to resemble him in the slightest. Bronson recounted the moment in an audio message he recorded for the premiere of the film. 'He's 'avin a f*****g laugh. No disrespect to Tom but I don't think he weighed 12 stone soaking wet. I'm 16 ? stone, solid muscle.' Tom reassured him that they were flying over his trainer to bulk him up and that, within weeks, he would have transformed to Bronson size. He didn't disappoint and Bronson was impressed when he next saw him a few weeks later: 'When he come back and seen me [sic] two months later, he was bigger than me... he had muscle where muscle shouldn't be!'

Over the course of several visits and phone calls, a friendship developed between the two men. The interaction between them, as well as being enjoyable and rewarding, was all grist to the mill for Tom who needed to hear Bronson speak and watch his mannerisms so that he could build a realistic portrait of the man to use on set.

When Tom spoke to the media about the film, the burning question on interviewers' lips always seemed to be: 'What was Charles Bronson like?' So much is written about him, but so few ever get to meet him that it was bound to be a source of fascination. Tom had been afforded a unique opportunity to meet first-hand a man whose reputation most definitely went before him. Tom was always careful to give a measured response to the question and to approach it from his position as an actor. He has said many times that he likes Bronson and finds him funny. But he was aware that there was a fine line to tread and he wasn't ever going to justify Bronson's violent actions. He also admitted that he learned a lot from the experience of meeting Bronson and that the man constantly surprised him. One unexpected moment of mirth between them came when the subject of Bronson's infamous moustache was broached. Tom recalled a conversation in which he had joked that he might not go with the moustache in the film, claiming it was 'a bit *Village People*' Luckily for Tom, Bronson thought this was hilarious and joined in the joke. Phew!

Although Tom was doing the best he could to understand Bronson and had quite a lot of contact with various underworld figures who knew him well, he was conscious that he was essentially an outsider. Bad boy he may have been, but deep down he was still the same frightened middle-class boy from the suburbs who was opening himself up to an environment he didn't really belong in. But he had a job to do and needed to be familiar with the world of Bronson in order to do him justice. 'I'm not there to be a gangster. I'm an actor. We're from different worlds. But there's a code of ethics about what they do, however immoral you think it is,' he told *Attitude* magazine.

Having recently lost weight, Tom now had to start piling it back on to be Bronson. For this actor, though, it wasn't enough just to bulk up and look a bit more like Bronson – he needed to transform into him. After *Bronson*, he would transform again for the film *Warrior* and, comparing the two he always said that changing his body for the cage-fighting role was a lot tougher and more disciplined. To get in shape for *Bronson*, he was able to eat foods that many of us would consider indulgent: ice cream, chicken and chips were all on the menu. As well as weighing more, he also had to make sure he developed muscles in the right places and proportions and for this, as usual, he enlisted Pnut's help. As Bronson only has a limited fitness regime within the confines of his cell, Tom and Pnut worked on a specific range of exercises that would have been possible for Bronson to do. Bronson is famous for the number of press-ups he can do in a minute, so they did a lot of those, plus dips and lifting. As Tom joked to Jonathan Ross in an interview, most of his training involved carrying Pnut up and down the stairs!

Tom had always thrown everything into his roles but with Bronson he went the extra mile. Opting to completely change himself for the part was something of a deliberate career move, too. Ultimately he wanted to be noticed for doing something remarkable and show that he could push himself as hard as he needed to for the sake of his craft. Ultimately, he wanted to establish transformational acting as a Tom Hardy calling card. 'I think there's a certain necessity to do that now, to establish myself as a serious actor. Nobody sits up and takes notice unless you do something extreme,' he told the *Irish Times*.

One of the big challenges in bringing the Bronson story to the screen was that Bronson had spent most of his adult life in prison – and most of his prison life in solitary confinement. Surely this would be rather limiting when it came to making a full-length feature? The solution lay in imaginative and creative film-making on the part of the director and the director of photography. For a start, the story wasn't told chronologically, it was carved up into bite-sized pieces. It also didn't attempt to plod laboriously through the whole of Bronson's life, only certain episodes were covered. The story-telling was stylised and varied and included close-up solo pieces to camera, imaginative and, at times, incongruous use of music, occasional use of real archive footage and scenes where Bronson would appear on a stage and deliver a monologue to an imaginary audience. As well as providing variety, it also, according to the director, was his way of taking Bronson outside the confines of his cell – even if he couldn't physically leave, he could escape in his mind and the stage was a fitting setting for the ultimate showman.

During filming, Tom continued to seek Bronson's approval as far as possible. Present most days on set was Bronson's close friend and link to the outside world, Mark Fish. If Tom or other members of the cast and crew had questions or wanted to find out how Bronson would feel about something, he would consult Fish, or Fish would somehow manage to contact Bronson to obtain his opinion. Equally, Bronson's family were often turned to for advice and approval. Tom was insistent that Bronson was on side with the film: 'You get into bed with the guy, with his family, and then you rob them? I ain't part of that. And not just because I don't want to be rolled up in a carpet and dropped to the bottom of the Thames,' he told *The Times*, in no uncertain terms.

The director and the star made no secret of their artistic differences about the film. They were approaching it from two contrasting standpoints and each had their own priorities. The director's focus was on making a film about the nature of celebrity, how one man managed to find it, and why. Tom was much more focussed, understandably, on Bronson the man and how he should be representing him on screen. Ultimately, though, they agreed that these contrasting points of view made for a richer, more textured film. There was also no question that the two men respected each other's work. Tom said it had been 'awesome' working with Winding Refn and recognised that the director was as dedicated to his craft as Tom was to acting, commenting that Winding Refn 'lives, breathes and doesn't sleep film'. In turn, the director confirmed that Tom's fascination with Bronson the man is what had made the character work on screen.

The way the film was constructed meant that it would stand or fall on Tom's performance – he was in every single scene and so was central to its success. And what a performance it was! The film's highly stylised nature meant that the actor was constantly adapting his style depending on what was required for a particular scene. In one scene he would be performing like a vaudeville entertainer; in another he would be delivering a monologue straight to camera in close up. Naturally, there were also scenes where he needed to act with extreme aggression and violence. Perhaps the most stunning achievement, though, was that he succeeded in giving his character humanity and a sense of pathos that pushes the audience to like him in spite of his actions. Tom succeeded in giving a rounded insight into a very complex man.

Even though Tom was the centre of attention in the film, he was by no means a selfish presence on set. Actress Juliet Oldfield who played Alison, the woman for whom Bronson stole the engagement ring, said that Tom was 'great to work alongside; he makes you feel extremely comfortable'. Hugh Ross, who played Bronson's Uncle Jack, was impressed with Tom, saying he was 'a dangerous, intelligent and exciting actor'.

The film opened in the UK on 13 March 2009 and its release date just happened to fall within a few days of a parole hearing for Bronson which, if successful, would see him moved to a lower-category prison. The premiere took place at Cineworld on Haymarket in London and a large contingent of the audience was a rogue's gallery of underworld faces. Prior to the screening, something else happened that generated even more controversy but which also drew the public's attention to the film. Somehow, Bronson had managed to record a speech to be played at the premiere and it had found its way outside. Contact with Bronson is strictly limited and only granted by approval of the prison authorities, who were furious when they discovered that, somehow, this had happened under their noses. An inquiry into what had gone wrong was demanded.

The audience were pleased, though, as it's rare that anyone gets to hear Bronson speak. In his message he said that he was sorry he couldn't attend the event and thanked everyone involved in the film. He of course paid homage to Tom, saying: 'What an actor, what a man – max respect.' He confessed that he had shaved off his moustache and sent it to Tom to use in the film, so that a little bit of him would be able to appear in it. He also expressed regret at his past acts of violence and stated that he had matured since then. He concluded by saying: 'I'm proud of this film because if I drop dead tonight, then I live on.'

Bronson was never going to be an easy film to defend and was always bound to attract a slew of media attention, much of it negative. Newspapers with right-of-centre tendencies were decidedly up in arms about it. The arguments were predictable: the film glorified violence, it gave a voice to a man who didn't deserve one, it neglected to show the harm Bronson had inflicted on particular people and it brushed his offences under the carpet. THE LIONISING OF A MONSTER screamed a headline in the *Daily Mail* in March 2009. The article quoted the National Chairman of the Prison Officers Association, Colin Moses, who was, unsurprisingly, opposed to the film. 'This film is glorifying someone who's spent his life attacking and assaulting prison staff and taking innocent people hostage for his own gratification. It's an outrage to decent, law-abiding people,' he said. The *Daily Mail* concluded its piece by branding the film 'tawdry, exploitative and indefensible'.

Nicolas Winding Refn chose to answer some of the criticisms by issuing a statement saying: 'I certainly would never make a film that glorifies violence or anything in that demeanour. On the contrary, all my films have always had a very strict moral code to them. I also think Bronson has.'

Other newspapers were more measured in their response to *Bronson* and chose to judge it on artistic merit rather than where they stood on the matter politically. Some understandably took issue with the fact that the film stood on shaky moral ground in that it seemed unapologetic about Charles Bronson's violence. Tim Robey in the *Daily Telegraph* found the film to have too much flamboyant style and not enough substance. 'Refn and Hardy are talented fellows but they've egged each other on to flaunt their gifts to excess, staging a loud but hollow tough-guy pantomime which has little, if anything, to say for itself,' he wrote.

Several critics chose to mark out Tom's performance as something worthy of attention. The *Daily Star* called it 'a considerable tour de force of acting' and the *Observer* said, 'It isn't… a pretty sight, but in a brave and bravura performance, Tom Hardy makes it a compelling one.'

Tom, in the meantime, put himself on the frontline to defend his work. As well as giving interviews for print media, he also made television appearances to promote the film and was inevitably called upon to respond to criticisms. When he appeared on *This Morning*, the presenters read out to him a 'charge sheet' of Bronson's crimes and Tom was asked how the man he knew differed from the man the press painted him as being. Tom reiterated that he is an actor and that his job is not to judge but to 'observe and reflect' the person he found in front of him. He hadn't met Bronson with an agenda, he just wanted to be able to listen to him tell stories and to pick up the rhythms of his speech. He added: 'The man I met wasn't a monster... [he has] massive anger problems and [is] incredibly charismatic, very, very funny, but very insightful and very gentle and calm too.'

In response to the common accusation thrown at the film – that it glorifies violence – Tom disputed this by explaining that ultimately Bronson's story was a tragic one. Every act of violence leads to him being incarcerated for longer. If anything, the film showed that 'fighting the system is not going to work – it's tragic, actually'.

Whatever the divided opinions of the world on *Bronson*, it proved a bold and wise career move on Tom's part. His performance didn't go without formal recognition: he won the award for Best Actor at the 2008 British Independent Film Awards and was nominated in the same category at the *Evening Standard* British Film Awards.

As he'd been at pains to point out, now that he'd done something extreme, people were starting to take notice of him. Thanks to making some noise with his talent, he was signed up by a big US agency who also represent the likes of Meryl Streep and Brad Pitt. In spite of this, Tom still had his feet firmly on the ground and was aware that he was still hovering around the bottom rung of the Hollywood ladder. As he explained, he'd have to 'eat a lot more dirt' before he could be considered on a par with Tinseltown's elite.

As well as helping to propel him towards the big time, *Bronson* had been a learning experience for Tom, one that had helped him to grow as an actor and expand his field of vision when it came to building characters. 'I've been somewhere I've never been before and I think it will help me

– and has done – to walk into rooms that I used to be frightened to walk into.'

Working on *Stuart: A Life Backwards* had made a deep personal impact on Tom and led to the development of a lasting relationship between the actor and a Cambridge-based charity called FLACK.

FLACK had its origins in a magazine produced by and for homeless people in the city called the *Willow Walker*. Alexander Masters at one point edited the magazine and, through his involvement in *Stuart*, Tom became a patron of the *Willow Walker*. Out of the *Willow Walker* grew FLACK, which expanded its services and ultimately replaced the magazine's role – Tom then continued his patronage for FLACK. 'I met wonderful people when filming *Stuart* and I feel supporting homeless issues in Cambridge helps make me part of a community and a responsible human being. And it keeps me healthy to be useful in other areas of my life that don't involve acting,' he told the BBC.

Tom supports FLACK in all sorts of hands-on ways. In May 2010, he took part in a charity screening of Bronson with a question and answer session in Cambridge, the purpose of which was to generate funds for the charity (at that point newly formed). The audience comprised homeless people who were involved with FLACK, Hardy fans and some Charles Bronson aficionados too.

At the start of 2012, Tom was called upon to help FLACK's urgent appeal for funds. FLACK had been founded on a grant of just £7,000 from the Kenneth Miller trust. The magazine had launched in October 2011 but by December of that year,

Space cadet. Tom first launched himself into Hollywood when he played Praetor Shinzon in the 2002 film *Star Trek: Nemesis*.

Above right: Separated at birth? Tom's character was a clone of Jean-Luc Picard, played by Patrick Stewart.

Below left: All smiles with co-star Dina Meyer.

Below right: At the London premiere with his then wife, Sarah.

Above left: On the road to recovery. The theatre work Tom undertook when he came out of rehab led to him winning the Outstanding Newcomer Award at the Evening Standard Theatre Awards in 2003.

Above right: Romance blossomed between Tom and Rachael Speed on the set of BBC television drama *The Virgin Queen*.

Below: Rake's progress. Tom as Dorimant in *The Man of Mode* at the Olivier Theatre in 2007. He is pictured here with Bertie Carvel.

Playing prisoner Charles Bronson was a career-defining role for Tom.

Above: Relaxing at the film's premiere with (left to right) Bronson's friend, Mark Fish, Kelly Daniels, director Nicolas Winding Refn and Rachael Speed.

Below (left to right): With Charles Bronson's brother Mark Peterson, mother Eira Peterson and his own mother Anne.

Inset: At a charity screening of *Bronson*. The event raised money for Cambridge homeless charity, FLACK, of which Tom is a patron.

Above: The *Inception* actors line up for a press call. *From left to right*: Tom, Joseph Gordon-Levitt, Juno Page, Leonardo DiCaprio, Ken Watanabe and Cillian Murphy.

Below: A family night. Tom with Charlotte Riley, his mother Anne and father Chips.

Above: The bat's back. This scene from the third and final instalment in Christopher Nolan's Batman trilogy, *The Dark Knight Rises*, was filmed on the streets of Manhattan in November 2011.

Below: Tom pictured with director, writer and producer Gavin O'Connor and actors Jennifer Morrison, Nick Nolte and Joel Edgerton at the premiere of *Warrior* in 2011.

Above: Best of British. Tom was delighted to work with such a talented group of actors in *Tinker, Tailor, Soldier, Spy*. *From left to right*: Tom, Colin Firth, Gary Oldman, Benedict Cumberbatch and John Hurt at the film's premiere in September 2011.

Below: Tom attends the London premiere of *This Means War* with co-stars Reese Witherspoon and Chris Pine.

Above: Tom and co-stars Anne Hathaway and Christian Bale attend the European Premiere of *The Dark Knight Rises* at the BFI IMAX in London in July 2012.

Below: Tom greets fans at the world premiere of *Jack Reacher* in Leicester Square, London in 2012.

Above: *From left to right*: Producers Paul Webster, Guy Heeley, director Steven Knight, Tom, Ruth Wilson and Andrew Scott attend a screening of *Locke* during the 57th BFI London Film Festival on 18 October 2013 in London.

Below left: Tom and Noomi Rapace attend *The Drop* premiere in New York on 8 September 2014.

Below right: George Miller, Charlize Theron and Tom grace the red carpet of the *Mad Max: Fury Road* premiere during the 68th Annual Cannes Film Festival in May 2015.

All images © *Getty Images and Rex Features*

according to creative director Kirsten Lavers, it had become clear that FLACK could not sustain itself on such a tight budget. The production of the magazine was putting huge time pressures on the staff and they were finding themselves with little time for crucial matters such as preparing funding bids. The trustees told FLACK that unless they raised £45,000 by January 2012, they would face closure.

Cue Tom. Lavers contacted him to inform him of their plight and the actor immediately swung into action. With his fame as his platform, he reached out to his fans and asked them, on his behalf, to donate to FLACK to help them reach their target. He and Lavers launched a Tom Hardy appeal page for JustGiving and Tom's message to his fans informed them that everyone who donated £2 would be entered into a prize draw to win signed Tom Hardy goodies and would also receive a thank you email from the actor. The response was overwhelming. Tom kept on posting updates on the page and on 9 January he announced the great news:

'100% thank you so much. FLACK is no longer facing immediate closure. Now their work really begins, FLACK still needs our support – if you haven't already donated please do.'

In just five weeks they had exceeded their initial target. 'Much of it is down to our patron, Tom Hardy, and his fans,' said Lavers to BBC News. 'They have sent donations from all over the world. It's really quite humbling.'

Tom didn't stop there, though. In February 2012, he announced that he would be embarking on a road trip – across Siberia – in order to raise money for FLACK. Again, his popularity meant the press were all too eager to run any kind of story he gave them so it didn't take long for his fans to learn of his latest fundraising venture. He said on his JustGiving page: 'So please do cheer me on as I brave the Siberian Steppes by donating whatever you can afford. I hope to send the odd pic from along the way if I can work out how to use my phone without taking my gloves off!'

FLACK isn't the only charity Tom is heavily involved in. He is also an ambassador for the Prince's Trust, a charity that helps young people to change their lives for the better. It offers practical and financial support and, since it was established in 1976, has helped more than 600,000 young people. It aims to reach out to those who have had problems at school, been in care, who are long-term unemployed or who have been in trouble with the law. In short, it gives a second chance to young people who have struggled – something Tom was bound to identify with.

In May 2010, The Prince's Trust announced Tom as one of its new ambassadors. To mark the announcement, Tom met eight young people aged between 19 and 24 who had turned their lives around with the help of the charity. They had all overcome their own setbacks which ranged from drug addiction to homelessness – areas familiar to Tom. He did some role plays with the group to help build their confidence and self-esteem. 'I find their enthusiasm incredibly infectious, partly because I can really relate to their struggles,' he said. 'It's great to be able to put my personal experience to some use, and help them build up some confidence.'

In March 2012, Tom presented an award at The Prince's Trust Celebrate Success Awards. He was joined by a host of other stars including Emma Bunton, Emeli Sandé and Ant and Dec – as well, of course, as Prince Charles with whom Tom had a chat in the obligatory star line-up. Speaking from the depths of his newly grown bushy beard, Tom said: 'I got involved with the Prince's Trust because I believe what they do is fantastic. I wanted to give back in any way that I could to my community and Great Britain, and I was looking for something to get involved with.'

It was great to see Tom using his fame to support two causes close to his heart. He knew he'd been lucky to get a second chance in life and wanted to help others to do the same. Soon his new lease of life would take him Stateside and a step closer to realising his dreams.

CHAPTER EIGHT

YOU MUSTN'T BE AFRAID TO DREAM A LITTLE BIGGER

If ever there was a leading character from English literature that Tom Hardy was born to play, it is Heathcliff from Emily Bronte's 1847 novel *Wuthering Heights*. Looking at the characteristics of Heathcliff is like reading a Tom Hardy attribute checklist: brooding, intense, passionate and menacing. In 2009, Tom won the role of Heathcliff for an ITV drama adaptation written by Peter Bowker and directed by Coky Giedroyc, with whom Tom had now worked a couple of times. Speaking of his motivation for choosing Tom as his Heathcliff, Bowker commented: 'Tom is the first Heathcliff I've ever seen who you honestly feel could beat the living daylights out of you. He brings great pain to the role.'

Adapting *Wuthering Heights* for the screen is no easy task: the timeline of the narrative is complex; the power of the wild setting of the Yorkshire Moors is an integral part of the book and, while it lives on the page, it is difficult to capture its magnificence when filming; it has a broad narrative that spans the themes of obsession, betrayal, revenge and class. *Wuthering Heights* has been remoulded for countless adaptations and Heathcliff has been played by a host of outstanding actors such as Lawrence Olivier and Ralph Fiennes – but no screen version has ever quite lived up to the original source.

Peter Bowker had enjoyed huge critical acclaim for several of his previous productions including *Blackpool*, a 2004 musical drama about a casino owner played by David Morrissey and *Occupation*, a drama about the Iraq war starring James Nesbitt. But how would he fare with condensing this classic and creating a programme suitable for prime-time transmission?

Bowker had his work well and truly cut out and made some fairly hefty changes to the novel for his screenplay. He dispensed with Mr Lockwood, thereby losing the story's narrator; he added several controversial elements such as Heathcliff digging up Cathy's grave so that he can lie next to her corpse, and committing suicide as opposed to simply passing away of an unknown ailment as he does in the book. He also chose to open the drama with scenes that occur some way into the book, such as Edgar bringing Linton back to Wuthering Heights, which may have been confusing for viewers, particularly those not already familiar with the characters in the book. A proportion of the violence in the book was also expunged for TV audiences.

One thing on which there would be no compromise, though, was the landscape that is so much a part of the atmosphere and mood of the story. Although at the time many dramas were being filmed in Eastern Europe because it is cheaper than filming in the UK, *Wuthering Heights* was filmed on location in Yorkshire. To have shot it anywhere but on the windswept, wild Yorkshire Moors would have been to deprive the drama of one of its vital components.

Various locations around Yorkshire were used for filming. The village of Halton Gill boasts sweeping views of the moors all around it, so was chosen for filming the scenes at Gimmerton fair, while St Oswald's Church in Arncliffe was recast as Gimmerton Chapel. Wuthering Heights itself is a central character to the story, so much care was taken to find a property with exactly the right appearance for the gloomy gothic farmhouse. There are, of course, no such houses perched up on the Moors so the production team found a house in Keighley to use for the exterior shots of the farmhouse. The magic of computer imaging was then used to place the Heights on top of the Moors for distance shots of the house in situ. The interior scenes were filmed at Oakwell Hall, in Birstall near Bradford, which closed for two weeks to accommodate the cast and crew. 'It was very exciting having the film crew here and it will be interesting to see how much of Oakwell Hall we can recognise. Many of the museum's historic items such as furniture, ornaments, paintings and wall hangings had to be removed into safe keeping to allow the crew to prepare the sets,' observed Kirklees museums operations manager Deborah Marsland.

At times, the Yorkshire Moors proved inhospitable for the cast and crew of *Wuthering Heights*. Transporting camera and sound equipment up to the moorland above Sheffield was by no means an easy task as the terrain was so rugged. The weather was also unpredictable (with plenty of rain making regular appearances) and predominantly windy – a lot of the actors found themselves suffering from wind burn and very tousled hair!

While Tom's profile had been increasing steadily over the past few years, the actress who was to be his Cathy was a newcomer. Charlotte Riley, originally from County Durham, had trained at LAMDA and won the role of Cathy just six months after she had left drama school. She remembers well the events leading up to discovering that she had been cast in the role. She was appearing in *The Cherry Orchard* at the Chichester Festival Theatre when her agent contacted her to let her know the good news. 'I remember running outside and into the courtyard where Diana Rigg and Maureen Lipman were standing talking, and I screamed with happiness. I couldn't believe it,' she told the *Daily Mail*.

Riley, of course, couldn't wait to share her news with her family and rang her parents immediately. Her father Michael is an engineer and her mother Margaret is a nurse and bereavement counsellor. She also has a brother, Simon, who is 10 years her senior. Before going to drama school, Riley had not strayed far from home when she studied English at Durham University and clearly remains close to her family. Between attending university and going to drama school, she taught drama to disabled children, and also won an award for a comedy she wrote called *Shaking Cecilia*.

Prior to working on *Wuthering Heights*, she had completed shooting on Stephan Elliott's adaptation of Noel Coward's *Easy Virtue*, in which she had starred alongside Colin Firth and Kristin Scott Thomas. Naturally, she had been nervous about the job: not only was she fresh out of drama school but she would be acting alongside luminaries of stage and screen. 'Working with actors of that calibre really made me step up to my game,' she said.

It is testament to her talent and determination that she won such a meaty role as Cathy so early in her acting career. It was a big challenge to be playing such an iconic character, but to Riley it was 'a dream come true'. Although she had not read the book prior to landing the role, she subsequently read it three times so that she could really get to grips with Cathy and was soon clear about how she wanted her take on the character to differ from others. 'I wanted my portrayal of Cathy to have an earthy feel about her. From memory, no one seems to have played Cathy as a northerner, so I felt I could explore this aspect of her.'

It might well have been daunting to be sharing the screen with an actor who has received as much critical acclaim as Tom and who is known for bringing so much to the characters he plays. For Riley, though, his earnestness proved to be inspiring rather than intimidating and his energy and dedication meant that those who acted alongside him were required to turn up the volume on their own performances. 'If you're playing opposite someone like that, you have to give as much as you are getting,' she observed. 'I knew there was going to be no holding back with his Heathcliff.'

As the two of them were to play a couple who shared so much passion and pain, it was natural for them to want to get to know each other before shooting their scenes. When she first approached Tom, she was a little taken aback when he greeted her with one of his Charles Bronson impressions – apparently a party trick he often uses to entertain those around him. But the pair soon bonded – apparently over many cups of tea – and it wasn't long before they were travelling to and from the filming locations every day. 'I hadn't met Tom before, so after the first day of rehearsals I thought, as we are going to fall so madly, deeply in love, we had better get to know each other,' she recalled to the *Daily Mail*.

As well as finding a companion in her co-star, Riley discovered she had a mentor in him too. She was new to television but Tom had been appearing in TV dramas for years so knew all about the technical aspects of putting them together. He helped her out and offered her advice to make the whole process easier – and so that she could concentrate on the job of playing her character. 'We were in an embrace and Tom kept turning me around in between takes. He explained that it was to keep me in full camera view all the time. Little things like that were so helpful and really generous.'

As for Tom, he was relishing playing the tough guy once again. He had the darkness of Heathcliff pegged and knew just how dangerous a character he could be. When talking about the role, he made it clear that when preparing for Heathcliff, he had drawn inspiration from contemporary references. 'If you put [Heathcliff] in Sao Paolo in the modern day, he's gonna be a bad boy. You put him in Cuba, in *Scarface* and he's gonna be quite a nice foundation for a gangster,' he told the *Telegraph*. Tom often pre-empts criticism of his work by openly declaring that he is expecting people to find holes in his acting. He had done so in the past when playing well-known characters, and Heathcliff was no exception. 'Everybody knows Heathcliff, so I know I'm going to take casualties on it.'

He needn't have been anxious. Four million people tuned in to watch the drama and there was plenty of praise for Tom's fierce and menacing Heathcliff. Some viewers and critics weren't keen on how the story had been carved up or that certain liberties had been taken with it. Some also found fault with the dynamics of the relationship between Heathcliff and Cathy and felt that Charlotte Riley's performance didn't capture Cathy's fickle nature well enough. They all, however, sang the praises of the leading man. The lauding of Tom's performances was beginning to make familiar reading as, for several years, he'd been getting exceptional reviews for his work. The *Independent on Sunday* described him as: 'One part smirking malevolence to two parts laser-eyed psychosis,' and Rachel Cooke in the *New Statesman* went so far as to say that Tom was 'the best Heathcliff I have seen'. She added that: 'There is something about Hardy's mouth – perhaps it is the unsettling contrast between his soft, pillowy lips and the teeth that they conceal, which look like mossy, tumbledown gravestones – that has you hanging on his every word, menace mingling with charm like the scent of cat's piss on roses.' The exact characteristics that had made Hollywood give him a swerve for Mr Darcy were now coming into their own and contributing to Tom's glowing notices. It was as if he was finally coming home.

Tom and Charlotte Riley meeting on *Wuthering Heights* was not just the start of a working relationship – over time, it developed into a romantic attachment. Although they became close on set, at this point Tom was still with the mother of his child, Rachael Speed, and both Riley and Tom were at pains to point out that they only started seeing each other after he had parted from Speed. The British press would have loved the story to have been different and desperately wanted a whiff of scandal but there was none to be had. At the time the press were trying to make something out of nothing, in the summer of 2009, to put any rumours firmly to bed, Riley stated: 'I share a flat in West London with three other girls. There is no man in my life.'

It wasn't long before matters changed, though, and in September 2010, Riley confessed that she and Tom were engaged to be married. Hardy fans would be forgiven for thinking that beautiful Riley was just another stepping stone in the serial monogamist's love life: after all, Hardy has something of a history of falling in love on set and dating his colleagues. And since the pair were both reticent to discuss their relationship, it was difficult to know whether things were serious or not. But it soon became clear that they were well-matched – Riley was as down to earth as her fiancé.

The daughter of an engineer and a nurse, it was playing Captain Hook aged nine in a school play that made Riley realise she wanted to act for a living. Like Hardy she relishes the freedom the career offers. 'I was like: "I can't get this wrong. It's just a matter of perspective",' she told *The Independent* in 2014.

But unlike Hardy, Riley is cautious and had a back-up plan: she decided to study linguistics at Durham University and launch her acting career by breaking into the university drama scene. She auditioned for Chekhov and Shakespeare plays, not having read either author's work. 'I was sitting there thinking: "Who are the three sisters?" I was 18 and I didn't know what I was doing and people were looking at me like,

"What the fuck are you doing auditioning for a play you know nothing about?"'

Confidence knocked, Riley began writing comedy sketches instead – with the now esteemed playwright Tiffany Wright. After graduating, she taught drama to children with special needs and continued working with Wright. Their first play, *Shaking Cecilia*, charted an agoraphobic's roadtrip from Surrey to Aberdeen. Performed in a pink Mini they found in a scrapyard, it got into the National Student Drama Festival and won the 2004 *Sunday Times* playwriting award.

The prize was a life-changing weeklong physical theatre workshop, which gave her the confidence to reapply to drama school. She got into LAMDA and within a year was playing Cathy to Hardy's brooding Heathcliff.

The couple like variety in their life and both try to live as much as they work. When she's not acting, Riley sings in a 1940s doo-wop band, paints, and runs a clowning workshop. You could say she's the light to Hardy's darkness. And they certainly make a good-looking couple.

After their engagement, the pair continued to keep a low profile and are hardly ever approached by fans. 'We're really quite lucky because when we're out and about, just getting on with life, people are super polite,' Riley revealed soon after the announcement. 'He doesn't get recognised a huge amount and I certainly don't so it doesn't affect us hugely.'

And they continued to work together. Though their next on screen pairing wouldn't be quite so romantic as *Wuthering Heights*.

When inhabiting the skins of some of his more brutal or

psychopathic characters, Tom Hardy builds these roles out of what he finds frightening himself. Those who interview him often want to know just what it is that inspires him to give such convincing – and at times terrifying – performances. His reply usually focuses on how he allows himself to delve into what it is about the character's actions that would intimidate him. Speaking about Freddie Jackson in *The Take*, he noted: 'A lot of the scary characters and scary moments I've played have come from what's scared me. I visualise these people doing it to me. So when I'm playing Freddie doing something – killing... that's some cold s**t and that would hurt me.'

The Take was Sky 1's big-budget summer drama serial of 2009. Based on the Martina Cole novel of the same name, it is a crime saga that follows the lives of a family of East London gangsters over the course of a decade. At the start of the action, 1984, Freddie has just been released from prison. While incarcerated he befriends crime boss Ozzy, who recruits him to the firm he operates from the inside. As well as being psychopathically violent, Freddie is power hungry and will stop at nothing to work his way up the criminal career ladder. Freddie's partner in crime is his rather more cerebral cousin Jimmy who is at first an idolising sidekick to Freddie, but ultimately proves to be smarter and more calculating than him. Freddie is married to the long-suffering Jackie whose sister Maggie also happens to be Jimmy's girlfriend. It's a tale packed with violence, sex, jealousy, betrayal and greed. 'It's incredible, dramatic stuff,' said Tom.

It was typical Martina Cole territory and her loyal readers (of whom there are plenty) were unlikely to be disappointed by the adaptation. Martina Cole writes a book every year and has an army of fans who delight in knowing that she will deliver exactly what they want with her books: gritty gangland crime fiction. Cole published her first book, *Dangerous Lady*, in 1992 – she had, in fact, written it some years earlier but had stuffed the manuscript in a drawer and forgotten about it. When she finally rediscovered it, she realised that what she had written was actually rather credible and so sent it to a literary agent. The agent recognised that her writing style and the subject matter were quite unlike anything else that was on the market and within days she had struck a publishing deal. Three of her books, including *Dangerous Lady* and *The Take* have been turned into hit TV dramas.

The drama boasted a fine selection of actors for its leading roles. Kierston Wareing, who had received critical acclaim for her role in Andrea Arnold's film *Fish Tank* was perfectly cast as Jackie, and Charlotte Riley, fresh from filming *Wuthering Heights* with Tom, was to play her more even-tempered sister Maggie. Jimmy was played by Shaun Evans and the legendary Brian Cox played Ozzy. It was Tom, though, who commanded the most attention with his seething, snarling, brutish Freddie.

Freddie is a horrific man with few – if any – redeeming features. He spends most of his time eliminating anyone who stands in the way of his advancement through the ranks of the East End underworld. He drinks heavily, gets off his face on drugs, has sex with countless women who aren't his wife and sets an appalling example to his children. Worst of all, in a particularly harrowing scene, he rapes his wife's sister. Charlotte Riley, in fact, described Freddie as 'like a rabid dog'. Could this character perhaps be the nastiest piece of work in Tom's expanding catalogue of dysfunctional, aggressive types?

Tom, as usual, wanted to find the heart of his character, to work out where he might be able to add layers of complexity to him in order to make him three-dimensional. 'Everyone has a point of view,' he explained to *indieLondon* website. 'So when approaching these characters – if they're soldier, terrorist, cop or criminal – you're going to find human traits in every walk of life, in every hole, under every rock. There's going to be a tale of hope or competition or love or rivalry – a human story.'

The actor was used to channelling aggression through the characters he plays and Freddie was no exception. There were scenes that required him to behave brutally and, as someone who brings maximum intensity to his work, Tom gave it his all. His co-star Kierston Wareing told of a scene they had to film where the couple are in the midst of an explosive argument. So completely immersed in the moment and fired up was Tom that Wareing said she at one point thought he might hit her. 'He slammed the door and the glass panel fell out, so the children were actually really scared and instead of stopping we both just carried on and got on with it, and I actually thought he might hit me. But I was quite prepared...' She was obviously aware that Tom would not have deliberately hit her, but she could see that his character had taken over and wanted to go with what was happening for the sake of making the action authentic.

Charlotte Riley, who had to film the rape scene with Tom, spoke of the trust between the two of them that helped to make the filming of the scene as painless as possible. The fact that they had worked together so closely on *Wuthering Heights* meant that they had an existing understanding of how the other worked and this made a complex and difficult part of the drama that bit easier for them to deal with. 'Because we'd worked on *Wuthering Heights* – when the love scene was really passionate – we had a good shorthand between us and knew what we were doing. But as well as we knew each other, it had to be handled with delicacy and trust,' she told the *Daily Mail*.

The series was a four-parter and had a strong narrative arc across the episodes. Reviewers were quick to praise Kierston Wareing's impressive performance, but they all seemed to be of the opinion that, out of everyone, it was Tom who shone. In what could have been an average television crime serial, his charismatic portrayal of Freddie had made *The Take* worth tuning in for. Matt Baylis of the *Express* called Tom's Freddie 'certainly the most arresting villain to grace our screens since Tony Soprano'. Kathryn Flett, meanwhile, found the character terrifying and said that he 'oozed psychoses'.

Tom was generously quick to give credit to others who had contributed to the success of the drama. 'If everything is all lined up – good writing, good directing, good DOP, all of that – then there's a profound story to tell and an opportunity for performers to come up with something good. And I do think *The Take* is that.'

Freddie Jackson was just one in a long line of threatening, intense characters to have been played by Tom, and he was now seen as the actor of choice when it came to such dark roles. Tom has always displayed a sense of humour about the fact that he is so often cast for these kinds of parts, and towards the end of 2009 fans were treated to a glimpse of a slightly different side to him when he appeared in the first-ever celebrity led advertisement for Kleenex tissues.

Kimberly-Clark, the company that manufactures the tissues, were aiming to create a TV campaign which would build on their 2007 'Let it Out' adverts. These had featured members of the public sitting on sofas and giving vent to their emotions. The idea driving the new campaign was to show certain celebrities revealing emotions not usually associated with their public personas. Bob Geldof is shown to be crying with laughter in an important meeting; Emma Bunton dances around the room like a rock chick and Sven Goran Eriksson is seen alone in a room playing keepy-uppy with a scrunched-up tissue. He heads it into the wastepaper bin and then runs around performing a goal celebration with his jumper over his head. For Tom's part, they wanted to show the softie behind the hard man and he is shown sitting on the sofa cuddled up to his dog, crying his eyes out as he watches something sad on television – and of course wiping away his tears with a particular brand of paper tissue. The advert was the brainchild of JWT Advertising and was filmed by none other than photographer and film-maker Rankin. It was an inspired and funny idea and can still be seen on YouTube if any Hardy fans missed it and want to see the gentler side of their hero.

The contrast between the two movies in which Tom appeared during 2009 and 2010 could not have been more marked. In February 2009, a film originally called *The Code* and subsequently renamed *Thick as Thieves* was released straight to DVD. The fact that it didn't warrant a theatrical release probably tells you all you need to know about it. To all intents and purposes, it looked to be quite an appealing prospect. It stars Morgan Freeman and Antonio Banderas and is the story of a master thief who undertakes the 'heist of a lifetime' to break into a seemingly impregnable vault and steal the last two original Fabergé eggs. Tom's role was as a cop called Daniels, who only appears in a few scenes of the film (with an American accent nowhere near as good as he had put on for many other roles). While those that made it declared it was a heist movie that transcended its genre, the end result seemed to be a tedious muddle of a film that didn't seem to really know what it was trying to be and failed to inspire emotion towards any of its central characters. In its review of the DVD, *The Independent* took a pretty dim view, stating, 'The dialogue is stilted, the plot is as thin as Banderas's hair, and even the plethora of twists can't rescue the movie from mediocrity.'

Heist movie *Thick as Thieves* may have been, but it couldn't have differed more from *Inception* – a high-concept, futuristic and accomplished movie from director/writer Christopher Nolan about a 'reverse heist' – with a big difference. The film tells the story of Dom Cobb (played by Leonardo Di Caprio), who is an expert in a special kind of industrial espionage: he is able to infiltrate people's dreams to extract information from their subconscious. He makes a living by doing this for rich business clients who are desperate for information on their rivals. He carries out his missions with his colleague Arthur (Joseph Gordon-Levitt). A wealthy Japanese businessman hires Cobb for a special assignment that is different from the ones he has carried out before: this job involves 'inception': entering the subconscious to plant an idea (as opposed to extracting it) in the mind of Robert Fischer (Cillian Murphy), heir to a large business empire. To carry out this reverse heist Cobb assembles a skilled team to assist him: Ellen Page (of *Juno* fame) plays the aptly named Ariadne, a gifted architecture student who will construct the landscape of Fischer's subconscious and guide the others around it; Tom Hardy plays Eames, a devious master forger with the ability to assume the appearance and personalities of those around him. The group undertake the daring mission to invade three layers of Fischer's subconscious and the result is a thrilling, imaginative venture into a state of unreality where the possibilities are endless – and high risk.

Nolan is an accomplished and gifted director who had ventured into the territory of the subconscious mind in his 2000 film, *Memento*. This cleverly constructed piece of cinema tells the story of a man who has lost his memory – but tells it in reverse, and through the lead character's eyes so, as he pieces together the fragments of his life, so does the audience; we are as confused and as desperate for clues as he is. Nolan had also been highly praised for breathing dark new life into the revitalised *Batman* films, *Batman Begins* and *The Dark Knight*.

A highly ambitious and big-budget venture, *Inception* was an idea he had been developing for many years and which he wrote as well as directed. 'This is a concept that has been locked in Chris's mind for eight years now so, for me, a lot of the preparation came from being able to sit down with him and understand that he had this extremely ambitious concept of doing a highly entertaining Hollywood film that is existential and cerebral and surreal,' explained the film's star, Leonardo DiCaprio.

In fact, it was necessary for the whole cast to sit down and talk face to face with Nolan about his vision for the film. So complex was the movie that it wasn't enough to go by what was written on the pages of their scripts – the director had to share with them what he was trying to achieve in each part of the film. Luckily, Nolan is so respected as a director that the actors who work with him trust his judgement implicitly. The whole project was his brainchild, so there was no room for individual actors to take over – they had to work as a team for the film to succeed and 'there was no ego on the set amongst all these very famous and brilliant actors. Because everyone just defaults to Chris. We're all very grateful to be here,' said Tom when speaking to *Cinematical*.

When talking about what inspired him to create the concept for the film, Nolan referred to his own ability to dream lucidly in the cryptic state that exists between sleep and wakefulness – and the infinite possibilities that being in that state presented. He was fascinated by the concept of being able to control the state through a shared virtual reality. 'You can look around and examine the details and pick up a handful of sand on the beach. I never particularly found a limit to that; that is to say, that while in that state your brain can fill in all that reality,' the director told *The Times*.

Tom has made no secret of his huge admiration for Chris Nolan, and he is not alone in being an actor who loves to work with him. And once you are on board the Nolan ship, it's usually a lasting relationship. Familiar faces reappear in his films as he likes to work with people he knows and trusts. Michael Caine, who had appeared in *Batman Begins* and *The Dark Knight* turns up in *Inception* as Cobb's father. Similarly, Cillian Murphy, who is Fischer in this film played the

Scarecrow in *Batman Begins*. When *The Dark Knight Rises* was announced, it was not unexpected for some of the names associated with it to be Nolan old hands – Tom Hardy and Ellen Page to name two. Tom and Nolan had not worked together before *Inception*, but Nolan had apparently enjoyed Tom's performance in *RocknRolla* and seen in him an actor with whom would like to work.

Eames was a part with which Tom could have a bit of fun and he certainly seemed to relish the chance to do so. He gave a lot of thought to how he wanted to craft this quirky character. To assist him, Nolan apparently gave him a book to read about the fake Vermeer paintings by forger Hans van Meegeren. Hardy also felt that the bond between him and Nolan as fellow Brits from similar kinds of neighbourhoods helped them to share common ideas for the development of Eames. Tom explained exactly what he thought Eames should be like: 'There's something very old school, MI5 about this guy as well. He's got the Graham Greene, *Our Man in Havana* type – old and faded, a slightly shabby down-and-out diplomat. A bit unscrupulous and off-the-radar.' He also maintained that Chris Nolan himself had been something of an influence on his character: 'I think Eames is Chris,' he stated, and admitted that he'd often adopted Chris's vocal mannerisms when delivering his lines.

It was new – and a little daunting – for Tom to suddenly be sharing a set with the cream of Hollywood. He'd done his fair share of work with the best British actors but these were his first tentative steps into the big-time. He was a fan of the work of those he was starring alongside such as Tom Berenger (a childhood acting hero of Tom), Ellen Page and

Leonardo DiCaprio, and the overwhelming desire to be a functional part of that great team, not to let the side down, helped motivate him to perform to the best of his ability. 'In my world these are very, very prolific people to do a good job with. I was concerned about letting the team down,' he told *Cinematical*.

The 'team' seemed to gel together on the set and Tom was able to teach some of the combat skills he'd learnt in *Warrior* to Ellen Page. The pair were photographed by paparazzi while they were practising their fighting and Page joked to Jonathan Ross on his chat show: 'It looked like he was beating up a little girl!' Tom also seemed to bond well with Leonardo DiCaprio, and their friendship continued off the set. Photos emerged of them in the crowd of spectators at a Lakers basketball game. When asked about the budding bromance by Alan Carr on his *Chatty Man* show in February 2011, Tom said of his new friend: 'He's really good, actually, he really looks after me.'

Filming *Inception* was a great experience for them all but hard work too. It took them to a variety of locations around the world including London, Los Angeles, Paris, Tangiers, Tokyo and Calgary in Canada (where the snowy chase scenes of the third level of Fischer's subconscious landscape were filmed). Some of the actors had to give a great deal in physical terms, but Tom maintained that they were all determined to push themselves as far as they needed to for the sake of their director. Thanks to the atmosphere that Chris Nolan had created on the set of his film, all of the actors were prepared to give just that little bit extra for him. Joseph Gordon-Levitt, for example, when filming the scenes in which the characters appear to be floating weightless in the hotel, had to be suspended on a wire for three weeks. This would be a challenge for any actor, but according to Tom they were all willing to undertake whatever was required for the film. Of Nolan, he said, 'That's a very specific human being that can not only orchestrate this kind of movie but get trust from people like that.'

Trust is key ingredient on any Nolan set. He is a director famed for keeping the details of his films locked down prior to release – and this could be one of the reasons he chooses those familiar and loyal actors for repeat performances in his movies. Try as journalists might to winkle any information out of cast or crew about his projects, they always draw a blank. The director is firmly of the opinion that the audience will gain so much more from his films if they walk into the cinema without prior expectations. He commented: 'I always believe that for me the most gratifying cinematic experiences as a viewer have always been films that I didn't know what to expect.' With a product as complex and innovative as *Inception*, it was easy to see why he wanted to keep an element of surprise up his sleeve. Would it be worth the wait?

The film came out in the UK in July 2010 and it was the most talked about movie of the summer. Although the Nolan shroud of secrecy had enveloped much of the detail of the film, in the months building up to the release, cinema audiences had been teased with enticing trailers showing phenomenal feats of CGI and mind-boggling special effects. Expectations were high and the film certainly delivered. The fact that it was a cerebral film with a challenging plot appealed to many of the critics and they were appreciative of how it

YOU MUSTN'T BE AFRAID TO DREAM A LITTLE BIGGER

performed on a technical level too. Philip French of the *Observer* remarked: 'The film is the stuff that dreams are made on, a collaborative work of great technical skill and imaginative detail where everyone is working to help the writer-director realise a personal vision... *Inception* demands and rewards our total attention as well as our emotional engagement. You'll want to see it again but not, I think, on the same day.'

Some found the film more an exhibition of style over substance and felt that, while it was visually impressive, the characters lacked emotional resonance. There's no denying that it was a film that demanded concentration from its audience, but there was a danger of some coming away from the film a bit confused. Philip French's comment that some might want to see it twice was pretty apt – the film moved fast and there was a lot of information to take in so it might have been necessary to watch it again to pick up things missed the first time around.

Although the film as a whole was a slick and impressive beast, oddly, it was Tom's understated and idiosyncratic performance that drew a great deal of attention from audiences. Many marked out one of his lines in particular as being a highlight of the film. The scene in question occurs after the team of dream-stealers has infiltrated the mind of Fischer – but the 'guards' protecting the victim's subconscious have detected the intruders' presence and are starting to attack them by opening fire. At one point, Arthur is firing his assault rifle on the 'projections' of Fischer's subconscious when Eames ambles over and says, 'You mustn't be afraid to dream a little bigger, darling,' promptly producing a rocket propelled grenade with which he blows up their enemies in one fell swoop. The line is classically delivered and is wonderful in that it sums up the whole essence of the film: that in your dreams, your subconscious is limitless and you can change events with the power of your imagination. The line is one that has gone down in film history and helped Tom gain recognition as an up-and-coming Hollywood star. The *Daily Telegraph* referred to his part in the film as 'a dry gift'.

Tom had been dying to make an impression in the USA for many years. *Bronson* had enabled him to put one foot on the ladder, but thanks to Chris Nolan he was now able to step up a rung. With the success of his performance in *Inception* came recognition on a larger scale and in February 2011, it was announced that Tom had been shortlisted for the BAFTA Rising Star Award. Tom being placed in this category was a bit ironic as he had been grafting away as an actor for many years and eight years previously had been earmarked as the 'next big thing' before his life had taken a very different turn.

The nominations for the BAFTA Orange Wednesdays Rising Star award recognise five international actors and actresses whose talent has captured the imagination of the British public. It is a special award because it is the only one voted for by the public and, for the first time in 2011, Orange Wednesdays customers were allowed to be part of the selection process too. Tom was up against some pretty impressive competition in the category, with the other nominees being Gemma Arterton, Andrew Garfield, Aaron Johnson and Emma Stone. Previous winners of the trophy had been James McAvoy in 2006, Eva Green in 2007, Shia LaBeouf in 2008, Noel Clarke in 2009 and Kristen Stewart in 2010.

Film fans voted in the tens of thousands in advance of the British Academy Film Awards on Sunday, 13 February 2011. At the star-studded ceremony, it was announced that the public had voted Tom their 2011 Rising Star. He wasn't actually there in person to collect his award on the night, but was genuinely delighted to have won and in his statement said: 'Thank you very much. This is very kind of you and much appreciated. I genuinely am grateful just to be working at all. I'd like to thank everyone who voted, everyone who loves a good story and every artist in the house tonight for the work they do.'

Spencer McHugh, Director of Brand at Orange said: 'We are delighted that Tom Hardy has been chosen as this year's Orange Wednesdays Rising Star. The support for our award, in its sixth year, particularly from Orange Wednesdays customers, has been phenomenal. Tom is one of Britain's most promising young actors and clearly has a glittering future ahead of him.'

The fact that Tom didn't attend the ceremony caused a bit of a stir in the press. The *Metro* newspaper claimed that the reason for the no-show was due to the actor ' dealing with the breakdown of his relationship with his TV actress fiancée Charlotte Riley.' Apparently, BAFTA officials had been unable to locate Tom prior to the awards and had been informed merely that he had 'personal commitments' which precluded him from attending. No one from either Tom or Riley's camp was able to comment on the story, but Tom put matters to rights when he resurfaced to appear on Alan Carr's *Chatty Man* show on 21 February. It was clear the stories about his relationship problems had been the fabrication of journalists, hungry for a story on the new star. Carr actually had the award to present to Tom and the actor expressed how chuffed he was that it was an accolade from the public. He went on to explain that the reason he'd not been at the ceremony was because he'd had only one weekend off in his shooting schedule and so had to choose between attending the awards or seeing his family – so it was understandable that he would want to prioritise time with his loved ones, especially his son. He joked that he and his family had watched the event on television and had become slightly anxious when it was announced that he was the winner.

Having won the award and with some fantastic new roles to get his teeth into – including Bane in *The Dark Knight Rises* and Max in *Mad Max* – Tom was well and truly deserving of his rising star status. Even with Hollywood stardom now a reality, Tom was not one to forget the less high-profile acting projects that were still so precious to him.

When actors start to hit the big time and take home substantial pay cheques, many of them express the desire to exploit their greater earning power by taking time off and indulging in smaller budget passion projects. Tom has made no secret of his wish to do this, time permitting. 'The American field is the place that I want to play on. The long-term effect is that smaller, independent films can be funded by greater exposure so I can go back to theatre or independent film.' Over the course of 2010 and 2011, he found himself in the position of being able to both perform on the stage again and to act in a short film.

The short film in which Tom played a part was *Sergeant*

Slaughter, My Big Brother, directed by renowned photographer Greg Williams. Ben Macleod played Keith, the younger brother of Tom's character Dan, an on-the-edge, violent young man who has decided to leave home and join the French Foreign Legion. Keith has his own issues in the form of a local bully who is picking on him. The short film, just over 12 minutes long, examines the nature of the relationship between the two brothers at this point in their lives.

The film was shown at various short film festivals around the USA, including the Palm Springs International ShortFest, the Sarasota Film Festival and the New York Digital Film Festival. Tom was great in the film (inhabiting his favourite territory of borderline psychotic characters), but what surprised some who saw the film – and has delighted dedicated Tom Hardy fans who might have the patience to seek out the short film online – was the full frontal nudity. In the second scene of the film, Keith walks into his brother's bedroom where Dan is sitting, making clay models, wearing only a beret and hunting knife tied to his shin. He doesn't stay seated for long, though and we are soon given an eyeful of Tom in the altogether. And it's not for just a few seconds, either. A very brave performance – his Drama Centre tutors should feel proud of how he'd succeeded in breaking down the fourth wall!

As Tom's profile has grown and he's been lucky enough to secure bigger and better roles, he's made no secret of how delighted he's been to be afforded the opportunity to work alongside some of his acting heroes. One actor who Tom holds in especially high regard is the supremely talented Philip Seymour Hoffman. In February 2010, Tom was cast in his US stage debut, *The Long Red Road*, at Chicago's Goodman Theater. The play was to be directed by Seymour Hoffman (and was coincidentally his Chicago directorial debut) and had been written by a playwright with whom Tom had found a great affinity earlier in his career, Brett C Leonard.

Brett C Leonard and Tom had first met several years earlier at the reading of Leonard's play *Roger and Vanessa* at the Royal Academy of Arts. They had made a connection and Tom had subsequently staged a production of *Roger and Vanessa* at the Latchmere pub, where his Shotgun theatre company had been in residence at the time. 'Brett and I spent a lot of time together and forged a really strong bond,' Tom commented when reflecting on that period of his life. The seeds of a friendship were sown and the pair were keen to create a situation where they could work together again.

The Long Red Road is a bleak play about the horrific impact of addiction within a family. Tom's role was that of Sam, an alcoholic who uses drink as a means to obliterate a past he is unable to come to terms with. Philip Seymour Hoffman, speaking to the *Chicago Sun-Times*, summed up the plot thus: 'The play is the story of two brothers and two families. Sam lives in a studio apartment on a South Dakota Indian reservation, where he and his girlfriend work as teachers and he drinks heavily. His wife lives back in Kansas with their 13-year-old daughter and with Sam's older brother. Nine years earlier, Sam was responsible for a terrible accident that left his wife severely maimed and one of their twin daughters dead.'

Leonard had written the part with Tom in mind and it suited him down to the ground. 'The role fits the actor... as snugly as the T-shirt Sam wears,' wrote the *Chicago Daily Herald*. Tom had played addicts before and, although he is able to draw from his own experiences when portraying these characters, he has often said that he knows how important it is not to impose himself on the part he's playing. 'We try to bring ourselves to the play without influencing or judging it,' he said.

Philip Seymour Hoffman was an actor with immense presence who, as well as starring in high-profile Hollywood films, was also a respected stage actor and director. Cinema audiences know him best from films such as *Mission Impossible III* and *Red Dragon*. In 1995, he joined the New York-based theatre group LAByrinth (of which Brett C Leonard is also a member), a not-for-profit company which numbers about 100 established and emerging theatre artists. It is a creative venture that encourages its members to explore their talents in all areas of the performing arts, including directing and writing. It was under the umbrella of LAByrinth that *The Long Red Road* was produced.

What did Tom make of being directed by one of his acting idols? 'On one hand, nothing could be more satisfying. But it is also difficult to deal with a guy who could do it so well himself,' he explained. In many ways Hardy and Hoffman were kindred spirits. Both had struggled with addiction and seen dark times. Both had turned their lives around and overcome their demons. Both were intense actors, who threw themselves into their roles. Hardy loved working with him and relished the opportunity to do so again. Sadly, they would never get the chance. The triumvirate of Hardy, Hoffman and Leonard proved an effective union and the play was positively received by Chicago's theatre critics. The *Chicago Tribune* hailed the work as 'intensely atmospheric' and called Leonard a 'fascinating and authentic writer'. The *Chicago Daily Herald* singled out Tom as giving a 'gritty, true performance'.

Two important film roles were just around the corner for Tom and would consolidate his position as the rising star in the Hollywood firmament. Plus, he was about to have the chance to star alongside another of his acting heroes.

CHAPTER NINE

THE YEAR OF TOM HARDY

By the time *Tinker Tailor Soldier Spy* hit UK cinemas in September 2011, there had been a long hiatus for fans awaiting their next glimpse of Tom Hardy in a new film role. As it turned out, this month would prove to be an embarrassment of riches as, the week following the release of *Tinker* also saw the opening of *Warrior*, a film in which Tom was to play a mixed martial arts fighter. Both films would garner a great deal of critical attention: in the former, Tom was part of a classy ensemble of British actors performing in one of the nation's best-loved spy stories; in the other, he would be afforded more of the spotlight as he proved his mettle in a supremely transformational role. The chameleon actor was showing once again that he could slip in and out of utterly contrasting roles with apparent ease.

The novel on which *Tinker Tailor Soldier Spy* is based – and follows faithfully in style and spirit, though not structure –

was written by John Le Carré and first published in 1974. John Le Carré is the pen name of David Cornwell who, in his own words, is 'a writer who, when I was very young, spent a few ineffectual but extremely formative years in British Intelligence'. The first three of Le Carré's novels were written while he was still in the pay of the secret service but, in 1964, he gave up his intelligence career to become a full-time writer. His spy novels are widely considered to be some of the best of the 20th century.

Tinker Tailor Soldier Spy features George Smiley, a spy who had been introduced to readers in previous books but who, in this story, takes centre stage. The plot concerns the discovery of a mole in the upper echelons of British Intelligence and the quest to root him out. It is Smiley who is called out of retirement to take on the task. The action takes place in the 1970s and, in order to build up the full picture that leads to the discovery of the traitor, characters recall events from their pasts in a complex series of flashbacks. Although this makes for an intricate and sometimes complicated narrative, it also gives the story a rich, layered feel, reflecting the maze of information that Smiley has to navigate before he reaches the truth.

Le Carré remembers how, in the early drafts of the book, he tried – without success – to make the story work without the flashback structure. Realising it wasn't working to his satisfaction, he took his manuscript into the garden and burned it. The phoenix that rose from the ashes was the book we have come to know and love and which has gone down as a classic.

Adapting such a well-loved book for the screen was not

going to be an easy task. Not only would the film have to contend with the scrutiny of fans of the novel, it would also have to stand up to comparison with the fondly remembered 1979 BBC TV series starring the late and revered Alec Guinness in the leading role. To so many viewers, Alec Guinness had been the quintessential Smiley and it would be hard to find an actor who could equal or better his performance.

By June 2010, it became clear that the film adaptation of *Tinker Tailor Soldier Spy* was more than just a rumour and would be going into production. In early reports, there were several high-profile actors linked to the movie but, as is so often the case, not all of them ended up on the final call sheet. Names who were originally attached but who, for whatever reason were never finally cast, included Ralph Fiennes, David Thewlis and Tom's fellow former Drama Centre student, Michael Fassbender. It was Fassbender, in fact, who was slated to play Ricki Tarr, the role that would eventually be filled by Tom. Always one to appreciate that the career of an actor relies upon good fortune as well as talent, Tom made no secret of the fact that he was not the original choice for the part. 'I got lucky to be in this film because it was Michael Fassbender's part and he couldn't make it, so I'm grateful for that,' he told ITN.

The character of Ricki Tarr is pivotal to the unfolding of the story. We meet Tarr, a disgraced field operative and former gun-runner, as he returns to Britain following an absence in Turkey (a change of location from the book, in which he returns from Hong Kong). Tarr has new information about the mole within the Secret Service (The Circus) who is passing information to the Russians. His information confirms and builds on suspicions earlier raised by the former head of The Circus, Control (in this adaptation played by John Hurt). Tarr's information starts the chain of events which sees Smiley retrace the past in order to lead him to the traitor, one of his former colleagues.

While the film is not an action spy thriller in the mould of James Bond or the Bourne series, Tarr is about the closest a character comes to having Bond-style adventures. He is a rogue and a ladies' man and Hardy was interested in the way his character differed from the other secret service types in the film. Against their drab buttoned-up natures, Tarr provides (in the film at least, and thanks to Tom Hardy's performance) a splash of colour and emotion. While Smiley is characterised by the repression of his feelings, Tarr's are on display from the outset as he recalls his encounters with Russian defector and lover Irina. The character is a wild card, but Tom's performance gave him some heart. Whilst admitting to never having read the book or seen the television series, Tom claimed he had formed his opinions about the story and the characters from his father, who was familiar with both. When speaking about Tarr, Tom has said he differed from other characters he had recently been playing because his vulnerabilities are on display from the outset – his performances as 'harder' characters had been more nuanced, with him having to find the light within the shade. Speaking to MSN, with his trademark wit he described this process as being like building 'a case around the soft centre – a bit like a Lindt chocolate.'

In the end, aside from Tom, the final cast list read like a who's who of the cream of British acting. Smiley himself would be played by Gary Oldman, Bill Haydon by Colin

Firth, Jim Prideaux by Mark Strong, Control by John Hurt and Peter Guillam by Benedict Cumberbatch. Kathy Burke would play Connie Sachs. The biggest challenge would be for Oldman, who would have to both differentiate his Smiley from that of Alec Guinness while at the same time paying his respects to the actor who had become so inextricably linked to the character.

Oldman, an extremely accomplished actor but one more recently associated with his roles in rather more fantastical productions such as *Harry Potter* and the *Batman* series, acknowledged that he would be judged in the shadow of Guinness's performance but maintained that an actor couldn't afford to let himself be haunted by previous incarnations of a character, however acclaimed they are. 'The ghost of Guinness was there,' he said. 'But you have to approach it like an actor would a classical role. If you do Hamlet, you've got the ghost of John Gielgud, Laurence Olivier and Richard Burton, but you can't let that get in the way.'

Smiley is described in Le Carré's book thus: 'Small, podgy and at best middle-aged, he was by appearance one of London's meek who do not inherit the earth.' He is, in appearance, unremarkable and would be the kind of person you would walk past on the street and not give a second glance – the perfect demeanour for a spy. This characteristic proved to be pivotal for Gary Oldman when it came to understanding Smiley. 'You're a bit like a nowhere man,' he commented to Baz Bamigboye of the *Daily Mail*. When it came to unlocking Smiley, Oldman also had a little help from a primary source in the form of John Le Carré. The pair met and Oldman drew on the former spy for inspiration: 'The voice is the signature of the character and really there's a lot of David in Smiley, so I nicked his voice.'

A lot of the news relating to the film indicated that it was going to be very much a European affair, with a large proportion of British input. The production company behind it was to be Working Title, which had scored a number of Brit hits including *Bridget Jones' Diary* and *Four Weddings and a Funeral*. Originally, Peter Morgan (the man responsible for the screenplay of *The Queen*) was rumoured to be the screenwriter but, in the end, the job went to husband and wife writing team Peter Straughan and Bridget O'Connor (sadly, Bridget O'Connor would pass away before the film was released.) Refreshingly – and unusually – the production was able to steer clear of any Hollywood involvement, having been financed by French company StudioCanal.

Another European element of the team was the Danish director Tomas Alfredson. Alfredson had recently made a name for himself with the vampire horror movie *Let the Right One In*, which was admired by critics and loved by film fans. It was noted for its atmospheric feel and pared-down style – but was a director who was noted for his success in the horror genre the right choice for this film? Speaking to *The Spectator*, Alfredson noted that 'horror' is something that is of the mind, not necessarily in the action taking place: 'Horror is 90 per cent inside people. The gap between reality and what's happening in their mind – that's what creates the horror. *Tinker, Tailor, Soldier, Spy* is a horror precisely because you do not know how far the conspiracies and lies stretch – it could be much worse than you think.'

There is no doubt that Alfredson turned out to be the

perfect choice for the film. True, his previous film had been a contrast but his style of direction was spot on in creating the right kind of atmosphere for the Cold War thriller. Gary Oldman offered his thoughts on how Alfredson's quiet, unfussy approach to filming had been key in creating the right atmosphere for *Tinker Tailor Soldier Spy*: 'It was as if he was eavesdropping, like a peeping Tom, which is what you sort of want for a spy film,' he commented.

With this outstanding team in place, filming got underway. As well as being filmed in London, location filming took place in Budapest and Istanbul. For Tom Hardy fans, a glimpse of him in character on set would come to light in March 2011. Photographed leaving his trailer, the ever-familiar tattoos were on display but there was a shocking new hairdo in evidence. Tom's usual locks had been replaced by a blond, ill-kempt seventies-style wig, which provided a clue as to how the character of Ricki Tarr was to be styled in the film. Speaking about the wig, Hardy revealed that it was modelled on Paul Hogan's hair in *Crocodile Dundee*. He also said that some scenes had required re-shooting with a toned-down wig as the first one had been, in his words, 'really fierce.' Hilariously, he also referred to sporting the wig as having 'a ferret' taped to his head.

Being a period piece, a great deal of care and attention went into the styling of all of the characters in the film. The person responsible for this important task was costume designer Jacqueline Durran, who had received acclaim for the stunning green evening dress worn by Keira Knightley in *Atonement*. One vital piece of wardrobe would, of course, be Smiley's overcoat. It is described by his creator as having 'a hint of

TOM HARDY: RISE OF A LEGEND

widowhood about it' and that 'either the sleeves were too long or his arms too short for... when he wore his mackintosh, the cuffs all but concealed the fingers...' The article chosen to be Smiley's outer garment in the film was an Aquascutum raincoat, apparently inspired by a photograph of Graham Greene which Alfredson gave to Durran. Smiley's glasses were also crucial to the character and many pairs were experimented with until it was Oldman himself who found the perfect pair in Los Angeles.

According to the *Observer*, which featured an article about the costume design for the film, Tom's character had 'the most interesting wardrobe' and it's fair to say that, amongst the sombre suits and muted colours, Ricki's clothes do stand out, in particular the sheepskin coat he is often seen swaggering about in. 'He is out shooting people, so we wanted him to be this manly action person. The first person we turned to was Steve McQueen,' Durran told the newspaper. Benedict Cumberbatch had his own take on Tom's look in the film. Speaking to the *Observer Magazine*, he joked: 'Tom did *Starsky and Hutch* via *The Sweeney* and I got the suits.'

Of course, much was being made of the stellar cast that the film had attracted. Many of them award-winners and all of them highly acclaimed, it was refreshing to read reports of both the high regard in which they held each other and also the rapport which emerged amongst them on set. Though Tom's star was undoubtedly already in the ascendant before *Tinker* came along, he was still appreciative of what an incredible opportunity it was to be part of something which had attracted such immense acting talent. 'All the other guys that were in it, all the big boys, the John Hurts and the Gary

Oldmans and the superheroes – to be able to work with them at all is incredible – it's like being a part of a huge slab of Italian marble in a beautiful kitchen.'

In particular, he was in awe of Gary Oldman, who he has often referred to as one of his acting heroes, even going as far as to admit that in the roles he had played thus far such as Stuart Shorter and Bronson, he had wanted to emulate what Gary had done before him. When they first met, Tom admits that he was star-struck by the older actor and remained so until he had grown accustomed to being in his presence. He also tells a heart-warming anecdote about the first scenes they had to shoot together. In the original scenes, Tom was sporting a beard which, it was later decided, was not appropriate for the character. During the initial shoot, he was so busy observing the way his idol worked that he became distracted from his own part and his performance didn't play out as he had intended it to. To Tom's relief, the scenes were re-shot minus the beard, and by the time of the re-shoot he'd had time to get used to the experience of working with the actor he had always held in such high regard.

Tom has made reference to the fact that he would love to be the counterpart to Oldman for his generation of actors. He has also said that he would 'chew his own arm off' for the chance to work with Oldman. Tom's lucky streak was set to continue and his wish was granted when the pair went on to work together on two more films back to back: *The Wettest County in the World* (renamed *Lawless*) and *Batman – The Dark Knight Rises*.

Though Oldman is an acting legend in his own right, he is grounded and considerate and clearly thoroughly enjoyed working with the new generation of actors in the film. 'It's fun when you get to work with good young actors who are coming up. There's some top talent in *Tinker*,' was his generous comment to the *Daily Mail*. He went on to pay Tom a huge compliment by saying that he thought 2011 would be 'the year of Tom Hardy'. What a fantastic accolade to receive from someone in whose footsteps you have always strived to follow.

Tinker Tailor Soldier Spy also saw Tom reunited with his old mate Benedict Cumberbatch, with whom he had co-starred in *Stuart, A Life Backwards*. Cumberbatch joked about the scene in which his character, Peter Guillam, has to trade blows with Tom's character. 'It was very enjoyable. He wanted me to hit him harder and I had to point out that I needed my hands for the rest of the day. Because he can take a bit of punishing, Tom. And it's probably, let's face it, the only time I'm going to really have a proper pop at him, in his current form. So it was good fun,' he commented.

Gary Oldman also revealed that during a lull in filming on the set one day thanks to bad weather, for want of something to do, the cast turned their hands to making the spy thriller into their very own musical. Speaking to the *Daily Mail* he said that all of the cast including Colin Firth, Kathy Burke and John Hurt joined in and 'we started imagining a musical with titles like *Where's the Mole?*' Apparently Benedict Cumberbatch's role in this spectacular piece of improvisation was as the impresario of the show. Film fans would have paid good money to see that behind-the-scenes gem!

Oldman was not the only actor to speak about the fun the ensemble cast had while on set. Colin Firth remarked, with typically British self-deprecating wit, in an interview with LoveFilm.com: 'If you get boys together, they regress ... we spent most of the time between takes inhabiting the age of 10. We ended up sabotaging ourselves... it was a pitiful spectacle.'

Over the summer prior to the film's release, anticipation grew as teaser trailers were released and the official artwork for the movie posters did the rounds on the internet. Neither the trailers nor the posters left fans disappointed: the film seemed as accomplished and stylish as they had hoped it would be.

The official release date for the film in the UK was 16 September, but its world premiere took place at the Venice Film Festival on Monday, 5 September. Early notices from the critics in attendance helped to build up the head of steam already growing about it. UK critics were clearly proud to have a film with home roots making such a strong showing at the event. The *Telegraph* awarded *Tinker* a five-star review and the paper's David Gritten called the film 'a British and European success story... it makes your heart pound, gets your pulses racing and sends your brain cells into overdrive.' It was widely agreed that the fine ensemble cast were, as a unit, triumphant, but Tom was singled out for praise in particular by several critics. *Empire*'s Matt Mueller remarked upon the contrast Tom's performance brought to the film when set beside the other characters: 'Besides Oldman, it's Hardy who makes the biggest impression, bringing a touch of humanity into this barrel of cold public-school fish.' The *Guardian*'s Xan Brooks stated, 'Tom Hardy raises the roof as Ricki Tarr,' and *IndieWIRE* went so far as to say: 'We're virtually past the point of having to say that Tom Hardy is brilliant in a film, but brilliant he is and once more showing new strings to his bow.'

The *Observer*'s Jason Solomons was so impressed with the film that he predicted it would be the frontrunner to win the Golden Lion, the top award of the festival. Sadly, the award was won by *Faust*, directed by Russian director Alexander Sokurov. The best actor award, ironically, was scooped by Michael Fassbender – the original name attached to the part of Ricki Tarr – for his performance in *Shame*.

Although the film didn't take home any prizes, the positive reports which emerged from Venice fuelled the anticipation of the film's UK release. Finally, on 13 September, fans gathered on London's South Bank to watch the cast arrive for the premiere at the BFI. Those who had patiently assembled were not disappointed as the stars of the film turned out in force, greeted their fans and gave their time happily to the press. The camaraderie between the actors was in evidence as they stood together for press photos to be taken. Tom spent a lot of time signing autographs and posing for photos with fans before being ushered away indoors.

John Le Carré was also present at the premiere and it was gratifying to hear his feedback on the film. Like any author, he'd had reservations about another adaptation of his work but admitted that he thought the finished product was 'wonderful' and that he was 'thrilled by it'. He referred to Gary Oldman as a Smiley who was 'waiting patiently to explode'. He said that he'd been involved but in a modest way – as 'a resource they could call upon' if needed.

'I approached the prospect of a feature film of *Tinker, Tailor, Soldier, Spy* with the same misgivings that would have afflicted anyone else who had loved the television series of 32 years ago... George Smiley was Alec Guinness, Alec was George, period. How could another actor equal, let alone surpass, him?

'My anxieties were misplaced. And if people write to me and say, "How could you let this happen to poor old Alec Guinness?", I shall reply that, if "poor Alec" had witnessed Oldman's performance, he would have been the first to give it a standing ovation.' Le Carré went on to say that Oldman 'evokes the same solitude, inwardness, pain and intelligence that his predecessor brought to the part – even the same elegance.'

He added that Gary Oldman's Smiley was more of a ticking time bomb than Guinness's version, somehow more dangerous.

The positive reviews that had poured in after Venice continued in the British press once the film had gone on general release in the UK. Jonathan Romney in the *Independent on Sunday* praised the intelligence and complexity of the film. 'You'll feel your own synapses working at full tilt as you watch this intelligent, bracing, consummately achieved entertainment,' he wrote. Chris Tookey of the *Daily Mail* was equally impressed, describing its 'expertly handled tension, subtle menace and superior acting by everyone involved'. He, however, also expressed concerns about the place that a film as cerebral and labyrinthine as *Tinker Tailor Soldier Spy* had in the modern age of effects-laden, action-packed movies. 'In these days of diminished attention spans, I worry whether audiences are willing to steep themselves in the intricacies of this complex puzzle. The movie requires concentration.'

He was not the first to raise such a point. The stars of the film had no hesitation in promoting the film as the antithesis of the kind of spy movies audiences had grown accustomed to watching. Gary Oldman had referred to it as 'a quiet movie. You have to listen, you have to focus.' In an interview with Sky Movies, Tom Hardy had highlighted the difference between this film and other films that took on a higher-octane approach to spying. '*Tinker Tailor Soldier Spy* is the spy movie without the gadgets – it's the footwork,' he said. John Le Carré praised potential British viewers and stated that the cinema audience is 'far more intelligent than it's given credit for'.

He was proved right. The film went straight to number one at the UK box office, becoming the third biggest three-day September opening on record. It wasn't just initial excitement, either: clearly positive reviews and word of mouth worked as the film held on to the top position for a second weekend, taking £2.1 million in the second weekend. In a triumph for the British and European production, in that second weekend it also beat the new Steve Carrell comedy movie and, ironically, Tom's next movie, *Warrior*.

Further accolades for the film came when both Tom Hardy and Benedict Cumberbatch were nominated in the Best Supporting Actor category at the 2011 British Independent Film Awards, for their work in *Tinker Tailor Soldier Spy*. Unfortunately, they both lost out to Michael Smiley for his performance in *Kill List*. Gary Oldman was nominated for Best Actor at both the BAFTA film awards and the Academy Awards in the USA but lost out on both gongs to Jean Dujardin for his part in *The Artist*.

Tinker Tailor Soldier Spy had been a triumph in every way, from the acting to the direction to the box-office figures. It was a movie any actor would have been proud to be part of – and Tom certainly was. Having received praise both as part of the ensemble and for his individual performance in *Tinker*, what would the critics make of his next, altogether contrasting part? Would this, as Oldman had predicted, really turn out to be Tom's year?

Warrior tells the story of two estranged brothers who are reunited against the backdrop of a Mixed Martial Arts (MMA) contest. It hit UK cinema screens just one week after *Tinker Tailor Soldier Spy*. Unusually, there had been a long lapse between the filming of *Warrior*, which had taken place in 2009, and its release in September 2011. The delay had been a result of the studio behind the film, Lionsgate, deciding to put back its release to avoid a head-to-head box-office battle with another prominent film in the same genre, *The Fighter* (starring Mark Wahlberg and Christian Bale). In a strange chronology, Tom had actually finished shooting *Warrior* before filming began for *Tinker Tailor Soldier Spy* and even before he worked on *Inception*, which had been released in July 2010.

In *Warrior*, Tom plays Tommy Conlon, a tormented ex-Marine who returns home to Pittsburgh after an absence of 14 years. He calls upon his father, Paddy (Nick Nolte), a recovering alcoholic, to train him for an MMA tournament with a winner-takes-all $5 million purse. Meanwhile, Tommy's older brother Brendan (played by Australian actor Joel Edgerton), is a former fighter turned teacher who has landed himself in financial straits and who concurrently embarks on a return to the ring – or more accurately in this case, the cage. Predictably, the two brothers meet each other along their respective journeys towards the contest and the fractured family is forced to face up to its troubled past.

Prior to *Warrior*, Joel Edgerton had been something of an unknown, particularly in Hollywood terms. The director and co-writer of *Warrior*, Gavin O'Connor, picked Hardy and Edgerton for their respective roles precisely because of their relative anonymity. 'I didn't want an audience to have any memories of these actors from other roles because I felt like that was going to get in the way of the performances,' he told the *Pittsburgh Post-Gazette*.

Ironically, in the lengthy period between wrapping the film and its release date, Tom's profile in particular had soared. In the interim, he had made audiences and critics sit up and take notice with his dazzling performance in *Bronson*, he had won the BAFTA Rising Star Award, he had been part of the highly respected Brit triumph *Tinker Tailor Soldier Spy*, plus it had been announced that he was to play both Bane in the new Batman film and Max Rockatansky in a prequel to the *Mad Max* film series. By the time of *Warrior*'s release, Tom had become hot property. Edgerton, meanwhile, had also had his share of plaudits as a result of his performance in the critically acclaimed Australian movie, *Animal Kingdom* and had been the subject of increased media attention when it was revealed that he had landed the role of Tom Buchanan alongside Leonardo Di Caprio in a forthcoming big screen adaptation of *The Great Gatsby*.

O'Connor was thus far best known for directing two movies in particular: *Pride and Glory* and *Miracle*. *Pride and Glory* is a familial tale of generations of New York cops which pits family members against each other; his earlier film,

Miracle, followed the fortunes of the 1980 US Olympic ice-hockey team. In *Warrior*, O'Connor would effectively draw from the two previous films and meld the themes of family dissonance and fierce sporting competition. For the director, it was the complexities of the relationship between the brothers and, in turn, their respective relationships with their father that would be at the heart of the film. 'This story is much more a life drama than a movie about Mixed Martial Arts. It tells the story of a family that has to overcome great challenges that everyone can relate to in these tough times, and the backdrop happens to be this particular sport … you don't have to be a fan of the sport to enjoy the story,' he said to Big Lead Sports website just before the film opened.

As cast and crew had intended, the film they had made was perceived as a story of dysfunction and separation within a family, which happened to be played out against a backdrop of sporting competition, as opposed to being solely a 'fighting film'. O'Connor was in some ways proved right about the perception of the nature of his film by the results of the screen tests. They returned surprising results: the best scores it received were from women. 'I remember after our first test screening, I went up to the studio and they jokingly said: "You made a chick flick." We were all shocked,' recalled the director.

Having established that he was not looking for big lead names to fill the roles of the warring brothers, what was it that Gavin O'Connor needed to bring the story from the pages of his script and to breathe life into his leading characters?

When Tom first read the script, the film was a very different beast from the final version. Initially, Tom felt he was physically too far away from the character of Tommy he was reading on the page, who was originally, according to the actor: 'Hispanic. He had long hair and a ponytail and went swimming every morning with rocks in a rucksack.' The script was re-drafted many times and, as part of that process, the character changed – as did the understanding of what was the central theme of the film. 'It started to add up to me that *Warrior* wasn't a kung fu martial arts kind of movie at all. This was actually a kind of family drama with a backdrop of the world of mixed martial arts,' Tom told Canada's *National Post*.

Tom was one of the last actors O'Connor met when looking for the right person to play Tommy. He needed to find an actor who could portray the complexity of the character, someone who understood the light and shade of the kind of human being who is outwardly aggressive but inwardly susceptible. 'I needed someone who had a very tough exterior and yet had a deep vulnerability. The character does a lot of bad things and the audience had to understand that what he was doing was coming from a place of pain,' reflected the director.

Initially, Tom was unsure as to whether he could portray all the elements of Tommy and needed reassurance that he would be able to give a complete performance. To do this, he and O'Connor had to be in tune about who exactly Tommy was – something which came about in a slightly unconventional way. O'Connor has recounted how, rather than a usual style of audition, the actor in his characteristically intense fashion, turned up on his doorstep late one Sunday night to speak to him. 'He was supposed to go to a hotel,' O'Connor said in an interview with *Wales on Sunday*, 'but instead stayed at my house for five days. He never left, so I got to know him very well. And the qualities he has as a human being are just right for the character.'

Indeed, who would be better able to inhabit the skin of a character like Tommy than Tom Hardy? On an emotional level, he is nothing less than a perfect fit for the role. He has referred to the character of Tommy as having 'no skin', which is also how he has referred to his own younger self. In the same interview, he said of Tommy: 'He's running from everything. He can't sit still ...', which again sounds rather like the Tom of a decade earlier. There were other personal experiences he could draw on too, enabling him to get inside the head of the man he needed to become on screen. He had first-hand experience of the immense strain that addiction can place on a family as well as the experience of recovery.

'I felt very much at home with the sadder side of Tommy, but it's not a territory I need to dwell in,' he told the *Daily Telegraph*. He went on to explain that, as well as finding the process of playing Tommy a cathartic one, he also felt that, by using his experiences to bring authenticity to the character, he might just be able to give audiences an insight, via Tommy, of the pain of this world that he himself had inhabited.

Edgerton's character, Brendan, while having his own issues with his family's ruptured past and undergoing his own personal crises, is a stark contrast to Tommy. While Tommy escaped his past life by joining the armed services, Brendan has chosen instead the path of suburban domesticity and has created the kind of family that his own never was. Brendan has a responsibility to his new family, both emotionally and financially. The actor proved a fit with the role and, according to O'Connor, he has 'integrity in spades. Joel, as a person, is a dynamic actor and you root for him and you like him.'

So far, so good – two actors had been found who could each turn in a performance which would highlight the divide between the two men who Tom Hardy has referred to as 'very different brothers. Cut from the same cloth, but very different.'

The next challenge was to get the two actors looking completely credible as MMA fighters – anything less would have done the film a disservice and been a distraction from the story. They both had to set about transforming their bodies and undertook rigorous training so that they would look authentic when sparring in the cage. This was no mean feat and required a great deal of dedication, determination and energy from the pair.

Originally, the characters in the film were to have been heavyweight fighters but it would have taken too long to get the actors bulked up to a degree where they would look like genuine heavyweights. Instead, they were cast as middle-weights and had to increase their bodyweight to a mere 84kg!

Tom is no stranger to transformation and much had been made of the extreme change he had undergone when switching between the roles of Stuart Shorter and Charles Bronson. As we know, Tom didn't find bulking up for *Bronson* too difficult but attaining the right kind of shape for *Warrior* was to be a very different prospect. Tom has made no secret of the fact that he found it a tough part of the preparation. 'Getting into a gym is something I'm not comfortable with at all, to be honest, so I was quite concerned by the whole thing. I was alarmed at the amount of exercise this demanded, and athleticism and discipline and structure. It wasn't up my alley at all,' he told ITN.

The process started 10 weeks before the cameras rolled, and to say it was demanding would be a huge understatement. Training was a full-time occupation and took place six or seven times a week. A typical day would consist of fight training at the gym from 7am until mid-afternoon; after lunch, there would be training in boxing, ju-jitsu as well as weights work and choreography – all of which would continue late into the night.

The actors have stated that they were 'side by side always' while they were in training and, as ever, Tom also had his great friend and personal trainer Pnut to assist him. It was Pnut who had helped Hardy to bulk up for *Bronson* and he now had an even greater task on his hands. 'Pnut had to pick me up off the floor after I finished *Bronson* and I had to strip away a load of fat and pack on muscle as fast as possible,' Tom told *Men's Fitness* magazine. True to form, Pnut was just the man Tom needed in his corner – he knew exactly what was required not only to get Tom physically in shape, but also to give him authenticity on screen. 'I didn't want to train Tom to look like he could fight – I wanted to train him to fight.'

Indeed, one of the key elements to the success of the film was that the fighting was as realistic as it possibly could be. To this end, training was also undertaken with MMA coach Greg Jackson and some UFC fighters too. Edgerton spent a good deal of time with Jackson and has credited him with being 'a real advisor for the integrity and detail of the sport'.

The stunt team, too, were a vital part of the operation and have been described by Tom as 'the glue for the fighting scenes of the film'. Martial artist JJ Perry, renowned for his work on a host of films including *Iron Man* and *Avatar*, was the stunt co-ordinator. Also on the team was fighter and stuntman Fernando Chien, who Tom states was 'responsible for the authenticity of the interactions that we had'.

Just as the two screen brothers have contrasting lives and personalities, so they have different fighting styles, which seem to reflect how they are as people. Tommy's fighting style is out-and-out aggressive and he often flattens opponents in just a few moves. Brendan, on the other hand, has to work harder for his victories and consequently spends a lot more time in the cage. This being the case, Edgerton was required to take on quite a bit more ju-jitsu and choreography training than Tom was.

Once on set, things proved no less exhausting. Long days of filming required just as much – if not more – energy and focus. It would apparently take about two days to film one of the rounds of fighting, so as well as having to dig deep physically, they also had to focus on maintaining the appearance of the aggression during the fight. At this point, the actors were also carb-depleted, sticking to a regime of eating chicken and broccoli every few hours, something which Tom has admitted wreaked havoc with his mood. Between takes, instead of resting, they had to get themselves in gear for the next round of fighting and could be found doing press ups, hitting pads or running up and down the stairs. And, while the rest of the crew broke for lunch, there was no such luxury for the two leads: you guessed it, lunchtime equalled another workout. There's no denying that the fighting was tough and took its toll. During the course of making the film, Tom broke a toe, two ribs and tore the ligaments in his right hand.

Did such an intense and testosterone-fuelled atmosphere on set lead to any kind of competitiveness off set? It would appear that quite the opposite happened and the two lead actors seemed to enjoy a happy working relationship and developed a mutual respect. They claimed, too, that due to the combative nature of the scenes they were filming, any negative emotion could be channelled into the fight, rather than displaying itself in other ways. 'There was no peacocking in the gym,' said Tom. In the inevitable press junkets the pair were subsequently required to undertake together, they appear totally at ease with each other and share a laddish, knockabout sense of humour. Edgerton has also generously described Tom as 'an exceptional actor'.

2011 marked the first annual CinemaCon exhibition in Las Vegas. The purpose of the event is to bring together cinema owners and operators from around the world and, with so many industry high-fliers together in one place, is the perfect opportunity to promote your film and get a buzz going around it. It was at CinemaCon that *Warrior* had its first public screening and it certainly initiated a flurry of activity on film websites and blogs. It wasn't yet the finished film that was screened but that didn't prevent it from causing a stir. *Firstshowing.net* called it 'incredible', while *slashfilm* gushed that it was one of the best films that they had seen that year. In the UK, meanwhile, where Tom had been recognised as a rising star for quite some time and was hardly lacking in a female fan base, excitement was growing at the sight of *Warrior* promo posters featuring the actor sporting a well-sculpted torso and looking menacing.

It helped that, by the time that promotion began apace,

both actors were becoming names on Hollywood's lips. Tom in particular seemed to fascinate fans and critics across the pond – people wanted to know more about this Brit actor with the intriguing past who directors seemed to be clamouring to sign up for their films. Everyone wanted to see what all the fuss was about.

With this positive buzz behind them, Lionsgate went all out to get their film talked about amongst cinema-goers in the USA. The studio set up a nationwide series of free screenings of the movie, with tickets being made available from 12 August. The promotion was deemed a success and the cinemas involved in the screenings reported good attendance rates, with the film being seen by over 17,000 people as a result of the scheme.

Warrior has firm ties to the US military because of the character Tommy's history as a US Marine, and the script had in fact been vetted by a Marine Corps liaison officer. In addition, though, the military were directly involved in the shooting of the film, and 200 real uniformed Marines appeared as spectators to Tommy's fights, backing their boy. In the summer months of 2011, prior to the film's release, Camp Pendleton in California hosted a screening of the film for the Marines based there. Tom was in attendance at the screening and took the time to sign autographs and meet some of the Marines at the base. He has spoken of how the presence of the real Marines in the crowd of spectators while filming the fight scenes helped him to get fired up for the scene ahead.

It's fair to say that the film had a mixed reception. Most agreed that, in plot and structure, it was somewhat flawed. It was definitely a film that was split down the middle, with the first half committed to painting the characters and their relationships; the second half committed to the unfolding of the brothers making their respective ways to the MMA tournament. Nicholas Barber wrote in his review in the *Independent on Sunday* that: 'For the first half of *Warrior*, you might be fooled into thinking that it's a gritty, blue-collar drama in the musclebound mould of *The Wrestler*, but once its heroes start their obligatory work-out sessions, it's clear that you're watching the most formulaic of Hollywood sports movies.' Indeed, once the contest in Atlantic City got under way, there was a strong sense of inevitability about how the second half of the film would play out.

There was one thing, though, on which critics were all agreed: barring any criticism of the film itself, the actors in it all turned in fantastic performances which were, arguably, its saving grace. Tom in particular was singled out for his outstanding portrayal of Tommy. It was widely agreed that he had succeeded in creating a character who, despite his out and out aggression, never loses the sympathy of the audience because we can see that underneath the hostile exterior lies a fragility. Barber referred to Tom as 'sensational' while *Screen* described him as 'arrestingly intense'.

Some critics went even further than that. The performance prompted several to compare him to a young Marlon Brando – and he had certainly shown he shared some of the brooding intensity and depth of Brando. When asked to respond to such comparisons, Tom was typically self-effacing and grounded about it all. Speaking to *Inquirer Entertainment* website he said, 'You're going to hate me. I've never watched *On the Waterfront*. I've seen *Apocalypse Now*. I thought he was wonderful in that. I feel a bit embarrassed when I'm compared to him. Marlon Brando is Marlon Brando. It's a tremendous honour to be compared to him. But I don't think I'm very good at what I do. I want to work harder at it.'

As 2011 drew to a close, it seemed as if Gary Oldman's predictions about Tom were coming true. He was turning in critically acclaimed performances; his openness, sense of humour and down-to-earth nature were gaining him fans the world over; and on a personal level, he seemed to be more than content: he was providing for his son and was settled in a happy relationship with fiancée Charlotte Riley. Now noted for his transformations, it seemed that our home-grown success was about to transform into a star of global proportions.

CHAPTER TEN

HOLLYWOOD

'I've got to earn my pipe and slippers and cardigan. The zenith of my attainment would be to be in a rom com and actually be passable.' The irony of this comment that Tom Hardy made to Jonathan Ross on his BBC1 chat show in 2010 lay in that, just weeks later, it would be announced that he was to star alongside Reese Witherspoon and Chris Pine in *This Means War*, a romantic comedy. While Tom's performance in the film may have been perfectly passable, unfortunately the film itself was far from it – in fact the premise and direction of the movie seemed to squander the considerable talent of those who starred in it.

Tom Hardy had been busily carving out a niche for himself as the best of baddies, but he was also trying to make a name for himself as a headline star – so the choice to act alongside one of Hollywood's hottest leading females in a film directed by the man behind *Charlie's Angels*, McG, seemed like a sensible step in the right direction. Tom's comedy roles on celluloid had been few and far between but he'd often brought humour to his more formidable roles in an attempt to present his characters as more complete and relatable.

Hardy fans would have had mixed feelings about the news that he was to star in *This Means War*. While it would be great to see him do something that, for him, went against the grain, everyone fervently hoped that it would turn out to be a film that showcased his diverse skill in a positive way. It would also be refreshing to see Tom looking his natural, handsome self as opposed to taking on the guise of a hard man.

This Means War is part action movie and part romantic comedy. In fact, at times, it doesn't seem to really know which genre it wants to fall into. The rather clunky and implausible story involves two best-buddy secret agents (Tom Hardy as Tuck and Chris Pine as FDR – yes, he is known by initials rather than by name) who happen to fall for the same woman – Lauren Scott, played by Reese Witherspoon. When they discover that she is the object of both of their affections, they try to outsmart each other in order to win her over. Being spies, they have a whole arsenal of tricks up their sleeves, which they utilise in an effort to gain the upper hand over the other. They end up spying on Lauren – and on each other when with her – which led many who saw the film to question its morally dubious storyline. It was certainly a bit of a questionable direction in which to take the story. One scene in particular which was commented upon is when Lauren is dancing around her apartment scantily clad, unaware that the two spies have broken in and are darting around planting secret cameras and bugs. The scene is played out for laughs in a comical, farcical style, but there is something decidedly off-key about it.

All of this monkeying about is building up, of course, to Lauren having to decide which man she wants to have a relationship with – which leads to another problem. Would this woman really have a quandary? Faced with the muscular, gorgeous Tom Hardy and the loaf-haired, wiry Chris Pine, in reality would there really have been a choice to make? Perhaps if the leading men had been more evenly matched we might have believed she was torn between them. There was also criticism of the way in which the film veered off into giving copious amounts of screen time to the 'bromance' between Tuck and FDR.

Director McG had admired Reese Witherspoon's work for a long time and knew that he would love to have her as his leading lady. She had just finished filming *Water for Elephants* when she got the call from Fox, telling her about his new project. She had admired McG's *Charlie's Angels* and was keen to know more about the film. When she read the script, she was attracted to the fact that it was a fun action movie and therefore something new for her to try her hand at. McG was clear from the outset that he wanted to present a different kind of Reese Witherspoon in this movie. Her usual characters are wide-eyed, sweet, girl-next-door types but McG wanted the world to see her sexier side. Recounting what he said to her at the time to *USA Today*, he said, 'I told her, "You're America's sweetheart. Women love you. Men like you. I want men to covet you."'

Having secured Witherspoon, McG set about finding his two leading men, who would need to be handsome and sexy enough to attract female cinema-goers to the film. He was clear about the kind of dynamic he wanted his leading men to have, too; it was to be a classic buddy-style partnership in the same vein as Butch and Sundance or Maverick and Goose from *Top Gun*. He also knew he wanted a blend of the classic American CIA agent (think Ethan Hunt in *Mission Impossible* or Jason Bourne) and the archetypal ice-cool British spy such as James Bond.

McG's meeting with Chris Pine took place at LA's A-list hangout of choice Chateau Marmont. Pine had thus far been best known for his role as the young Captain Kirk in the rebooted *Star Trek* movie of 2009. In Pine, the director knew that he had found an actor with the right qualities for his FDR: he needed to be supremely confident but ultimately likeable too, assets he'd shown he possessed in abundance when he played Captain Kirk. Speaking to website *Movieclips.com*, McG said of the actor: 'By his own admission, he does everything in a sort of decidedly self-assured way. The ability to do it with such self-assuredness and still be charming, that's a real gift; most people can't do it. Chris Pine, he's a young actor who has that rare skill set.' Witherspoon echoed these sentiments, describing Pine as having 'a Cary-Grant-type quality, sort of effortlessly charming'.

Onwards McG went with the search to find Pine's British counterpart, someone who would be contrasting yet complementary. Though Tom has legions of fans who consider him to be the sexiest man on the planet, he doesn't quite fit the Hollywood mould for a leading man. Handsome, yes, but in a rather un-American way – and there was still the age-old wonky teeth dilemma. But McG knew that Tom had what he was looking for as the flipside to the all-American Pine. 'He was the only choice for Tuck,' he later confirmed. The director travelled to London to speak to Tom about the part and to show him some initial scenes. He knew that Tom's catalogue of past work was quite different from what he was proposing, but felt he'd found his ruggedly charming man. 'The guy's a monster. We know what he can do with his acting... he looks like the love child of Marlon Brando and Paul Newman,' McG said to *USA Today*.

Tom was fascinated with the nature of the film and the fact that it seemed to mix up traditional genres. 'I really like to play against the fact that we're doing a spy movie in a rom-com,' he commented. Plus, starring opposite Reese Witherspoon was bound to be an attractive prospect for a young male actor. 'It was awesome to work with Reese as she is clearly the queen of the genre – she was really the draw,' he told the *Sunday Mirror*. In turn, Witherspoon was pleased to have Tom as part of the team as he brought his usual staunch work ethic along to the set with him: 'Tom is a very intense, focused actor. His mind races with thoughts and ideas. He was writing his own lines and helping us construct narrative. He's smart – always adding to the process,' she commented generously.

The final piece of the casting jigsaw was to find the right woman to play Witherspoon's character's best friend, Trish. Trish is smart, wisecracking and her circumstances are very different from Lauren's. She is married with kids and so delights in living vicariously through Lauren's love life. Lauren often turns to her for advice, which she willingly dishes out – and it's often quite terrible counsel! Witherspoon was desperate for Chelsea Handler to fill the role of Trish. As well as being an actress, Handler is a comedienne and writer but best known for presenting her own talk show, *Chelsea Lately*. Witherspoon knew that Handler would bring just the right kind of caustic ballsiness the role required. Handler was a perfect fit but the two actresses were, by their own admission, polar opposites in their approach to work. Witherspoon is the consummate professional, always coming to work prepared, whereas Handler had a rather more off-the-cuff approach to things. Handler would often ad lib in her scenes and make up jokes, causing Witherspoon to have to fight back laughter when filming. Witherspoon has referred to Handler as 'uncontrollable and a genius' and the pair clearly had a lot of fun when on set together.

Chris Pine reported that the wisecracking banter between the two women was often in evidence, but that because he and Tom were rarely involved in the same scenes as them, they would usually miss out on the jokes. The following day, though, the boys would get to see what had transpired on set when watching the scenes played back and were astonished and entertained by what had been going on. 'It was inevitable that Tom and I would come to set, and Reese and [Chelsea] would have shot a scene the day before and everybody was talking about what they'd shot yesterday. We'd watch playback and from poltergeist [jokes] to urethra [jokes]. It was just incredible,' he told *USA Today*.

Hilarious though Handler's improvising was, some of her jokes were deemed a bit too near to the knuckle for the censors. Fox was anxious to get a PG-13 rating for the film in the USA so that it would reach as wide a demographic as possible. In order to do this, some of her racier sexual jokes had to be removed. The film had originally been given an R rating but, deeming this too restrictive, the studio appealed to the board of censors to lower it. When the appeal was turned down, they made the cuts to ensure they succeeded in getting the film rated as a PG-13. The bawdy jokes stayed in for British cinema-goers, though!

Fun on set was by no means just the preserve of the two women. All those involved seemed to have a great time during the course of shooting. Although Tom and Reese Witherspoon hadn't worked together before, they broke the ice on their first day in a rather unconventional manner. The first scene they had to film involved Lauren shooting Tuck in the crotch with a paintball gun. Ouch. 'I just thought she's sexy. But paintball in the nuts hurts,' joked Tom.

The pair also had a lot of fun filming the scene in which Tuck takes Lauren on a date and arranges for them to swing on a circus trapeze. Apparently Tom dedicated a lot of time to perfecting his trapeze skills so that it looked effortless when doing it for the cameras. 'He practised for at least a month ahead of time,' revealed Witherspoon to Front Row Features. 'He rehearsed a lot, and he'd wake up super early in the morning. He had a trapeze installed in his hotel room. He did a great job. We're very proud of him.'

Reese has also made no secret of the fact that turning up to work on *This Means War* was by no means a chore. She loved the fact that she was getting to work on an action movie for the first time and delighted in learning how to use weapons – she even begged McG to write in more situations where she could use them. Having two good-looking and charming leading men also had its upside for the actress. 'I had such a great time making that movie. It was interesting to get to fire guns! It was a lot of fun making out with two very handsome guys like Chris and Tom, a girl couldn't ask for more than that,' she explained to *GT* magazine.

Pine's experience was equally positive and he said the film was 'a blast to shoot'. He was also in awe of how Reese threw herself wholeheartedly into the action part of the movie, stating: 'I have pictures of Reese suspended in mid-air on a studio backlot.' As for the 'bromance' between Chris Pine and Tom Hardy, did it extend behind the scenes? Tom clearly has a lot of respect for his co-star, saying 'he's hot as hell and really lovely. He's a very funny guy so the banter with him was fun.'

According to Reese Witherspoon, the cast was kept in the dark as to the ending of the film. As the conclusion would be such a crucial part of the film, it was essential that no information about which agent Lauren would choose – if indeed she did choose one of them – leaked out in advance. In order to prevent this from happening, the studio opted to play it safe and shoot a variety of endings for the film. 'We shot endings where I could end up with Tom, or I could end up with Chris, or I could end up alone. Or I could end up with Chelsea Handler,' she joked to *Total Film* magazine.

For a change *This Means War* didn't require a huge physical transformation for Tom. Having really piled on the muscle for *Warrior*, he'd actively been trying to lose some of the bulk since the film had wrapped. Now, he needed to put a little bit more back on so that he looked like a strong, fit spy. His preparation, then, wasn't too demanding and, according to the actor, involved eating quite a bit of cake and other sugary foods. Chris Pine decided that to play FDR, whom he saw as a 'hedonist', he would need to stop lifting weights so he too lost quite a bit of his muscle mass.

The US release date for the film had been slated as 17 February 2012, but Twentieth Century Fox made the decision to pull it forward in the schedule and try to hang publicity on the peg of Valentine's Day. The president of Fox Distribution, Bruce Snyder, issued a forthright statement about the change, declaring: 'Starting Valentine's Day, we're making war, not love. We're armed and ready with the perfect movie. This is a picture that has it all – humor, charm, wit and action – and it plays through the roof.'

If using cinema-goers' and critics' reactions to the film as a yardstick, the studio's apparent confidence in their movie could be construed as a bit misplaced. Many felt that the plot of *This Means War* was just a stretch too far and that it had failed to maximise the talent its cast had to offer. In particular, many singled out their disappointment that a powerhouse actor such as Tom had found his way into what they considered to be a below-par film. *Newsday* summed up matters quite neatly when it referred to *This Means War* as 'less than the sum of its parts' and went on to express a hope that Tom Hardy had a twin and it was he who had in fact played Tuck, as 'the guy in this alleged comedy has drunk the Hollywood Kool-Aid'.

In spite of the film not being a big hit, Tom had made his first foray into the world of the big-budget, star-studded, glossy Hollywood romantic comedy. Now that he had one foot firmly planted on American soil, the projects he was taking on were bigger and he was starting to become a name people would remember.

Bigger – in every sense of the word – was most definitely the order of the day when it came to Tom's next job. In fact you can't really get much bigger than the third and final instalment of Christopher Nolan's *Batman* trilogy. The excitement, the budget, the hype, the cast were all huge – and, as it happened, so was Tom's character!

In his original form, Batman was a DC Comics superhero. He has been brought to life in various guises, first in two 1940s films and then in the 1960s television series in which Adam West took the title role. The television series bore little resemblance to the dark nature of the original comic book stories and was bright, colourful and camp. In the 1980s, Batman was brought to the big screen over the course of several films. The first, *Batman*, came out in 1989 and was directed by Tim Burton, with Michael Keaton in the title role and Jack Nicholson as The Joker. The film was deemed a success, both critically and commercially. The 1989 film was followed in 1992 by *Batman Returns* which boasted villains in the form of Michelle Pfeiffer as Catwoman and Danny de Vito as The Penguin. In 1995, the shine of the new *Batman* films faded a little when Joel Schumacher took over as director and Michael Keaton was replaced by Val Kilmer in the lead role. The series limped to a close with the fourth and final film, *Batman and Robin* in 1997. Val Kilmer couldn't commit because of scheduling conflicts and was replaced by George Clooney and Schumacher once again took the helm as director. The tone of the film was too light-hearted and silly, probably thanks to Schumacher's decision to pay homage to the 1960s television series, and was far from beloved by critics or fans.

Thank heavens for Christopher Nolan, who has proved himself a trustworthy custodian of the caped crusader. In 2003, Nolan and co-writer David S. Goyer began work on *Batman Begins* for Warner Brothers. They knew from the start that they wanted the film to have a dark, brooding atmosphere and to be more realistic than the previous attempts. *Batman Begins* went back to the start of the Batman story and showed how he made his initial journey from Bruce Wayne to adopting his alter ego. The film was a fine achievement and was helped by having a perfectly cast group of actors working on it. Christian Bale – another actor known for his transformations and for the intensity he can bring to his characters was cast as Bruce Wayne/Batman, with Michael Caine as loyal valet Alfred. Tower of strength Gary Oldman was weary, morally upstanding Commissioner Gordon and Cillian Murphy was superb as the villainous Scarecrow. Katie Holmes brought just the right blend of strength and vulnerability to Bruce's love interest Rachel Dawes. Released in 2005, the film was applauded by reviewers and restored the faith of audiences in a superhero movie franchise.

The winning formula was repeated in the second instalment in 2008, *The Dark Knight*. Bale, Caine and Oldman all reprised their roles and they were joined by Aaron Eckhart as Harvey Dent/Two-Face and Heath Ledger as The Joker. Tragically, Heath Ledger died of a sleeping pill overdose shortly after he'd finished shooting his scenes. His performance as The Joker was one of the many highlights of the film, which was lauded both by critics and fans. *The Dark Knight* was a runaway success and, as well as being the highest-grossing movie of 2008, is the eleventh-highest grossing film of all time. This paved the way nicely for the third part of the trilogy in 2012.

Fans were desperate to hear any news about the final film of the series and their patience was finally rewarded at the end of April 2010 when Warner Brothers confirmed that the film was underway and would be released in July 2012. Granted, there would be two agonising years to get through, but if Nolan's previous form was anything to go by, it would be worth the wait. In October 2010 came the announcement that the title of the film would be *Batman – The Dark Knight Rises*.

Gradually, over the course of the next few months, pieces of information about the film were fed to the press. It was confirmed that Christian Bale, Gary Oldman and Michael Caine would be returning for the conclusion, but one of the biggest questions on fans' lips was which villains were going to be making an appearance. Nolan is famed for keeping his powder dry and, at this early stage, gave away very little of his plans. One thing he did confess to, though, was that the villain in his film would categorically not be The Riddler. Speaking to the *Los Angeles Times Hero Complex*, he did say: 'We'll use many of the same characters as we have all along, and we'll be introducing some new ones.' Not many clues there!

In January 2011, more news was forthcoming and it was announced that one of the villains of the piece was to be a character called Bane – and he would be played by none other than Tom Hardy. Anne Hathaway was confirmed as Selina Kyle/Catwoman and Joseph Gordon Levitt and Marion Cotillard were both definitely to be in the film, but who exactly they would be playing remained the subject of debate.

Nolan said at the time: 'We're very much excited about really finishing a trilogy and giving a conclusion to our story. And that's what we're doing.'

Tom, needless to say, was delighted to have secured such a major role and wasn't afraid of showing his excitement when asked about it. '*Batman* is such an amazing franchise that I honestly feel overwhelmingly privileged to be part of it. It's such an amazing cast to work alongside, they are all so talented. I loved being able to play a baddie and, coming from East Sheen in South-West London, that doesn't come easily to me. I actually had to work on not being very nice,' he explained to the *Mirror*. He was understandably anxious, though, because he knew that comic-book fans had strong opinions on Bane and didn't want to be the one to let them down. 'So many people love him, and when you step into that role – you are going to fail. And be judged,' he told *CineMovie*.

The icing on the cake for Tom was to be working with Christopher Nolan again. He'd been lucky enough to work with the director on *Inception* and has the greatest respect for him. Tom often makes reference to the esteem in which he holds the director when he gives interviews and has variously said that he would read anything Nolan asked him to, including a shopping list or a telephone directory! 'When Christopher Nolan throws a ball, I go fetch. I feel incredibly lucky to be working with a man of such imagination and technical ability. Long may it continue. He's on a roll,' he said in an interview with *Huffington Post*.

Tom also feels indebted to Nolan as the director has given him two very big opportunities to showcase his talent in front of a much bigger audience: first in *Inception* and now in *Dark Knight Rises*. 'I owe an awful lot to Christopher Nolan, because he put me on a massive platform and trusted me twice. I'm very grateful for it,' he told the *Daily Telegraph*.

Nolan had wanted Tom to play Bane from the start, but feared that his filming commitments on *Mad Max – Fury Road* would clash with filming for *The Dark Knight Rises*. When he heard that *Mad Max* had been delayed, he made the call to Tom who didn't need to be asked twice.

It's noticeable that, besides using actors who had appeared in the previous *Batman* films, for the new characters he ended up casting quite a proportion of actors with whom he had worked on previous projects. Tom, Joseph Gordon-Levitt and Marion Cotillard had all been in Nolan's *Inception*. As well as being familiar with these actors' work and knowing what he could achieve with them, perhaps the director's penchant for remaining tight-lipped on his projects means that he likes to keep a close and trusted circle of familiar faces around him. The strategy seems to work and they all remain loyal to the cause – even if they themselves are often kept in the dark about what is happening in the film. 'Chris Nolan doesn't tell you anything,' said Tom. 'So I don't know what I'm doing or who I'm playing until the morning that I'm working.'

When it came to *The Dark Knight Rises*, Nolan was refusing even to let the actors know how the film would end, to minimise the risk of any details slipping out into the public domain. He apparently sent scripts out to some of them with pages missing. Gary Oldman received his script with the final few pages missing and had to go and see Nolan in person to find out what would take place in the final scenes. 'Christopher doesn't want anyone to ruin it and I completely understand that. The newer people on the film go to his office to read the script.' According to Oldman he has the details of the ending 'locked away in his head'.

When the press attempt to get any information out of cast members about the content of the film, they are met with a wall of silence. Tom and Joseph Gordon-Levitt have both invoked the 'just trust Christopher Nolan' mantra when confronted by media speculation. The only small slip-up came when 12-year-old Joey King, a young actress in the film, revealed that her character was to be the young Talia al Ghul. She then, however, went on to say, 'I can't give too much away because I promised Mr Nolan I wouldn't say anything. There are too many secrets about the character and the movie.'

The fact that King revealed who she would be playing was deemed a spoiler as it hadn't been confirmed that the character Talia al Ghul, daughter of villainous Ras al Ghul (played by Liam Neeson in *Batman Begins*) would be appearing in the film. It had long been rumoured that Marion Cotillard might be playing the older version of the character and the statement from King confirmed that the character would be making an appearance. And if she was to play 'the young', who would be playing the older incarnation?

So who was this baddie that Tom would be inhabiting? Bane was indeed a villain taken from the Batman comic books. He was created in 1993 by writers Chuck Dixon and Doug Moench, along with artist Graham Nolan (no relation to Christopher). Bane's sole purpose was to destroy Batman and he is legendary for being 'the man who broke the bat'.

The character was born and raised in a high-security prison. Thanks to his background, he turned into a vicious but clever assassin who, thanks to having had experiments carried out on him using a derivative of the drug Venom, has superhuman strength. He is the most powerful and cerebral enemy Batman has ever come up against. 'Yes, he's even smarter than Bruce Wayne, with six languages at his disposal and a photographic memory. A superb detective, he's able to deduce Batman's secret identity in just one year. Even scarier? Unlike The Joker and Two-Face, Bane is completely sane,' wrote *Total Film* in October 2011.

Bane had appeared in Joel Schumacher's *Batman and Robin*, but justice wasn't done to the character and he was used as a camp sideshow to Uma Thurman's Poison Ivy. Thankfully, the Bane of Chris Nolan and Tom Hardy's imagination looks set to be something larger than life and utterly terrifying. Speaking to *Empire* magazine in January 2012, Tom gave his appraisal, as far as he was permitted at that stage, of Bane. 'He's brutal. And, you know, he's a big dude. He's a big dude who's incredibly clinical... it's not about fighting. It's just about carnage with Bane. He's a smashing machine.' And while he was prepared to talk about how Bane fights, lips were firmly sealed on any other aspect of the villain.

Tom would once again have to beef up big time to transform into Bane. And, once again, Pnut would be by his side, helping him to build muscle in all the right places. For *Warrior*, Tom had bolstered his muscles to such an extent that he weighed 179 pounds. For Bane, he upped his body mass even more and weighed in at 190 pounds. He wanted to grow as big as he possibly could to try and live up to fans' expectations of the enormous hulk. Those fans apparently would have loved Bane to be 400 pounds, as per his comic book incarnation, but this was just a bit too much of a stretch for poor Tom. Even the king of transformation has his limits!

Of course, for Tom, the transformation wasn't purely physical. Christopher Nolan knew that he was an actor easily talented enough to take on all the challenges that playing a villain such as Bane presented. For a start, he would have to wear a mask which, as well as being uncomfortable, would conceal a lot of his face and therefore a great deal of facial expression would be lost. 'I felt that if I could get somebody as talented as Tom to agree to hide himself in the character I would get something very special,' Nolan told *Empire* magazine. He went on to compliment the way in which Tom can play a big brute of a character, but is still able to pull back those raw characteristics when he needs to. 'He's found a way to play a character who is enormous and powerful with a sort of calm to it.' To those familiar with Tom's acting this would come as no surprise – he has shown time and again that he will always find a way to portray the light and shade in any character he plays.

Aware of the fans' insatiable appetite for information about the film, the press were keen to run any stories associated with it as they knew whatever they printed would be devoured hungrily. One angle they seemed to like was constantly publishing pictures of Tom's ever-expanding physique leading up to and during shooting of the film: there were photos of Tom arriving on US soil and even photos of him 'showing off his bulging biceps' whilst out shopping in LA.

It wouldn't be too long before fans were given a small

concession to their curiosity. In May 2011, the internet was abuzz with news of an official 'leaked' photo of Tom Hardy as his Bane character. The week prior, the official *Dark Knight Rises* website had been launched and had mysteriously consisted of a black screen and some background chanting noise. While some may have thought there was a glitch with the site, clever fans figured out that if the noise was played through a programme that can visualise audio files, it would display a Twitter hashtag. Fans who tweeted the hashtag then found that their Twitter avatars were used to build a mosaic on the website which, when complete, revealed the Bane photograph. The first reaction was that fans had got the better of website security and leaked the photos, but it was in fact an extraordinarily clever viral marketing campaign on the part of Nolan and Warner Bros.

The photo was the first glimpse of a new character from *The Dark Knight Rises* and, though not especially revealing, was atmospheric. The image showed Tom as Bane, photographed from behind, with his head turned about 90 degrees back over his shoulder so that you can just make out Bane's mask, shaved head and some of Tom's facial features. The huge expanse of back and shoulder on display gives a good idea of just how vast and imposing this villain is going to be. His elbow also appears to be resting on a wide, powerful-looking leg. It wasn't much to go on but it did the trick and started to build excitement on fansites and in the press. The *Independent* newspaper noted that Warner Bros had used a similar campaign when promoting *The Dark Knight* in 2007, ahead of its 2008 release. 'For more than 14 months, fans were encouraged to participate in a series of interactive marketing exercises designed to promote the film, including: sending emails, submitting photographs and joining scavenger hunts. When the film eventually did screen in the US in July 2008, it smashed the box office record for the biggest opening day and the biggest opening week.' Whether the phenomenal success at the box office was helped by the marketing campaign is open to debate but there's no doubt these interactive tools, while not giving much away, help the fans to feel a little bit of ownership towards the film.

It was probably also a wise move to do the Bane 'reveal' at this point as, when shooting got underway, it was inevitable that some photos of the cast in their costumes would find their way out into the press – and indeed they did.

Shooting for *The Dark Knight Rises* took place at a variety of locations. Early on in the shooting schedule, location filming took place in Jodhpur in India and from there the cast and crew went briefly to London to film at the Farmiloe Building on St John Street in Clerkenwell, which had been used as Gotham City police station in both *Batman Begins* and *The Dark Knight*. Nottingham's Tudor mansion, Wollaton Hall, was also used as a location, which brought some unexpected benefits. In preparation for filming, the production company paid for The Great Hall and the Entrance Hall to be redecorated and regilded. *My Nottingham* website also revealed that: 'A number of windows at the back of the property were specially wood-grained, and a new carpet is currently being woven for the Salon to replace the old 1980s carpet, which was removed for filming.'

Then, for 18 days in August 2011, the cast and crew were to be found in Pittsburgh. They shot at various locations around the city and residents were told to be prepared for fake gunshots, explosions and assorted chaos as filming took place. The emergency services in the city braced themselves for a high number of emergency calls from those who weren't expecting the unfamiliar noise. The local emergency management spokesman told residents: 'If you hear shots fired or a disturbance or gunfire... call 911 and report it and we'll figure it out.'

Other disruption on the streets of Pittsburgh came about following the closure of some streets for filming, the use of fake snow and the felling of some trees in order to create the appearance of Gotham City. When filming finished in the city, Nolan and the crew took out an advertisement in the *Pittsburgh Post-Gazette* to thank the city for their patience and co-operation during filming. Nolan and the producers also then donated money to the Tree Pittsburgh group and paid for the trees they'd removed to be replaced.

Tom Hardy spoke of the problems when filming at locations such as these. Clearly, the public would be able to see what was going on and were likely to want to take pictures. 'I think there's a certain inevitability if you're going to shoot in the middle of the street,' he told *Access Hollywood*. 'It's very hard to block off the entire street from people taking photographs... but that doesn't mean it's going to be anything like the film.'

The other location that featured in the Pittsburgh shooting schedule was Heinz Field, the home of the Pittsburgh Steelers football team. Heinz Field was used to film a football match between Gotham City Rogues and the Rapid City Monuments (shots from this can be seen on the extended trailer for the film that has now been released). Local residents were recruited to be extras for the scenes and, in spite of it being summer, had to be kitted out as if it were a Gotham City winter. One of the extras who was present on the day said that, even when it began to pour with rain, Christopher Nolan was far from deterred and wouldn't let the weather interfere with his work – he apparently 'put on his raincoat (although he didn't bother with the hood) and continued to work on getting the right camera angles and directing the crew,' she told *Patriot News*. Another extra present on the day described Tom as 'truly larger than life'. Photos from the various shoots in Pittsburgh did leak out, so fans were able to get a clear idea of what Bane would look like in the film.

In October, two weeks of filming in New York got underway. The cast and crew braved Wall Street (which had been home to the Occupy Wall Street anti-capitalist protests) to recreate Gotham's police department and also to shoot a fight between Batman and Bane. The fight scenes were filmed at City Hall and over 1,000 extras were used. Reportedly, Warner Bros picked up the tab for police and fire officers to be on the site. A spokesperson from the Mayor's office said: 'There are thousands of jobs attached to the production and we are thrilled that those jobs and this production are in New York.'

Tom spoke of the difficulty of filming his more aggressive scenes in the midst of so many extras. In one of his scenes, he needed to fight with a number of policemen in the crowd but was concerned about making sure he picked out the ones who were the trained fighters. Rehearsing the fight was no problem and Hardy had his moves blocked but when it came to doing it for real, matters got a little trickier. 'That's all right in a rehearsal room, but then you add 1,000 people that are all dressed the same as the seven you're supposed to hit – because they're all police officers – and I don't know where *my* police officers are,' he explained to *Empire* magazine.

The filming, of course, attracted a great deal of attention and photos appeared of the Batwing on a crane over Wall Street. Joseph Gordon-Levitt and Christian Bale (in his Bruce Wayne guise) were spotted and photos also appeared of the hyped epic fight between Batman and Bane. Amongst the combat photos, a lighter moment was revealed when a photo of Christian Bale and Tom Hardy sharing a macho hug turned up in the press.

It was refreshing to see that the two actors – who seem to have similar approaches to preparing for their roles – had only positive things to say about each other. Speaking on the ill-fated *Jonathan Ross* show, Tom said of Bale: 'He was a massive draw to work with.' He went on to add that, when he'd first seen Bale on set, he thought that he would be no competition for him as man mountain Bane. However, when Bale appeared in his Batman gear, he revised his opinion, saying to Ross that Bale is 'a really tough boy'.

The compliments were reciprocated when Bale described Tom as a 'phenomenal actor. I like working with him a great deal. He goes the whole hog. I know that Bane has been seen in movies before but in my eyes, Tom is essentially creating Bane for the first time, so there's a great deal of freedom for him to be able to do so.'

Filming together didn't always run smoothly for the two actors, though. When both in their respective costumes, they realised that they were struggling to communicate when filming scenes together. As Batman, Bale is subsumed beneath his mask, which covers most of his head, including his ears, and Tom obviously had most of his face obscured by Bane's mask. For Bale, trying to hear what we can only assume will be the very muffled voice of Tom must have been really tricky. Tom explained to *Total Film* magazine that while the parts of the costumes they had to wear on their faces were great at establishing their physical presence on screen: 'The only downside is you can't hear a word anyone is saying. Batman can't hear me and he can't see me speaking so we sort of stand there looking at each other... we've been doing hand signals. I put my thumbs up when I finish my lines or I wink. And he sort of wiggles his fingers out of shot...'

One other small problem that Tom probably wasn't prepared for was during one of his fight scenes with Christian Bale. Apparently Bale got a bit too heavily into the fight and left Tom with a pair of ripped trousers. The fight was, according to the *Express*, part of a 'prison breakout storyline'.

Before 2011 came to a close, more morsels of information about *The Dark Knight Rises* were revealed. Speaking to *Empire* magazine, Christopher Nolan confirmed that the third part of the trilogy would pick up eight years after the conclusion of *The Dark Knight*, which according to the director left our hero with 'his reputation in tatters, on the run'. Wayne would therefore be considerably older in *The Dark Knight Rises* and would also apparently appear more in the daylight than he had in the previous two films. 'The character himself has the reputation now, so he's able to expose himself more and still intimidate people. And with the third film we're just pushing that further.'

The first teaser trailer for *The Dark Knight Rises* had been released in July 2011, but hadn't given a great deal away. At only just over a minute long, it showed Commissioner Gordon in a hospital bed saying that Batman needed to return because evil was on the rise. It also gave us the first glimpse of Bane in his mask as well as a brief shot of what seemed to be Bane and Batman gearing up for a fight with each other. The second trailer, a full-length one, was unveiled in December of the same year and provided a better glimpse of Bane (and his rather muffled voice), our first taster of Anne Hathaway as Selena Kyle and, excitingly for those who like a film with boys' toys, a glimpse of the Batwing in action and Bane's Tumbler. The trailer was the most watched trailer on iTunes, with 12.5 million people viewing it in just 24 hours.

The marketing campaign stepped up a gear when, just days after the release of the second trailer, a preview of the first six minutes of the film was shown at IMAX cinemas in the UK with screenings of *Mission Impossible: Ghost Protocol*. It was fitting that it was shown on IMAX screens – Christopher Nolan had steadfastly refused to shoot *The Dark Knight Rises* in 3D, as is now the norm, but had opted to stick to shooting as many scenes as he could using the large format IMAX cameras. For *The Dark Knight* he had shot about 25 minutes-worth of footage as IMAX, which works so well for action-packed, cinematic sequences. Apparently, for *The Dark Knight Rises*, he'd managed to shoot about twice as much in the larger format. Although the results using IMAX cameras are spectacular, Nolan maintained that the cameras are very noisy to operate, so not suitable for use when filming dialogue scenes.

As the sneak preview was only available via IMAX cinemas,

of which there are relatively few in Britain, not that many people saw it. There was much written about it in the press, though, which helped to keep the film at the forefront of people's minds. Unfortunately, the aspect of the preview that most occupied journalists' column inches was the fact that Bane's dialogue was difficult to understand thanks to his speech being muffled by his mask.

The concern about Bane's lines being unintelligible didn't at first seem to bother either Nolan or Tom Hardy. Nolan has apparently refused to re-record or edit the dialogue but it has been suggested that a re-mastered version of the audio has been made available. When asked about the issue, Tom shrugged off any criticism saying: 'I trust Christopher Nolan implicitly. I'm not worried at all about people understanding him [Bane] mumbling away.'

As the world counted down to the next Batman instalment, hype around the movie only grew. It had a lot to live up to: its predecessor had set a new bar for what a comic book movie could be, blowing critics away, bagging two Oscars and taking over a billion dollars at the box office in the process. The new film would either be a real turning point in Hardy's Hollywood career or turn him into a laughing stock. Which would it be?

The Dark Knight Rises officially premiered in New York City on 16 July 2012, before hitting cinemas around the world a few days later. Fans watched a reclusive Bruce Wayne have his fortune wiped out by new nemesis Bane, who beats him to near paralysis before throwing him into the almost inescapable South American underground prison that he himself grew up in. 'Almost' being the key word...

The film is cinematic and sweeping. Fans and critics agree

that it is a fitting third part to Nolan's tryptic. 'Many critics and cinema-goers have wondered whether or not *The Dark Knight*, Christopher Nolan's second Batman film, was really, in its essence, a superhero film,' wrote *The Telegraph*'s Robbie Collin. 'The key ingredients were all there on a superficial level – the costume, the techno toys, the cackling baddie bent on citywide destruction – but Nolan had stirred and synthesised them in new ways to craft a lucid, sinewy crime epic closer to Michael Mann's *Heat* and Coppola's second *Godfather* film than anything Marvel Studios has yet produced.'

Nolan had wanted Hardy's Bane to be the complete opposite of his manic predecessor – the late Heath Ledger's Oscar-winning The Joker. Bane is the brute force to The Joker's unpredictable lunacy. 'The Joker didn't care,' Hardy told *Entertainment Weekly*. 'He just wanted to see the world burn, and he was a master of chaos and destruction, unscrupulous and crazy. Bane is not that guy. There is a very meticulous and calculated way about Bane. There is a huge orchestration of organisation to his ambition. He is also a physical threat to Batman. There is nothing vague about Bane. No jokes. He's a very clean, clear villain.'

Indiewire's Todd Gilchrist was totally won over by the film. 'Tom Hardy's Bane is a different sort of villain – a focused and more ideologically-developed version of Heath Ledger's anarchist – but one with equally ruthless charm.'

'Hardy does make Bane a creature of distinct malevolence with his baroque speech patterns and rumbling bass tones, provoking a sort of lower-register duet when pitted against Batman's own voice-distorted growl,' decided *Variety*'s Justin Chang.

But hearing – or more accurately not hearing – Hardy's voice was still an issue, which is a shame, because a lot of work went into its development. 'Bane is somebody who's in tremendous pain all the time,' Hardy explained to *Business Insider*. 'So he had an older voice. Which is sort of Richard Burton. Slightly florid, camp English villain ... in many ways, but just off-centre.' There was also, he told the *Wall Street Journal*, a hint of French Revolution Robespierre. But the character needed to be of Latin descent – Bane's origins in comic lore are rooted in a South American prison, after all. So Hardy looked at original Latin too, exploring the Romany Gypsy accent.

He found the bare-knuckle fighter Bartley Gorman to be an inspiration. Gorman was once the bare-knuckle boxing champ of the world – referred to as the King of the Gypsies. He died in 2002 but clips of him speaking can still be found on *YouTube*.

He sounds nothing like Hardy's Bane – Gorman's is an aggressive voice, the combination of many accents. But our boy is no mimic. And it would be a huge over-simplification of Hardy's talent to say he merely copied the Irish traveller's voice. So Bane's hard-to-hear growl is a special Hardy-style mix of all of the above influences.

As well as muffling his speech, the iron-looking spider-like mask wasn't exactly comfortable to wear. Neither was the rest of his attire: just as Bane himself suffers in it, so did Tom!

The mask is intentionally animalistic but functional – it masks Bane's identity but also keeps him alive by pumping a painkilling gas into his body. It had to look metal but couldn't be black so it was different from Batman's cowl. The end result took hours to create and was digitally mapped to Tom Hardy's face as a prosthetic.

Costume designer Lindy Hemming researched Bane's whole outfit meticulously to make sure that it reflected his backstory. It's a hotchpotch of influences from the different parts of the world the character had visited as a mercenary. 'I was looking at two main areas, firstly his military surplus scavenging, which has gone into making up his entire wardrobe and breathing equipment,' explained Hemming in an interview with *ClothesOnFilm*. 'I fell in love with a very old, matted Swedish army sheepskin arctic wear coat with huge collar and lead weights as buttons, a great characterful garment.'

She also had to think about Bane's idealistic, revolutionary aspirations. 'This led me to think about the French Revolutionary style/military greatcoat look with ample collars. We also had a feeling that this garment could be a "sign/ signal" of the change for the mania in his behaviour of and his worsening destructive megalomania.'

But despite an exhaustive search, she couldn't find anything like what she was envisioning. The battered shearling coat had to be made from scratch instead, and finding someone who worked with sheepskin in perennially sunny LA was no small feat. As a result, Bane's jacket took the longest out of every outfit in the movie to make.

'The outfit was an extra hot, heavy horror, as he was already facing torture by face and mouth with the covering mask,' explained Hemming.

Hardy didn't disagree. 'It's uncomfortable because your body's really restricted,' he said. 'It's heavy and it's tight and the costumers need it to look good and solid. So it looks great when it's tight but it's not practical to move it, and you need a couple of hours of moving about before the suit will then move with you. You got zips and undershorts, underarmour – body armour – under that. It's all a bit of a faff. Forget about taking a shit, that's not happening.'

Whoever played Bane was always going to be in for a tough time – Nolan knew from the very start of production that the costume would be uncomfortable. When he approached Hardy to take on the role he made it very clear that he would have to wear the mask for long periods and it wouldn't be nice. 'I think he worried it would be something I might not consider because wearing a mask might damage my career or something. He thought I'd be worried that the audience couldn't see my beautiful face,' he joked to *Entertainment Weekly*. But Hardy was undeterred. 'Like I care. It's Chris Nolan! I would wear a paper bag over my head for that man.'

Hardy had bulked up for *The Dark Knight Rises* and the Bane outfit was designed to make him look even more of a muscular juggernaut. But even after gaining pounds for the role he was no match for his old *Inception* co-star Christian Bale.

'He's a big lad, Christian. He's not messing around. I just pull faces and wear tights for a living, do you know what I mean? I'm not a fighter,' he told *Empire Magazine*. 'He's tougher than I am. In real life.'

Hardy has great respect for Bale, who has in the past been described as being tricky to work alongside. 'I love Christian. He's brilliant. He's really good fun. He's a brilliant character actor, and not at all alpha male in the way that there's not enough limelight for everybody to shine around him. He has a tremendous humility as a performer. It's a breath of fresh air to work with somebody like that.'

The Dark Knight Rises was both a financial success and a critical one. It took over $248 million on its opening weekend and broke the record for the fastest movie to make over $50 million in IMAX theatres. It was the thirteenth film in history to cross the $1 billion mark and is the tenth highest grossing film of all time.

It more than lives up to its marketing hype. Nominated for a staggering 42 awards it won 7, including *Movie of the Year*, *Best Supporting Actress* and *Best Action Actress*, both of which went to Anne Hathaway for her portrayal of Catwoman.

Hardy was nominated for *Best Villain* at *The MTV Movie Awards*, but was narrowly beaten by Tom Hiddleston for his work as Loki in *The Avengers*. Maybe the loss had something to do with the tragic Aurora massacre, which took place in Colorado just days after *The Dark Knight Rises* release.

On 20 July, during a midnight showing of the film, 24-year-old James Eagan Holmes entered the town's Century 16 cinema, where Batman fans were enjoying the new film. He was wearing a mask that witnesses likened to the fictional Bane's, leading some to at first think he was part of a publicity stunt organised by the cinema's management. Others thought he had simply dressed up for the movie – until he lifted up a gun and opened fire on the horrified audience, killing 12 people and injuring 70 others.

Three of the dead were young men who had shielded their girlfriends from the spray of bullets. One was a six-year-old child. Her pregnant mother survived but was critically injured during the shooting and miscarried a week after the attack.

Initial reports stated that Holmes identified himself as The Joker when he was arrested but police later retracted this claim. One officer, who searched Holmes' explosive-riddled home to collect evidence, said they found a Batman mask inside the apartment. It was an horrific and tragic event.

Warner Bros. – acting swiftly and sensitively – cancelled the film's planned Paris, Mexico and Japan premieres and several broadcast networks suspended TV ads for the movie in the US. Christopher Nolan released a statement on behalf of everyone involved in the film. It read: 'I would not presume to know anything about the victims of the shooting but that they were there last night to watch a movie. I believe movies are one of the great American art forms and the shared experience of watching a story unfold on screen is an important and joyful pastime. The movie theatre is my home, and the idea that someone would violate that innocent and hopeful place in such an unbearably savage way is devastating to me. Nothing any of us can say could ever adequately express our feelings for the innocent victims of this appalling crime, but our thoughts are with them and their families.'

As the remarkable trilogy came to an end, Christopher Nolan admitted that he would be sad to see the conclusion of his superhero franchise. Speaking to *Hero Complex* he confessed: 'I tend not to be too emotional on the set, I find that doesn't help me do my job. But you definitely get a little lump in your throat thinking that, OK, this is going to be the last time we're going to be doing this. It's been quite a journey.' It certainly had: the legend had ended.

CHAPTER ELEVEN

LOCKED & LAWLESS

When it comes to Hollywood big cheeses, you really can't get much bigger than Harvey Weinstein. Originally known for being one of the founders of the film distribution company Miramax (eventually bought by Disney), in 2005 he founded film production company, The Weinstein Company, with his brother, Bob. Weinstein has been a producer on some of the biggest movies of recent years, including *The King's Speech*, *The Fighter* and *My Week with Marilyn*. He also took a huge – but very canny – gamble and invested in a black-and-white French film about a fading silent movie star... Meryl Streep has jokingly referred to him as 'God'. In short, when Weinstein speaks, the movie world listens.

At the start of 2012, it was reported that the cinematic release of *The Wettest County in the World*, a film distributed by Weinstein, was being pushed back in the schedule from April to August. The reason? Weinstein was of the opinion that one of the actors was about to make it very big indeed and because of this, it would make more sense commercially to delay the project and cash in on the forthcoming celebrity. 'We have a star in Tom Hardy, who's completely anonymous right now,' said Weinstein, when quizzed about the revised date for the opening. He went on to qualify this by stating that *Batman – The Dark Knight Rises* would bring Tom to the attention of the world: 'He's going to be a huge movie star by August,' he added. That's quite an accolade, coming from one of the most powerful men in Hollywood.

Weinstein wasn't wrong. Everyone was talking about Bane and the man behind the mask – the Batman film had brought Hardy to a wider audience and he was now a big draw. It was a shrewd move. He also renamed it *Lawless* – a bolder title than the 2008 book on which the script is based. Written by Matt Bondurant, the novel has its origins in the true story of his grandfather and two great uncles, Prohibition era bootleggers who took the law into their own hands. The screenplay is by multi-talented musician Nick Cave, while John Hillcoat (*The Road*) serves as director.

Lawless had suffered years of financing issues and faced a significant amount of studio apathy before Hardy came on board. Many actors were linked to the film in its early days – including Ryan Gosling and Scarlett Johansson – but the production seemed doomed never to see the light of day and one by one, the big names dropped out.

One remained a constant from the start – Shia LaBeouf, the young actor who had recently found fame playing the lead (human) role in the *Transformers* movie and also starred alongside Michael Douglas and Carey Mulligan in *Wall Street: Money Never Sleeps*, the sequel to *Wall Street* (1987).

While producers Lucy Fisher and Doug Wick tried to source financing, Shia was equally determined to make the film happen: he told them he would explode if he had to do one more *Transformers*' CG-heavy scene (acting opposite a green tennis ball) and that he was desperate to do something real.

Then he saw Hardy act in *Bronson*. 'That shit changed my life,' he told *The Hollywood Reporter*. 'I went home and wrote Tom a letter saying I was a fan. He sent me a script, and I sent him *Lawless*. He called me back and said, "This is fucking amazing."'

Unbeknownst to LaBeouf, Hardy was already on Hillcoat's radar – the director visited him on the set of *This Means War* and signed him on the spot. From there, things slowly began to come together and by the time filming started in early 2011 the assembled cast was as stellar as the script deserved.

Tom plays Forrest Bondurant, the almost mythical eldest of the three bootlegging brothers. Crazy middle brother Howard is portrayed by Australian *Zero Dark Thirty* star Jason Clarke, while LaBeouf plays cocky young upstart Jack, the youngest of the trio.

Gary Oldman and Guy Pearce provide the heavyweight casting, while the film's female presence is represented by Mia Wasikowska, the young, up-and-coming starlet who shone in *Alice in Wonderland*, with Jessica Chastain as the main romantic lead.

There were no studio perks during the shoot. Everyone stayed in a cluster of cheap condos in Peachtree City, a far-flung suburb of Atlanta. Filming took place in various rural locations in Georgia, including Newnam, Grantville, Haralson, LaGrange, Carroll County's McIntosh Park and the Red Oak Creek Covered Bridge, near Gay. To save costs, they used existing locations – covered bridges, churches, gas stations, outside spaces, the Cotton Pickin' Fairground – apart from Blackwater Station, which the production built especially.

There was a real sense of camaraderie on set and the cast grew close. Hardy and Chastain, who played lovers in the film, had a particularly strong bond. But there was tension between Hardy and LaBeouf: their real-life dynamic seemed to mirror an on-screen brotherly tension and it was widely reported that the two men eventually came to physical blows.

'It's such an intense thing to make a film,' director John Hillcoat told *Digital Spy*, confirming the altercation. 'So when you're shooting, often with serious actors who are fully enmeshed in the roles, it'll start to play out in ways. So yeah, there was a bit of that mirroring.'

'There were no shoot-outs,' he hastened to add. 'Shia's so enthusiastic and chomping at the bit, and Tom has this kind of stoic power to him. So they're quite different energies.'

Screenwriter Nick Cave joked that what had made Hardy and LaBeouf the best choices for their roles in the first place was 'that they were gonna beat the s**t out of each other.'

Hardy had no problem confirming the story either. In an interview with *Den of Geek* he was very candid about the whole thing: 'I got knocked out by Shia LaBeouf,' he said, matter-of-factly.

Despite this statement being met with incredulous laughter from the assembled journalists, Tom was serious: 'No, he did.

He knocked me out sparko. Out cold. He's a bad, bad boy. He is. He's quite intimidating as well. He's a scary dude.'

Describing how the fight came about, Hardy said: 'He just attacked me. He was drinking moonshine. I was wearing a cardigan, and er, went down.'

He revealed that he regained consciousness in the arms of his personal trainer and friend Pnut, saying: '[Pnut] was concerned for me. I was like, "What was that? It was lightning fast". And he said, "That was Shia." I said, "Fuckin' hell. Can we go home now?" "No, we've still got three weeks to finish."'

Fans were shocked that anyone could beat Hardy in a fight and the revelation prompted a flurry of explanatory rumours about why the two had come to blows. One rumour that gained legs was that everyone on set was discussing their fast cars and LaBeouf, whose own wealth and fame has never quite sat right with him, was angered by the ostentatious conversation. But LaBeouf himself just blamed the scuffle on brotherly love.

'That wasn't moonshine related at all,' he said, when asked to clear up the rumours. 'That was straight love. There was a lot of love on that set in general. There was a lot of aggression in me and a lot of aggression on Hardy's side. We were playing brothers. There was a constant finger-in-the-ear [teasing] thing going on. But it was all love. I love the dude like a brother, straight up. The man's a genius. I think he's incredible.'

Whatever the reason, LaBeouf said Hardy 'never did that roughhousing thing' with him again.

Although the film was made independently, it was one of

the hottest properties at the Cannes Film Festival that year. At its premiere screening, it received a ten-minute standing ovation.

Weinstein snapped up the distribution rights for a reported $5 million, after a bidding war between his company, CBS Films, and Relativity Media, and the film landed in cinemas in August 2012.

Hardy plays his Forrest Bondurant as a kind of taciturn patriarch – very quietly, and very still. He speaks very little but with great patience and communicates mostly through a series of well-timed grunts. He is passive in all respects apart from one – his capacity for brutal vengeance. 'Tom really interpreted the character in such a different way than what was on the page,' Nick Cave told *The Guardian*. 'It confounded John Hillcoat to begin with, but he really created something interesting. I was totally impressed by his unique way of thinking. At one point, he said to me: "I just want to play it like an old lesbian." That blew me away. He saw the role as being essentially maternal.'

Hardy also cited Tweety Pie's cartoon gran as inspiration for the role!

Alongside a superb Hardy, Gary Oldman stands out as Floyd Banner, the city gangster whose criminal empire is spreading into Franklin County, where the Bondurants are revered as local legends. But it's the arrival of Guy Pearce's sinister Special Agent Charlie Rakes that sparks the all-out backwater war that escalates in the film.

As Weinstein predicted, it was a huge hit. *The Telegraph* singled Hardy out for praise, saying: 'By far the most intriguing character is Forrest (Tom Hardy), their notional leader, a bear-like man with a mesmerising gaze just below a tall, broad-rimmed hat – and a cigar stub wedged between surprisingly full lips, placed there by a hand adorned with knuckle-dusters.

'The running joke about Forrest is that he's indestructible, and Hardy portrays him with a subtle sense of fun. When he speaks at all, it's indistinctly; mostly he emits low, animal grunts with meanings that require guesswork.'

The Hollywood Reporter's David Rooney wrote: 'If *Lawless* doesn't achieve the mythic dimensions of the truly great outlaw and gangster movies, it is a highly entertaining tale set in a vivid milieu, told with style and populated by a terrific ensemble. For those of us who are suckers for blood-soaked American crime sagas from that era, those merits will be plenty.'

Meanwhile Mike D'Angelo of *The A.V. Club* called it 'a thoroughly familiar – but flavourful and rousing – shoot-'em-up.'

Owen Gleiberman from *Entertainment Weekly* gave *Lawless* a B grade, writing: 'Hardy's presence is compelling, but the film comes fully alive only when it turns bloody. At those moments, though, it has the kick of a mule.'

Lawless more than doubled its $26 million budget to take $56 million at the box office. It was nominated for four awards, including a Cannes Palme d'Or for Hillcoat and three nominations for Nick Cave from the Georgia Film Critics Association. In the event it won none at all, which was surprising.

Also surprising was the amount of column inches devoted to Forrest's tatty old cardigans.

Hardy had actually filmed *Lawless* before working on *The Dark Knight*, but had been training hard and bulking up in preparation for Bane. It wasn't ideal – 'I wanted to be skinny,' he told *Vulture*, 'but Batman came in, and then I needed to be bigger. I had six months to train, but there was a three-month period where *Lawless* was being filmed at that time, so I had to train during *Lawless*, so that's why I was physically the size that I was. Luckily, Shia was physically big as well so it kind of worked, but I would have preferred to be more Billy Bob Thornton-sized.'

Men in prohibition-era America were not muscle-bound, or thickset. Most men of the time were strong but wiry, so Tom knew that his recently acquired thick neck and bulging biceps were totally out of keeping. This proved problematic for *Lawless* costume designer Margot Wilson.

'Forrest was the most challenging character,' she explained to *ClothesOnFilm*. 'When I first saw Tom very briefly at a script reading he was bigger than I had imagined. So my task was to make him fit into our world and make him visually work with his brothers.'

Hardy also had to look different to the others, which was a challenge when working with the basic and very plain rural clothing of the time. For inspiration, Wilson asked the director how he was going to direct Tom. When he described the still, quiet way that he wanted his character portrayed, she fought hard to put the leading man in a cardie.

It worked better than she anticipated.

The real Forrest would have been living in battered and dirty cardigans for years. In Chicago or Atlantic City – as seen in shows like *Boardwalk Empire* – moneyed gangsters wore fine suits and colourful silk shirts but in the country this was seen as frivolous and sissy. Not so with the cardigan, particularly when shabby and distressed.

'I love the fact that it puts the audience into a comfortable mindset and then it is surprised by the explosive behaviour of the one who wears a cardigan,' she declared.

The Telegraph wrote: 'It's ghastly, yet implausibly renders him even more endearing.'

Hardy had proven himself in gritty character portrayals, mainstream blockbusters and arty gangster flicks. He was clearly popular, talented and versatile and his schedule, once so clear, was now jam-packed.

From now on, if you wanted Tom Hardy to star in your film, you had better be prepared to book him early, maybe even years in advance. Unless you were prepared to base the whole production schedule around him, that is.

If you were to predict our boy's next career move, what would it be? Another Hollywood blockbuster? A gritty biopic à la *Bronson*, but with a bigger budget? Tom Hardy definitely had all those things on his horizon, but first he had something completely off the wall to sink his teeth into: a mesmeric slice of life film called *Locke*.

Writer and director Steven Knight had admired Hardy since first seeing him in *Inception*. The pair initially met at the tail end of 2012 to discuss a project that ultimately never came to fruition, but Knight was undeterred and wrote his very next script with Hardy in mind.

It's a crazy concept: a film that consists solely of a man making phone calls while driving. 'There's something about phone calls where people are saying one thing but their faces are saying something else, which is such a gift,' Knight explained to *The Washington Post*. 'And if you're going to have one actor on screen for that length of time they better be the best. And in my opinion Tom is the best actor we have.'

He knew that Hardy was the only man to play the character of Ivan Locke. All he had to do was convince him. 'It'll be over quickly,' were the words he used. But he needn't have worried: after hearing the premise of the movie Hardy was immediately enthusiastic, and offered up the only free time he had in his schedule: two weeks in February. For both rehearsals and filming.

'Of course, Tom's not available for about eleven years because he's on big films, back-to-back,' said Guy Heeley, who co-produced *Locke* with his colleagues Paul Webster and Joe Wright at Shoebox Films. 'So we reverse-engineered it around the only two weeks he was free.'

It was tight, but all they needed.

'It was the fastest turnaround I've ever been involved in,' Webster told *Screen Daily*. 'This was an inkling in Steve Knight's brain in November 2012, and we were shooting the movie by February 26. Steve said, "I want to do something quite different, in a confined space, about a guy whose life changes during the course of one car journey. And we never leave the car."'

Webster and Heeley made a call to Stuart Ford of IM Global, who had just worked with them on Knight's critically acclaimed directorial debut, *Hummingbird*. 'We got it financed off the idea of Tom being in it,' Heeley told the *Evening Standard*. 'We pitched over the phone, we outlined the basic finance structure, and on that same phone call he said, "I'm in."'

IM Global stumped up the entire budget – less than £1 million – while Lionsgate UK quickly came on board for UK rights. The project also took advantage of the UK film tax credit. Now, all that was left was to film it.

Cinematographer Haris Zambarloukos had just shot a Jack Ryan action film so he knew a thing or two about shooting moving cars. The team mounted the BMW X5 on a low-loader, and rigged three cameras to ensure different angles, as well as lots of subdued lighting. Knight wanted to make a film where sound was secondary to the visuals, and he credits Zambarloukos for realising this vision: 'He is a hero. He rediscovered a reflective device that hasn't been used since the 50s to enhance the amount of reflection we'd get on the screen.'

Production was scheduled to take place on the M1 between four junctions, but two weeks before shooting began the Highways Agency reversed their permission to film there and the production nearly folded. Fortunately they discovered that the A13 from Docklands going east is privately owned, so for five days filming took place there and on London's famous North Circular Road. Each night, Hardy and the production crew would drive and perform the script from beginning to end. Then they would do it again... and again.

'We basically shot it sixteen times beginning to end and cut it together,' Knight has explained. 'The best take was at 3 a.m. when everyone was exhausted.'

Shooting took place in real time and the film-makers only took breaks to change the camera memory cards – every thirty-seven minutes. The production had a police escort, but no one could control other drivers hooting, or traffic jams. Everything became part of the film.

For the last three days of production a scaled-down crew took two cars up to Birmingham, where the film begins. With a Hardy double at the wheel, they shot bits of hands, windscreen views, signage and all the crucial parts of the London approach that signify the end of Ivan Locke's journey.

The whole project was a real experiment. Hardy had just five days to rehearse and mostly read the script off an autocue in front of him. 'That's the closest I've ever been to a writer's absolute word,' he told *The Washington Post*. 'Right up to the letter, to the full stops.'

The result is an absolute triumph. Hardy's Ivan Locke is an ordinary guy – a construction director, with a family waiting for him at home. At work he builds his foundations with concrete, but the solid world he has constructed for himself at home is starting to crack. He has huge problems at work to resolve and problems at home that are similarly distressing. At the end of a work day, on the eve of a multimillion-dollar industrial concrete pour, Locke leaves the Black Country construction site and turns right towards London instead of left and home. He's driving both away from something and towards something, determined to do the right thing, no matter the consequences. Throughout the course of the film the audience learns why, as he exchanges calls with his wife, his son, his boss, and other key people. There are no high-speed chases. No car crashes. No flashbacks to help explain what's going on. Just Hardy's face, lit by the ethereal glow of the motorway lights and a phone that keeps ringing.

This is the story of an ordinary man's crisis. 'It's the end of the world for him but he doesn't have a superhero suit and he's screwed,' Hardy told *Entertainment Weekly*. 'You have to get from A to B. You have to put out a lot of fires, and you're not allowed to lose your [mind]. You have to be really normal.'

He chose to portray Ivan Locke with a Welsh accent – to emphasise the measured, calm demeanour his character hopes will get him through his journey. For the voice, he borrowed the composed speaking style and temperament of a Welsh friend of his and then listened to Richard Burton reading Dylan Thomas's *Under Milk Wood*.

'It was calming and at the same time commanding,' he told *The Wall Street Journal*. 'I wanted him to be unflinching in many ways, but not insensitive. [Ivan] tries to leave each conversation a little better than how he found it. I thought you need a calming, mellifluous voice to do that.'

Hardy was suffering from a cold while filming, but he didn't try to hide it on screen. Instead he worked it in as one of his character's many stressors: his Locke is a solid, patient man, and only once or twice shows any sign of the strain he is under. It makes the film tenser, as does the constant expectation that the car will crash or swerve.

All unseen, Hardy's co-stars include Olivia Colman, Ruth Wilson, Andrew Scott, Ben Daniels and Tom Holland – the friends, family and colleagues who call Locke on his journey home.

All of the actors were Knight's first choice for the roles.

For *The Lone Ranger* actress Ruth Wilson it was the combination of Knight's reputation and the novelty of the project that proved irresistible. 'I go for things that are different from the norm, challenging in a different way,' she told the *Evening Standard*. 'I hadn't read anything like this before but I knew Tom's work and lots of people signed onto it were brilliant. I thought, "What a great endeavour for Steve to be doing and what a great thing to be part of." Also, it wasn't a huge time commitment...'

In the same interview, *The Impossible*'s Tom Holland echoed her sentiments: 'I had never read anything like it.'

His was one of the hardest roles – having to maintain a believable filial relationship with Hardy – solely over the phone. 'It was tricky at first but it didn't have to be totally natural because we were on the phone,' he explained. 'There was room to make things more heightened here and there.'

To add to the drama, Hardy never knew when the all-important phone calls were coming. Most directors would have pre-recorded them, but Knight put his actors in a nearby motorway service station conference room, with some red wine and biscuits. On cue they'd go to a microphone to talk to Tom on the phone.

It was the first time Hardy had done such an intense, straight drama. Although a tough, reactive way to work, he thrived on the adrenaline-fuelled situation. 'He's one of the best actors in the world at the moment,' Webster told *Screen Daily*. 'He's got incredible charisma, he just holds the screen beautifully... It's a real challenge for him, it's only him on screen, the other actors are offscreen. It's unadorned, it's relentless... He's a powerful film presence.'

Everything about the creation of Locke was quiet and low-key, including the largely non-existent press surrounding its premiere – at the Venice Film Festival in September 2013. 'We wanted it to be a complete surprise, and it's a movie that should be discovered by people,' explained Webster. The film had a limited release in the UK in April of the following year.

'Tom Hardy isn't supposed to be this good an actor,' declared *The Wall Street Journal*. 'He's that guy built like The Hulk who bashes people in the face, right? He's the metal-masked villain Bane in *The Dark Knight Rises* and the brutal Virginia moonshiner Forrest Bondurant in *Lawless*. He's the destructive Pittsburgh cage fighter Tommy Conlon in *Warrior* and "Britain's most violent prisoner", bloody and naked much of the time, in *Bronson*.

'But now here he is in *Locke*, driving a BMW in a yuppie sweater delivering one of the most subtle and powerful film performances of the year.'

'*Locke* is the most singular, arresting and surprisingly British film you will see this year,' wrote Nick Curtis of the *Evening Standard*.

'Till now, Tom Hardy's best-known performances have tended to project the image of the movie star most likely to headbutt someone on the red carpet,' wrote online critic Jonathan Romney. 'Hardy's roles don't often give him the chance to work in a minor key, but here he shows a mastery of small, telling gestures – gently furrowing his brow, putting a hand to his mouth – all suggestive of a man constantly tamping down his inner tension. He speaks quietly, slowly, with pauses and dips of volume accompanying smooth, Richard Burton-like Welsh cadences – as if Locke, a master persuader of others, is also trying to hypnotise himself into believing that all is well.'

Even *The Guardian*'s Peter Bradshaw – never a huge fan of

the actor – admitted it was time he jumped on the Hardy train: 'For years, I remained stolidly baffled while all around, critics simpered and swooned at the words "Tom Hardy". The mere mention of his name caused hardened reviewers to whinny ecstatically as they slid to the floor. Well, it's time to do some swooning and simpering and whinnying and sliding of my own. Hardy gives us a masterclass in less-is-more acting for this absolutely engrossing, stripped-down solo piece.'

Locke wasn't a huge box office hit when it was released, making just $5 million in both the UK and the US, but both critics and fans loved it.

'Because of technology a lot of films invite the audience not to use their imagination, which invites people to create the characters themselves,' Knight told the *Evening Standard*. 'We didn't know if there was an audience for this, but what's great is that it's people who are the furthest thing from art-house lovers who respond the most. A lot of middle-aged men who don't usually go to cinemas end up with tears in their eyes. I think once people engage with the story, the character, they forget this is an experimental, unusual format. Once the story gets them, that's it.'

Theatre directors in three different countries have since approached Knight about adapting *Locke* to the stage, but those productions won't benefit from Hardy's presence carrying the story. For his portrayal of Ivan Locke he was given a Best Actor award by the Los Angeles Film Critics Association in 2014.

The world had seen yet another side to the versatile actor, who continually seems to surprise audiences with his performances. Critics and fans alike had even begun calling him the next Marlon Brando, after the iconic movie star.

From the moment *A Streetcar Named Desire* hit screens in 1951, Brando became a cultural archetype, an actor known for his blend of beauty, animal magnetism, danger, vulnerability, emotional commitment and sly playfulness.

Viewed by so many as the finest actor of his generation, critics have been on the hunt for someone with his unique mix of talent ever since his death in 2004. And every actor secretly wants to be that someone. In the past, there have been some epic contenders: Robert De Niro, Paul Newman, Mickey Rourke, Sean Penn, Nicolas Cage, Daniel Day-Lewis, Johnny Depp, Leonardo DiCaprio and now Tom Hardy.

The two actors definitely share a brooding demeanour and the tendency to communicate on screen with a grunt rather than an eloquently delivered line. In her review of *Lawless* for *The Wrap*, Sasha Stone wrote: 'Hardy can't help but steal every scene he's in. Bulked up for his Dark Knight role, Hardy seethes, grunts and stalks around – reminiscent of Brando.'

'There is something so charismatic about his screen presence that he reminds me of the young Marlon Brando,' agrees Chris Marloch from *Outword Magazine*.

'It's the nick on the eyebrow that's the giveaway,' Leah Rozen mused in *Anglophenia*, referring to Hardy's portrayal of Tommy Conlon in *Warrior*. 'Tom Hardy is making like Marlon Brando, or at least paying tribute to him.'

'Actors like Tom Hardy are rare. His technique harkens back to the old-school masculinity of stars like Marlon Brando,' film critic Karen Kemmerle wrote of *Locke*.

But the comparisons make Hardy nervous. And not everyone thinks they're a good thing.

Hardy's friend Jessica Chastain told *The Guardian* in 2014: 'It is actually really embarrassing when those comparisons start to come forward. I think Tom will always be plagued by that. But I actually hope he's not the next Marlon Brando, because even though Brando was brilliant, he had a troubled life and I'm hoping that Tom won't. He has a beautiful fiancée and they're really happy together. He's able to play these troubled characters now and have a stable life.'

Hardy admits he hasn't even seen the iconic films that made Brando such a star and shies away from the pressure that such a comparison obviously carries with it. 'You're going to hate me. I haven't even seen *The Godfather*, I haven't seen *On the Waterfront*, I haven't seen *Streetcar Named Desire*,' he revealed at the Cannes press conference for *Lawless*. 'I've seen *Apocalypse Now*, I thought he was wonderful in that. I feel a bit embarrassed when I'm compared to him. Marlon Brando is Marlon Brando. It's a tremendous honour to be compared to him. But I don't think I'm very good at what I do. I want to work harder at it.'

CHAPTER TWELVE

HIGHS AND LOWS

There were pups in the script and pups on the set but Tom Hardy felt like his next movie could accommodate one more canine companion: in April 2013, he was in New York filming *The Drop*, when his co-star and good friend Noomi Rapace took him to Sean Casey's animal shelter, near Brooklyn in New York, to research their roles.

You can guess what happened next.

'I knew the minute we walked in there, he'd be walking out with a dog,' Rapace told the *LA Times*. And so dog-lover Hardy introduced another canine – Carol – to the already animal-heavy set, before finding a 'forever home' for her soon afterwards.

This is not unusual behaviour for the star. Tom has two dogs already and it wasn't the first time he has picked up a stray while on a movie. In fact he is well known for it.

'I'm the finder of dogs, you know what I mean,' he told

Vulture. 'My missus, she's like, "You're not allowed to bring another dog back from a job." But I'll always find one. On every job we go on, I'll either find someone's dog and look after it, or I'll take my own dog, or I find a dog and we home it.'

Hardy's current dog, Woody – a lab cross – was found on the set of *Lawless*. Driving with Jessica Chastain in Atlanta, Georgia, Woody, then an eleven-week-old nameless stray, was dodging traffic on the motorway. Tom almost ran him over – with a Prius. He chuckled as he told journalist Jada Yuan the story: 'Of all things. What would be worse: to be run over, or to be run over by a Prius?'

As they watched the tiny pup hare across the honking traffic, Chastain feared for his life and urged Tom to pull over and try to coax him to safety. Woody became the film's on-set dog and when filming was over, Tom couldn't bear to part with him. So Jessica's mum looked after him for six months while he cleared quarantine, and Woody eventually became part of the Hardy family in London. He often goes on set with Tom, and even to press events.

Tom has always identified with dogs. 'I see myself as a dog inside in many ways – that's the way I am,' he told *Vulture*. 'It's like, I bark a lot, and I can bite, but I don't really. You know, they've got an energy. I just have an affinity with a dog. I'm very, very loyal, but, you know, I will piss on the carpet. I will chew your sneakers! And sometimes I look like I'm going to bite, but actually, if you know me, I'm not like that.'

It was his love of dogs that drew Hardy to *The Drop* in the first place. Based on the short story, *Animal Rescue* by Dennis Lehane, *The Drop* centres around Bob, an awkward loner with a secret who works in his cousin Marv's Brooklyn bar – and also as a money runner for the Chechen gangsters who've overtaken it.

His world gets turned completely upside down when he finds an abandoned pitbull puppy in a dumpster and takes him home. In Tom's words, 'It's a movie about a guy who's never had interaction with another human being since a period in his life, and a dog opens up his entire world and his heart.'

He had heard about the role from his good friend Noomi Rapace, of *The Girl with the Dragon Tattoo* fame. The pair had met on a project that never came to fruition, but admired each other so much they were determined to find the right thing to work on together. When Rapace read the script for *The Drop*, she knew she'd found it.

It was lucky she was on the case, because Hardy admits he's not very proactive in his script scouting. 'No one auditions at the top level,' he told *The Independent*. 'It's a conversation with a director or other actors as people discuss a project that's in the ether. And Noomi is awesome at finding stuff. She's ahead of the game; she knows everything about everyone, whereas I'm not so good at that. I do sitting down and waiting.'

'If I don't know who a director is,' he explained, 'I'll text Noomi and go, "who's this dude?" "Oh, he directed *The Godfather*." "What's that about?" So, I'm a prick. But getting me in the room with a director is key because I'm not a great reader or watcher of films.'

But the pair still had to convince the director, Michaël R. Roskam, that they were right for the roles. Roskam wasn't even sure he wanted European actors to headline the film. 'But when I found them, it made sense,' he told *The Phillippines Star*. 'New York is a city full of nomads. It's a gateway to the rest of the world. There are so many nationalities represented here. Probably 40 percent of the people I met during location scouting spoke with an accent that wasn't purely Brooklyn.'

Rapace forced a meeting with Roskam and outlined how she saw Nadia, Bob's love interest in the film. 'I told him that I thought Nadia is a very beautiful, wounded soul and we started from that,' she explained. 'She's gone through a lot. It's like she's backed into a corner, living a quite protected life and sticking to the same routine. She and Bob are both quite lonely, but deep down they dream of meeting someone who understands.'

The pair chatted for ten hours and Roskam was more than convinced.

During a Skype call with Roskam, Tom displayed similar enthusiasm, which cemented him in the role. When Roskam asked if he really 'felt' Bob, Hardy simply lifted up his shirt and showed him the huge pitbull tattoo on his back.

For the character of Bob, Hardy says he set out to explore 'the layers of denial and the masks that you have to create in order to participate in life on life's terms, whilst trying to deal with having done something so heinous that you can't forgive yourself, but at the same time you can justify. The complexity of that I found fascinating; that was a big challenge in its own right.'

Though by now a seasoned actor, Hardy admits he didn't exactly read the script properly before shooting began. And this led to him missing a crucial part of his character's motivation. Without giving it away, it's pretty central to the film...

'It was a big miss,' he told *The Independent*. 'I like to think I'm confident and pretty good at what I'm doing – and I missed that key thing! Three weeks into the shoot, Noomi turns to me and says: "You do realise what's in Bob's basement?" I said: "That's a very good point, Noomi. Why is it in my basement?" And Noomi says: "I love the way you're living Bob because he would shut it out too." I was like: "No, Noomi, I just didn't read the script properly."'

Shot entirely on location, in and around the neighbourhood of Marine Park, near Brooklyn, the film also stars the magnificent James Gandolfini in what would be his final role – as the bar's beaten-down owner, in over his head with the Chechen mafia.

It was a tight production schedule. Hardy was single-minded in his approach to working with the famously self-critical Gandolfini. And he certainly wasn't bashful in offering suggestions as he watched scene playbacks at the end of each day. In fact, he convinced Lehane and the producers to rewrite a more ambiguous ending into the script.

He also injected some much-needed playfulness into the serious production: on one afternoon, when Roskam yelled 'cut', he reportedly chased co-star Matthias Schoenaerts around the set in a game of unrequited tag. Hardy feels letting off steam is important. 'I joke around because if I don't let it go, it has a counter-intuitive effect on the work,' he said at a press event in Toronto.

'Some actors, they can stand still behind a string,' Roskam

added. 'And with some actors, it's like they don't want to over-concentrate and be good when you're not shooting, and then you say action and they lose it. Tom is one of those actors.'

Working together was as good as Rapace and Hardy had expected it to be. 'I'd been wanting to work with Tom for a while,' Rapace told *The Phillippines Star*. 'He's a one-of-a-kind actor who always brought something to the table that I hadn't thought about. That forced me to dig into things, to think and to be open. Each scene could go in any direction because he has a completely different take on it.'

'Noomi is capable of doing anything she puts her mind to,' he said about her in return. 'She's unstoppable – full of courage, truth and heart. If you want to put a team together, Noomi is the way to go. She keeps the flag flying when everyone else is tired and out of ideas.'

And then there were the puppies, of course.

Somehow, Tom managed to convince the film's dog handler, Kim, to let him take all five of the cute little actor pups home with him for cuddles over the course of the production.

'I was a bit lonely in New York and I worked closely with the Roccos: T and J and Pups and then Ice turned up and another called Indigo,' he explained to *Vulture*. 'T was the first one we had, then he started to grow, then he started to get bigger, so J came in, and they had two different personalities – all dogs have different personalities.'

'But it was hard,' he admitted. 'I was getting favourites. T was my favourite, and then T started getting boisterous, he didn't really care so much, so I found J. J was really cute and he wanted to just kiss all the time, and like, lick. He was the one that came back with me, and then T got upset because I was taking J back, so I had to take T back, and I was like, I've gotten really on with these dogs.'

He even took them to the pub with him to meet Roskam and Rapace for drinks – tucked inside the hood of his coat to keep them warm.

Back on set, Tom was often in fits of laughter while filming alongside James Gandolfini. 'There's a scene where he said to Bob, "It's just a dog, it's not like your long-lost relative that turned up with a colostomy bag hanging out of his ass, saying, "I'm yours now,"' Hardy told *Digital Spy*. 'And the way he said it, even in the cut of the movie, you can see that I can't hold myself together. Normally I'm very good at keeping a deadpan face but Jimmy was funny in a way that was electric.'

This charming anecdote is now bittersweet.

Weeks after filming on *The Drop* wrapped, Gandolfini flew to Rome with his family for a short holiday. He was on his way to Sicily, where he was to be honoured with an award at the Taormina Film Festival, and had stopped in the city for a quick break with his wife, Deborah Lin, his thirteen-year-old son Michael and baby daughter Liliana.

After a day of sightseeing in the sweltering June heat, his son found him unconscious on the bathroom floor. He had suffered a massive heart attack and died shortly afterwards.

His death shocked the whole world.

Roskam had been due to meet with Gandolfini soon afterwards in Brussels, for a catch up. Plunged into mourning, he locked himself away in his editing suite and focused on making the actor's last movie a fitting tribute. 'I do hope that I'll bring honour to his last performance,' Roskam said in September 2013, on the eve of the film's first screening at the

Toronto Film Festival. 'Not just for him but for his fans and all the people who loved him... I think I'm just waiting until the movie premieres and when I let the film go, I think I'll finally experience that he's gone. I went to the funeral, but I would see him every single day in editing. I still forget that we're walking the red carpet without him. I still kind of expect him to show up.'

Rapace reminisced about the first time she met the late actor – when he entered the Brooklyn restaurant where she and Roskam were eating one night. 'I wanted to tell him I was a fan or that I admired him, but I couldn't say anything,' she told *The News*. 'He was one of those people that when he came in a room, you just felt his presence. I don't get starstruck with a lot of people, but I couldn't say anything to him. I felt like a teenage girl.'

Ann Dowd, who plays Gandolfini's sister in *The Drop*, was a lot more blunt: 'He had a tenderness to him and he was sexy as hell, I mean that completely. You kind of got a crush on him the minute you were in his presence.'

When Hardy began doing press for the film at the festival, a young Michael Gandolfini was by his side. He'd let the youngster – who aspires to work in film some day too – shadow him at the event.

In his interview with *Vulture*, Tom had some beautiful words to say about the actor. 'I met him just in this movie, but he was the full, real deal,' he said. 'He had everything, and he was the funniest guy to work with. He'd work on levels that were deep and metaphoric. He can laugh, he can joke. He had a huge range of intelligence, and he was a very instinctive performer, and I just loved him. Such a tragic loss. I won't even … it's not my place to say, because they have families who miss them and I can't speak … I'm just somebody who met them and worked with them. So to watch the movie now, in that light, of course there's a sadness there … but it was a true honour and a true privilege.'

The Drop made $18,658,381 at the box office, out of a budget of $12 million. Part of its success was undeniably audiences flocking to see Gandolfini's last performance, but critics and filmgoers alike agreed that the film was a standalone triumph. And they definitively singled Tom Hardy out for the best praise.

'It's Hardy's performance, above everything else, that sneaks up on you,' wrote Tom Robey for *The Independent*. 'Following his sterling work in *Locke*, this trudging, subdued characterisation is another mettle-testing triumph. It's his most Brando-esque performance to date, without making a great show of its craft or virtuosity.'

Empire gave the film 3 out of 5 stars and said: 'The cute puppy almost steals the show but Hardy is ace and quite the watchable chameleon in his surprising switch from lovable dumb ox to cannier-than-we-thought. It's Hardy's deceptive, sympathetic performance that really distinguishes this from any number of competent but routine crime-gone-awry dramas.'

But Justin Chang, *Variety*'s chief film critic, summed it up best when he wrote: 'For all the moderately surprising twists served up in *The Drop*, the big revelation turns out to be no revelation at all: Man, that Tom Hardy can act. Like an adorable puppy that turns out to boast an extremely sharp set of teeth, Hardy's skillfully restrained performance as a mild-mannered Brooklyn bartender who finds himself an unwitting pawn in all manner of crooked schemes isn't just the film's strongest element; it's the reason this serviceably constructed thriller remains as absorbing as it does.'

After Hardy finished filming *The Drop*, he spent the summer of 2013 filming *Child 44*, another movie with Noomi Rapace. This one, however, would not be so well received by the press. After a run of exceptional successes, this next project would break his winning streak – but importantly not his stride.

Child 44 is based on a fictional book of the same title from author Tom Rob Smith, which in turn is inspired by a real series of gruesome murders in Russia: by the serial killer Andrei Chikatilo, who assaulted, murdered and mutilated fifty-two women and children.

Filmed in Prague, the mystery thriller is set in the 1950s during Stalin's Soviet Union rule. Hardy plays MGB agent Leo Demidov, who loses everything when he refuses to denounce his wife Raisa – played by Rapace – as a traitor. Exiled to a grim provincial outpost, Leo and Raisa join forces with Gary Oldman as General Mikhail Nesterov to capture a serial killer who is preying on young boys. They soon find that their investigation threatens a system-wide government cover-up...

Directed by Sweden's Daniel Espinosa and produced by Ridley Scott, the film's stellar line-up and $50 million budget predicted good things. Alongside Hardy as the lead and Oldman as Nesterov, the movie also starred Joel Kinnaman, Paddy Considine, Jason Clark and Vincent Cassel. It was the fourth time that Hardy had worked with Gary Oldman and by now the two got along famously.

Tom's friend and mentor Philip Seymour Hoffman was also set to star in the film, but had been replaced by *Ocean's Twelve* star Cassel at the last minute. Hardy would never again work with Hoffman, who died of a drugs overdose just a few months after filming wrapped on *Child 44*.

Like Hardy, Hoffman had struggled with drug abuse. After twenty-three years clean, he had suffered a brief relapse in early 2013 – while Hardy was filming *The Drop*. He'd checked himself into rehab for ten days and when he came out, he was open about his struggles to the press. It appeared to be a minor slip-up and his friends and family thought his demons were back under control. But on 2 February 2014, Hoffman was found dead in the bathroom of his New York apartment. He was just forty-six and left behind a young family.

Hardy found the news devastating. *Moviepilot* reported him as saying: 'I loved Phil, he was my North Star of standards – he was brilliant – funny and full of wisdom and eccentricities and love – he nurtured talent and believed in team. I had the pleasure of being "Judged!" by him... he... taught me so much and continues to do so. I felt he believed in me in a way that few have ever and took the time and effort to show me the road. Above all I will miss Phil more than it is possible to say.'

When the first trailer for the film appeared, the press were hopeful. 'Tom Hardy looks to have another box office hit on his hands with the Ridley Scott-produced crime drama *Child 44*,' wrote *IndieWire*. But from the moment of its release in April 2015, it was clear that it was not going to be anywhere near as successful as Hardy's past projects.

First, Russia pulled the film from all its cinemas after the country's culture ministry deemed it 'historically inaccurate'. Pavel Stepanov, head of the movie's Russian distributor, told the RIA Novosti news agency that he was 'unsatisfied' with the film, and called for 'more government control over the distribution of films which have a socially important context to them'.

Then *The Guardian* panned all the actors' Russian accents as fake – and not even golden boy Tom Hardy escaped criticism. 'Hardy, who plays Smith's hero, Russian homicide cop Leo Demidov, has dazzled us with accents before, becoming plausibly Welsh in *Locke*, while his Brooklyn accent in *The Drop* felt flawless and lived-in. I have no doubt that to some ears, his Russian accent will feel persuasive too,' complained broadsheet journalist John Patterson. 'But sometimes it feels as if we've moved not one inch forward from Derren Nesbitt in *Where Eagles Dare*, clicking his heels together, chuckling darkly and savouring the sheer blackness of his SS uniform, while throwing out a few "achtungs" and "Heil Hitlers" to persuade us that it's 1943, not 1968.'

Empire Magazine gave it a meagre 2 stars out of 5, while *The Guardian*'s Phil Hoad said that while Hardy's performance, accent aside, was strong, 'pulling in a meagre $600,000 from 500 theatres in the US and $2m globally from 25 markets, the $50m film is looking like it will, unfortunately for studio Summit Entertainment, vanish without a trace.'

The Independent also praised Hardy's performance. 'Once we get used to Tom Hardy's Russian accent (reminiscent of the one John Malkovich attempted as Teddy KGB in *Rounders*), his performance is stirring enough,' wrote Geoffrey McNab.

'He has the physique and intimidatory quality that has made him such a menacing villain in *Bronson* and *The Dark Knight Rises*. Hardy plays him in the same conscience-torn way as he did the husband whose marriage is unravelling in *Locke*.'

As did *The Telegraph*, who said both he and Oldman were on 'glumly good form'. 'Usually when a film is described as novelistic it's meant as a compliment,' Robbie Collin declared. 'But *Child 44*'s script feels like a straight transcription of the book, and the resultant lack of focus means the film starts to drag before it's had a chance to begin. When Gary Oldman first shows up some way into the second hour as a crumpled bureaucrat, you're surprised the actor has taken such an incidental role in a mid-tier film – until it becomes clear that he hasn't, and the film has simply taken far too long to introduce him.'

Somehow not even Hardy and the rest of the A-list line-up had saved the movie from a critics' tongue-lashing. It would go down as a rare misstep in the actor's film footnotes but nothing that would prevent the Hardy train from continuing to gather pace.

Our boy wasn't worried. When asked on the red carpet about the origins of his much-maligned Soviet twang, he even joked: 'I watched *Sesame Street*. The Count speaks just like it.'

CHAPTER THIRTEEN

FAMILY AFFAIRS

In February 2014, it was announced that Tom Hardy would join the series two cast of *Peaky Blinders* – Steven Knight's Birmingham-based gangster drama. Set during the aftermath of World War One, the BBC2 drama follows a gang of Brummie racehorse racketeers as they manipulate their way to the top of the criminal underworld.

He wasn't the only member of his household to bag a role in the popular show either: his fiancée Charlotte Riley joined him on the Black Country set. Surprisingly, neither knew the other had been cast when they took the roles. 'I got the job and I rang Tom up to tell him and he said, "That's really weird. Steve has just asked me,"' Charlotte told *The Independent*.

The pair didn't share any scenes, either. In fact, the only reason they saw each other at all on set that spring was down to Woody – the loved-up couple took it in turns to dogsit while the other was shooting their scenes.

Hardy plays Alfie Solomons, a Camden don who runs his bootleg distillery under the cover of a legitimate bakery. Riley plays May Carlton, an aristocratic widowed racehorse trainer.

Woody was supposed to be there for moral support only but he had other plans: early on, when it was Riley's turn to look after him, Woody escaped and nonchalantly began following Hardy as he filmed a scene. The cast and crew were amused but the director saw potential and after a few test runs Woody won himself the part of Solomons' dog.

Cillian Murphy, who plays the lead role of Tommy Shelby in the phenomenally successful series, was pleased to be starring opposite Hardy again – the pair had worked together on both *Inception* and *Dark Knight*. 'He's a brilliant man and he's a good pal and I always enjoy working with Tom,' Murphy told *Den of Geek*. 'When you work with great actors you have to step up and we've always enjoyed that, and I think we work well together.'

Hardy and Murphy are the latest in a long line of Hollywood actors to make triumphant returns to the small screen. The traditional trajectory for an actor's career has been from TV to film but with the rise of *Netflix*, *Amazon Prime*, *NOW TV* and other online platforms – along with viewers' increasing appetites for binge-watching good television – actors are now performing U-turns and snapping up plum roles in riveting and award-winning TV series.

Matthew McConaughey and Woody Harrelson were in *True Detective*. Zooey Deschanel was in *New Girl*. Kevin Spacey was in *House of Cards*... the list is endless. 'Gone are the days when television was reserved for lesser actors,' wrote *Harper's Bazaar*. 'Recruiting Irish actor Cillian Murphy –

whose most recent roles include Christopher Nolan's *Batman Begins*, *The Dark Knight Rises* and *Inception* – was quite a feat for BBC Two gangland drama *Peaky Blinders*. The addition of Tom Hardy for season two is a veritable coup.'

'What makes TV so attractive to actors and to writers is the long form nature of it,' Murphy explained in his *Den of Geek* interview. 'The idea of playing and developing the character over six hours and now we're in the second series doing it for another six hours is a real gift. Any actor would kill to spend that time and go so deep within that character. You get to explore parts you wouldn't get to do in a two-and-a-half hour film.'

For an actor like Hardy it was a tantalising opportunity and one he took full advantage of. Sporting an impressive beard, when *Peaky Blinders* aired in autumn 2014 it was to rapturous applause. With the right kind of swagger to make his mark on the series, he strode back onto British TV screens uttering the whisky-slurred words: 'I once carried out my own form of stigmata on an Italian. Hammered a nail up his nose. It was fucking biblical, mate.'

It was a role he was clearly born to play. As the website *EntertainmentWise* summarised: 'Cillian and Hardy are clearly a well-matched team on screen and the gutsy Solomons is such a huge character that his performance seems to lift Murphy's as well. Last series it was almost inevitable that he'd overcome his almost comical foes, but Hardy is finally a worthy adversary for both Tommy and Cillian to bounce off.'

Hardy's Solomons was such a success that he was immediately snapped up to appear in series three of the drama too. In April 2015, to the excitement of *Peaky Blinders*' fans, he was spotted filming on Dale Street in Liverpool, a location used in both the previous two series.

'I'm not going to put too much pressure on myself, I just want to have some fun. The more of a challenge I give myself, the easier it is to take on more projects which are complicated in the future.'

Wise words from Hardy, considering the breadth of his next project. It may have been well trodden ground for the actor, being a gangster film, but that didn't mean it would be an easy gig: Hardy had agreed to play both the infamous Kray twins in a new biopic of the East End gangsters.

Ronnie and Reggie Kray were celebrity gangsters who ruled London's East End in the Swinging Sixties. Born in October 1933, they grew up in a slum area of Bethnal Green. Talented amateur boxers, the pair developed impressive hard-man reputations before their twenty-first birthday. With their gang, 'The Firm', the Krays led armed robberies, arson, protection rackets and even committed murder – by the early 1960s they were making up to the equivalent of £10 million a year. But their crimes did eventually catch up with them and they were jailed for life in March 1969.

As well as the dark deeds they were eventually imprisoned for, the pair moved in important social circles – partying with the likes of Barbara Windsor, Diana Dors, Frank Sinatra and Judy Garland at their popular London club, Esmeralda's Barn.

The club is no more – in its place is the smart Berkeley Hotel – but the twins are still revered. They defined a movie-like era of sharp-suited gangsters vying for turf and control, where innocents all too often got caught in the middle. Legends in their time, they are revered to this day: when Reggie passed away in

2000 – five years after his brother suffered a fatal heart attack in Broadmoor Hospital – his funeral was marked by hundreds of people who came to pay their respects. Even now, their family in the East End vehemently protect the name of Kray.

Legend is based on best-selling author John Pearson's trilogy of the Krays, *The Profession of Violence: The Rise and Fall of the Kray Twins*. With a screenplay from *L.A. Confidential*'s Brian Helgeland and Hardy in the lead roles the film is sure to be a winner. But it has not been without controversy.

At the time of writing, the plot is said to focus on the Krays' dodgy dealings in the fifties and sixties and more specifically, Reggie Kray – older by ten minutes – as he fights to keep his psychotic younger brother (rumoured to be a paranoid schizophrenic) under control. It's also rumoured to portray Reggie as gay and his short-lived marriage to Frances Shea as a sham. Reggie married Shea in 1965, but two years later, aged twenty-three, she committed suicide.

As filming got underway in June 2014, various gangland figures interviewed by famous Hollywood director Helgeland as research began speaking to the British tabloids.

Freddie Foreman, an ex-enforcer for the Krays' 'firm', told *The Sun*: 'The marriage was never even consummated. That poor girl was a trophy wife, nothing more.'

Kray family members still living in the Bethnal Green area were unimpressed. 'What they told the film-makers is a load of filth,' eighty-nine-year-old Joe Lea – first-cousin to the Krays – told *The Docklands & East London Advertiser*. 'People are spreading all this muck about.'

But it's all great publicity for the film, set for release in autumn 2015.

Previously, the Kray brothers were immortalised in the 1990 film starring the famous Kemp brothers from eighties band Spandau Ballet but no one has single-handedly tackled *both* brothers before. And though playing ex-boxers and hard-men isn't straying too far from Hardy's comfort zone, playing two at the same time won't be easy. Luckily it's just the kind of challenge he relishes.

Despite looking so similar, Ronnie and Reggie were very different personalities, so in his preparation Hardy was going to have to find subtle ways to distinguish them on screen. And the shoot was always going to be logistically tricky too. 'It's quite technical and I'm a bit of an anorak,' he told the *Daily Mail*. 'There's a physical transfer; we'd have to shoot one bit, go away, come back and shoot it all again with another part. I've never dreamt of playing two people on the screen!'

To physically look the part, he trained with Freddie Roach, former coach to World Champion boxer Manny Pacquiao. He was dedicated, as he always is for his roles. Roach even says that Hardy was so good he could have been a professional boxer in another life.

By the time the press began eagerly publishing pictures of Tom on set, he was looking and acting the part. Hair slicked back and sporting thick-framed glasses to play Ronnie, he looked menacing as he filmed in Borough Market in the summer of 2014. In a slick suit, puffing away on a cigar, he was every inch a Kray; even Freddie Foreman, who gave Hardy tips on how to play the twins, was convinced. He admitted to *The Sun* that the actor had 'nailed the part' and said that being on set with him was like being with a Kray twin in the flesh.

Filming took place at various locations in east London and during breaks astonished bystanders even got to see Hardy playing in the sunshine with Woody. The dog was – of course – on set with the actor.

Also spotted on set were Hardy's co-stars, including Emily Browning (playing tragic Frances), David Thewlis, Christopher Eccleston, Chazz Palminteri and Tara Fitzgerald.

When filming finally wrapped towards the end of the summer of 2014 Hardy took a clapperboard from the set as a keepsake. It remains to be seen whether *Legend* will be another smash hit for him, as at the time of writing it has not been released. But let's face it: it certainly seems likely.

While many rising Hollywood stars are photographed with a succession of beautiful women on their arms, Tom Hardy has been in a solid relationship with Charlotte Riley for a number of years now. So it was no surprise that reporters were always asking the down-to-earth pair the obvious question: 'When's the wedding?'

'You'd have to ask Charlotte when we're getting married,' Hardy told one inquisitive journalist in early 2014. 'She's a difficult woman to pin down, as she's always so busy with work.'

Riley just laughed when she was told what her fiancé had said. 'That's not true at all. He's a cheeky bugger,' she told *The Telegraph*. 'We are desperate to do it, but I'll never have a celebrity wedding. It will be low-key, with family and friends.'

The couple may not have been splashed all over the pages of *HELLO!* magazine but Hardy never missed an opportunity to sing Riley's praises. In April 2014, he was speaking at The

Cinema Society in New York when he said something that excited the gossip columnists. Gushing about Riley's supportiveness, he said: 'Well, my wife is an actor so she sort of gets it.'

Wife? It would be just like the media-shy and romantic pair to marry in secret and not tell anyone. Riley had even hinted as much when she revealed it would be low-key. Had the couple eloped and not told anyone?

A few days of frantic enquiries to publicists revealed that they were still engaged to be married but it was no simple slip of the tongue: that autumn, *The Sun* revealed that the pair were officially husband and wife. And they'd managed to keep it quiet for months!

Hardy had obviously had wedding plans on his mind when he had jumped the gun and referred to Riley as his wife in the spring, because in July – during a break from filming *Legend* – the pair had snuck away to be married.

The ceremony took place at the romantic eighteenth-century Château de Roussan, a beautiful country estate in the South of France. A source told the newspaper: 'It was a beautiful, low-key day made even more special because they just had their closest friends and family around them. Tom's son Louis played a key role during the ceremony. There was nothing flash about the wedding, they always said they wanted it to be about the two of them and their family rather than any grand gesture.'

Sorry, ladies – Tom is now firmly off the market.

CHAPTER FOURTEEN

MAD MAX
AND BEYOND

On 14 May 2015, the much-anticipated *Mad Max* reboot was screened at the prestigious Cannes Film Festival. *Mad Max: Fury Road* had been a long time coming but the world would now see Tom Hardy take on one of the most iconic roles of the 1980s.

It was way back in October 2009 that George Miller confirmed he would return to the directorial helm for a fourth, updated instalment of his cult *Mad Max* films. At that stage not a great deal was known about the production, but that did little to stop the rumour mill from going into overdrive. Several actors were touted as being in the running to take over Mel Gibson's role as Max Rockatansky, including Sam Worthington, Jeremy Renner and of course, Tom Hardy.

Being an Australian, Worthington was the favourite choice down under, but it was suspected he might have a schedule clash with another production. Charlize Theron had already been confirmed as having won a part in the film – as Furiosa – and as she'd already worked with Renner in *North Country* it was whispered he might have an advantage over the other actors. But after a few weeks of speculation, it emerged that Tom Hardy was to be the new Max.

Even those who were at first sceptical about the part not being played by an Australian seemed pacified by the news that the role had been taken by Tom – he'd shown how strong and accomplished an actor he was in *Bronson* and film fans were keen to see more.

The first *Mad Max* film had been released in 1979 and starred a young Mel Gibson in the lead role. Directed by George Miller, who went on to direct two sequels in the 1980s, the film was set in a dystopian future Australia, where law and order have broken down. Max is a policeman whose wife and child have been murdered by a vicious motorcycle gang. The enraged protagonist eventually tracks down all the members of the gang, killing them as revenge.

At the time, Mel Gibson was a complete unknown and the films were responsible for launching his career. In 1981, *Mad Max 2: The Road Warrior* came out, followed by *Beyond Thunderdome* in 1985. The series attained cult classic status and the films have been recognised as having a profound influence on the now hugely popular post-apocalyptic genre.

The fourth instalment had been a long time in the offing. For over a decade Miller had been in possession of a script he was satisfied with, but filming stalled in 2001 because of global security issues and economic turmoil. While drumming his fingers waiting to start work on *Mad Max 4*, Miller veered off on an unexpected course and directed the animated musical features *Happy Feet* and its successor, *Happy Feet Two*. All the while, though, the director was honing his next *Mad Max* movie and paving the way for when shooting did eventually begin. 'All the time I worked really hard to get the screenplay right and really prepared the film very well,' he commented.

With Hardy in the lead role and Theron secured as the terrifying Furiosa, the rest of the casting went smoothly. Nicholas Hoult from *Skins* and *About a Boy* would play Nux, Zoe Kravitz was picked to be Toast and beauties Rosie Huntington-Whiteley, Riley Keough and Megan Gale would also feature.

Miller had originally hoped to start shooting in the second half of 2010 but he was stopped in his tracks by something over which he had no control: the weather. The Australian outback at Broken Hill – a location sometimes referred to as 'the end of civilisation' in Australia – with its harsh wasteland-like appearance, was the perfect backdrop for the apocalyptic landscape of *Mad Max*. That part of the country had, however, been subject to unexpectedly high rainfall, which meant the scenery changed beyond recognition.

'We were all set to shoot in the Australian desert and then unprecedented rain came and what was the wasteland – completely flat, red earth – is now a flower garden...' explained Miller at the time.

While good news for Australia, it was bad news for the progress of the film and a major rethink was needed. The solution was located many miles away in the south-west African nation of Namibia and so the whole production was moved, delaying matters for a year. That delay meant Hardy could also do *The Dark Knight Rises*, so ultimately it was no bad thing for the actor.

Leaving Australia certainly didn't mean leaving behind some of the most important stars of the film: its vehicles. Miller confessed to *The Frame* that 150 vehicles had been especially constructed for the film – most of which would be destroyed during the course of shooting. The vehicles, designed by Ford Australia's Research Centre, were shipped from Australia to South Africa and transported overland to Namibia at the start of 2012.

It also transpired that the film was going to be a physically demanding one for the actors and would involve a lot of stunts. To this end, Charlize Theron and Tom Hardy were undergoing exacting training. Speaking to ABC News, Miller said: 'The reason the movie is so big is that it's just got a huge number of stunts and we're trying to do stuff that I believe people haven't done before.'

Hardy says the shoot was difficult and dangerous. 'We were in the middle of nowhere,' he told *Esquire* magazine, 'and just getting things to and from the set was a nightmare. We'd lose half a vehicle in sand and have to dig it out. It was just this unit in the middle of x-million square kilometres of desert, and then this group of lunatics in leathers, like a really weird S&M party, or a Hell's Angels convention. It was like Cirque du Soleil meets fucking Slipknot.'

Despite the extensive safety precautions there were, he says, a lot of accidents. 'Luckily nobody died.'

Always anxious to perform at his very best and to do his utmost to keep fans of the original film happy, Tom's excitement at landing such an iconic role was tinged with the nerves he so often had to combat when taking on a big new part. He knew what he was taking on and how much pressure he could be under to live up to expectations. 'The guy's an Australian icon, I'm s******g myself,' he admitted to *The Sunday Telegraph*. 'I feel bad I'm not Australian, really. But look, I'm gonna come and represent and do my best.'

Already he'd given a huge amount of thought to his character. As well as wanting to appear strong and lean physically, he described the Max he wanted to create as being like a hungry wolf. 'This is the kind of guy who's not well. So I have to create that reality.'

If past form was anything to go by, Max was in a safe pair of hands with character actor Hardy. George Miller was excited about having found a new actor to fill the role of Max. He calls him, 'one of those special actors who comes along' and says that Tom even met with Mel Gibson to discuss the part.

Tom knew he had big shoes to fill so it must have been reassuring to have the older actor's blessing but he later revealed that the meeting didn't go quite so smoothly as imagined! Speaking about the exchange to *Details* magazine in 2015, he said: 'I met Mel. I needed to meet Mel purely from a young man's perspective. I wanted to touch base with the previous Max and just say hello. And is it okay? Because I'm taking on Max, I have to meet Max. It's awkward. "You're Mad Max. I'm Tommy Hardy, and I'm playing him."'

Hardy says he got a little over-excited. 'He was bored with me. He said, "All right, buddy, good luck with that." Bless him. I made him a bracelet. And then we talked for a couple of hours about all kinds of stuff. I left, and that was that. And then he called up my agent and said: "I think you found someone that's crazier than I am."'

Despite this awkward but sweet exchange, Hardy was clearly excited about the role and for fans to finally see him take it on. 'Mad Max is, like, the coolest superhero that a boy could get,' he said. 'Cause there's no cape, there's no rubber suit. There's no flying. Nothing really hurts Batman or Superman. Everything hurts in *Mad Max*. Those kind of heroes, they excite me because they are ordinary people in extraordinary circumstances. They are fallible. And when they jump, they're not sure if they're going to make it to the other side.'

After months of filming in the desert, Hardy returned to the UK. Years passed and still there was no sign of a release date. He was kept busy working on other projects but as filming periodically stopped and started up again he must have been wondering if it would ever be finished.

The production remained shrouded in secrecy, with everyone involved keen to keep it as much of a surprise as possible. Various news outlets reported that the film would be one long road trip, with little dialogue. George Miller himself eventually revealed the basic storyline: 'Mad Max is caught up with a group of people fleeing across the Wasteland in a War Rig driven by the Imperator Furiosa. This movie is an account of the Road War, which follows. It is based on the Word Burgers of the History Men and eyewitness accounts of those who survived.'

When the first pictures from the film were finally released in July 2014, appearing in *Entertainment Weekly*, fans were delighted with what they saw: Hardy was suntanned, bloody and weather-beaten, dressed in a steampunk outfit that looked as if it was moulded to his body. His beard was full, his eyes blue pools of rage and sadness.

Images of the vehicles showed them to be twisted, sharp and spiky hunks of metal, kicking up dust and smoke in their wake. Theron's Furiosa was shaven-headed and dirty, dressed in rags, while Hoult's Nut was scarred, mangled and unrecognisable. In short, clearly a lot of work had gone into the movie to make it visually epic. And it finally had a release date: May 2015, a whole six years after production had started. It would be an epic summer blockbuster, pitted against Marvel's *Avengers: Age of Ultron* and *Ant-Man*, Disney's *Tomorrowland* and many more releases set for the season.

So, how did it fare?

When the trailers began to appear, fans were overcome with excitement. Set to a soundtrack of classical music, Max and his co-stars look impossibly badass, covered in dirt, sweat and oil as they rumble through the dusty landscape. Explosion after explosion lights up the desert. There were epic fights, incredible stunts and breath-taking scenery.

'Our world is reduced to a single instinct: survive,' says Hardy in one voiceover.

It may have been a long time coming but it certainly looked as if it was going to be worth it: early test screenings proved positive. Miller had finally managed to whittle his film down from a mammoth 480 hours of footage to an acceptable length. All that remained for him and the cast was to see what the critics and fans thought of the epic reboot, which cost an eye-watering $150 million to make.

And they weren't disappointed. Most reviewers awarded

the action-packed epic 4 or 5 stars, with *The Daily Telegraph* describing it as a 'Krakatoan eruption of craziness'.

Den of Geek was particularly gushing in its praise: 'At a time when expensive summer movies seem increasingly formulaic, *Mad Max: Fury Road* tears up the rulebook. It feels like Miller going for broke – holding nothing back for a sequel, but instead throwing every ounce of creativity and imagination into one compact slab of sound and movement. *Mad Max: Fury Road* is a brutal, breathtaking work of pop art.'

They singled out Tom's performance, posting: 'Hardy's an effective replacement for Mel Gibson as a very different kind of Max; one who communicates largely through grunts and gruff utterances, yet always with a glimmer of humanity behind his eyes.'

Awarding it 5 stars, *Time Out*'s David Erlich said the film was like 'a tornado tearing through a tea party', writing: '*Fury Road* steers this macho franchise in a brilliant new direction, forging a mythical portrait about the need for female rule in a world where men need to be saved from themselves.'

Variety's Justin Chang wrote that the 'word-of-mouth excitement over the film's beautifully brutal action sequences should lend it tremendous commercial velocity.'

Jamie Graham from *Total Film* said that the blockbuster had some of the greatest action ever put on screen and wrote: 'In the battle of the 2015 behemoths, the maxed-out madness of *Mad Max: Fury Road* sets an extraordinarily high bar – then pole-vaults clean over it and smashes the entire rig to smithereens.'

And *The Guardian*'s Peter Bradshaw awarded it 4 stars,

describing it as 'like Grand Theft Auto revamped by Hieronymus Bosch'. After the screening, Bradshaw even tweeted: 'Slightly embarrassed with myself at how very much I enjoyed the barking Mad Max: Fury Road.'

Hardy has announced that he is attached to star in three more Mad Max movies but nothing is set in stone – it will all ride on the overall success of his first outing as Max Rockatansky.

'Everything's based on figures and how things are perceived. Inevitably it's a business,' he told *Esquire* magazine.

Based on the first wave of reviews, *Mad Max* business is booming. And it's a safe bet that it won't be long before we see the next instalment in production.

So, what's next for Tom Hardy, the hottest new talent on the block? Great things, and after years of laying the foundations, that's no less than he deserves. Over the next few years we're going to see him play everything from an outlaw frontiersman to a singing cabbie and we'll even see him produce his own content.

The Revenant, based on the Michael Punke novel of the same name, will reunite him with his *Inception* co-star Leonardo DiCaprio and team both with fabled Spanish director Alejandro González Iñárritu. Hardy thinks it was DiCaprio who gave him the nod for the project, due to hit cinemas in 2016. 'I shamelessly don't read scripts,' he told *Esquire* magazine. 'But Leo called me up and said, "Dude, you have to check this out, I think it's a brilliant piece and Alejandro's a genius – will you read it?"'

He was supposed to be filming *Splinter Cell*, a film based on Tom Clancy's successful black ops novels and computer games. 'I was like, "I'm going to jump out of helicopters, mate. I want to go and play soldiers!" and he said, "Just read it, you idiot!" I was like, "Mmm, all right."'

Hardy was instantly hooked and though he's still attached to *Splinter Cell* – which is now due to start filming at the end of 2015 – he signed up for the extra project at once.

The sweeping Western centres on DiCaprio as 1820s fur trapper Hugh Glass, who is mauled by a grizzly bear, left for dead and then robbed by his three friends – played by Hardy, Will Poulter and Domhnall Gleeson. When he survives, he goes on a journey of revenge.

Filming began in remote locations in Canada in late 2014, and continued until mid-2015. Hardy, of course, had a canine companion for the shoot: not Woody this time, but Georgia, a St Bernard he 'borrowed' from a local animal shelter. The film is sure to be a corker.

He has also managed to fit in a cameo in the 2015 big screen adaptation of *London Road*, a movie that began life as a unique musical stage play. Director Rufus Norris is tackling the project, which centres round the community of Ipswich, devastated after the real-life 2006 murders of five women by serial killer Steven Wright.

The play – which tracks the community as it tries to rebuild itself – was a huge hit during its run at The National Theatre in 2011 and 2012, with Hardy one of many fans, so when he heard about the movie he made it known that he was keen to get involved. The result is a scene where he plays a cabbie called Mark, who sings about a troubling passion he had as a teen.

It might sound bizarre, but Hardy can sing. Otherwise there's no way he would have won his next part – playing

Elton John in *Rocket Man*, a biopic of the singing legend! 'It's all sort of a bit under the radar at the minute, but yeah, I am speaking to Elton,' he told *Digital Spy* in 2013.

'Tom is quickly becoming known as one of the world's most versatile actors, and like others at the top of their craft, he has proven his ability to transform himself completely into the character or subject found in the material,' co-executive producer Peter Schlessel told *Variety* magazine, making the news official. 'We are confident that Tom will embody the physicality and spirit of Sir Elton.'

Hardy admits he's a bit nervous about it. When asked by *The Wall Street Journal* if he would be singing in the new film, he replied: 'Yeah, I hope so. Otherwise I'll have probably failed, right? But that's terrifying me. God knows how I'm going to do that.'

The project is currently still in development.

His fans would agree that Tom Hardy can do anything he sets his mind to – and that includes activity behind, as well as in front of the camera. In 2012, without much fanfare, he and his friend and production partner Dean Baker set up their own production company, Hardy Son & Baker. Their aim is to create films, TV and documentaries and it's an ambition they're well on the way to fulfilling: in 2014 they signed a two-year first-look deal with NBC Universal International Television Productions. It was a surprise to many, but showed just how far Hardy has come since the days when he knew nothing about studios and production and thrived off his raw talent.

JoAnn Alfano, head of scripted programming at NBCU-ITVP, described Hardy and Baker as 'passionate storytellers with a talent for telling original unconventional stories', with the ability to attract 'first-class talent' to their projects.

Hardy released a statement saying: '*NBCUniversal* is a great fit for Hardy Son & Baker, and this partnership is a fantastic next step in the endeavour to build our company into a major international TV drama producer.'

The company has already produced *Poaching Wars*, a documentary series on ITV, fronted by Hardy himself, and is co-producing *Taboo* with Ridley Scott for BBC1 and FX.

It's clear Tom is still fiercely loyal to those he trusts: *Taboo* is being directed by *Locke* director Steven Knight and is based on a story by Hardy and his writer father, Chips. The series will see him play nineteenth-century adventurer James Keziah Delaney, who returns to Europe from Africa with fourteen ill-gotten diamonds and seeking vengeance after the death of his father.

Hardy says: '*Taboo* is the first major production our company, Hardy Son & Baker, is setting sail on, and it gives me great pleasure to know that we are in partnership with FX and the BBC. I believe with the high standard of creative talent – with Steve Knight and Ridley Scott at the helm – and with the support and backing of these two great broadcasters, we have found the perfect home and team for *Taboo*.'

It will likely debut in mid-2016.

Tom has now firmly established himself as a leading Hollywood name, but how has this changed his life? He claims his introduction to the big time will not affect him – he's still Tommy Hardy from East Sheen. 'If I want to go down with my little boy to *Crock A Doodle* and paint ceramics, I'm doing that,' he told *Esquire* magazine emphatically in 2015. 'And nothing's going to stop me. Because I'm financially secure enough to say that, within my means. I'm not a multi-multi-millionaire; I haven't got enough money to survive my whole life and look after my friends and family, but I would rather be able to go to *Crock A Doodle*, and be with my dogs, and walk down the street, and people know me and say hello. That's great, it's like being a local in an old-fashioned sitcom, *Cheers* or whatever, but in real life. You know me? Great. That's cool. Totally. Brilliant. Love it. At least I know I'm not alone in the world.'

Hardy is anything but alone. And it's pretty much a sure bet he'll continue to entertain his family, friends and fans for many more years, both in front of and behind the camera. He deserves his success, as we deserve the chance to watch the most impressive acting talent of a generation doing what he does so well.